Hearing the Noise

Hearing the Noise

My Life in the NFL

Preston Pearson

William Morrow and Company, Inc. New York

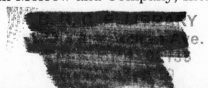

Library of Congress Cataloging in Publication Data

Pearson, Preston.
  Hearing the noise.

  Includes index.
    1. Pearson, Preston.   2. Football players—United
States—Biography.   3. National Football League.
I. Title.
GV939.P43A35   1985   796.332′092′4 [B]   85-5054
ISBN 0-688-04191-4

      Printed in the United States of America

      First Edition

      1 2 3 4 5 6 7 8 9 10

      BOOK DESIGN BY JAYE ZIMET

To Gregory Keith and Matthew Jay,
and especially to the memory of my mother.

Acknowledgments

I want to thank the Colt, Steeler, and Cowboy organizations; Tom O'Malley; Ed Pearson; Rufus Pearson, Sr.; Rufus Pearson, Jr.; Mary Pearson; Alice Collier; Pearlee Brooks; Kellen McClendon; Steve Sokol; Judy Hoffman; Linda Tipping; Janie Tilford; Kathy Junell; Gail Servatius; Linda Finley Pearson; Hazel Finley; and Sherman Finley.

Contents

Hearing the Noise

1
Getting Ready for the Jets and Joe Namath

The Baltimore Colts were confident and had every reason to be. We had gone 13–1 in the 1968 regular season, defeated a tough Minnesota team, 24–14, in the playoffs, then clobbered the Browns, 34–0, in Cleveland for the NFL Championship. A writer for *The New York Times* said we might be "the greatest football team ever," stronger even than the champions of Super Bowls I and II, the mighty Vince Lombardi-led Green Bay Packers. Yes, we were confident; no way on earth existed to lose in Super Bowl III to the New York Jets of the AFL, referred to by some players as the Mickey Mouse League. There was no way to lose, but we did, in one of the most startling upsets in football history, in a game which, amazingly, is more controversial today, at least in some circles, than when it was played. Today there is talk that the fix was in, that the Super Bowl, the most important single sporting event in America, was rigged.

Jimmy "the Greek" Snyder, now a CBS sports commentator, was in 1968 *the* individual who established odds for athletic contests in the United States. The Greek said the Colts were seventeen-point favorites or, if you wanted to bet straight—just on which team would win or lose—the Jets were 7–1 underdogs. Very seldom has a professional football team been so prohibitively favored, and *never,* not before or since, in a Super Bowl. But many bettors thought the point spread wasn't high enough. The large amounts of money wagered on the Colts soon shot it up to eighteen and a half.

It was as it should be, I thought. The Colts had better players than the Jets, a simple matter of fact. We had the great Bubba Smith, big, strong, smart, mean, a defensive lineman just couldn't be better than he was—God simply gave him more talent than the others; Mike Curtis, aptly named "Mad Dog," intense, vicious (but a pussycat off the field), one of pro football's premier linebackers; Bobby Boyd, in my opinion an all-time, all-pro cornerback, so smart and quick, savvy, he could play an unheard-of ten yards off *any* receiver and still cover short passes in front of him; Lenny Lyles, intimidator extraordinaire, no talker he, just a hitter, a defensive back who once told me he wanted to "be as hard as the ground"; and Ordell Braase, experienced, one of the best pass rushers in football, a man who had been in the famous 1959 Colt overtime championship victory over the Giants, called by many the greatest football game ever played.

That was just the defense. On offense was John Unitas, nonpareil quarterback, able to throw long, short, soft, hard, a tough guy, smart (on the sidelines with Don Shula it was Unitas who did most of the talking), a Hall of Famer in absolutely everyone's opinion; John Mackey, prototype tight end, could catch a ball alone or in a crowd, fast as a sprinter, strong as a lineman, devastating blocker, 235 pounds of perfect football player; Willie Richardson, wide receiver, in a class with Paul Warfield and Otis Taylor, which means he breathed in rarefied atmosphere, able to make utterly spectacular catches, a gamebreaker of the first rank; Tom Matte, dubbed "a garbage player" because he was always there to turn loose balls or other mistakes into scores, an above average running back but also smart, almost as if he were another coach on the field; and Bob Vogel, a number one draft choice out of Ohio State, not a big offensive lineman (he was 245 or 250), but a student of his profession, very strong, he understood leverage and was an excellent blocker, for the run but especially for the pass few people ever got by Bob Vogel.

Even the Colt backups were outstanding, and I say this not because I was part of the team, but because it's true. Certainly our superb personnel, as I look back on Super Bowl III, only makes the memory of that loss to the Jets more unpalatable. It was just my sophomore year—I would play fourteen seasons in all, in three different decades—but later I was privileged to be part of some of the unquestionably great teams of all time, and believe I'm qualified to write about gifted athletes. Just such were many of the Colt reserves.

There was wide receiver Ray Perkins, who came in the same year I did (along with Bubba Smith, Charlie Stukes, Rick Volk, Ron Porter—clearly a vintage draft for the Colts), later coach of the New York Giants and now the successor to the legendary Bear Bryant at the University of Alabama. Perkins was a sophomore at the University of Alabama when Joe Namath was an all-America senior, and Namath's description, offered just a few days before Super Bowl III, of his former receiver's ability was a succinct single word: "Terrific." And Timmy Brown, backup to Tom Matte, formerly a big star with the Philadelphia Eagles and a slightly smaller one in the television series *Wild, Wild West* and the original movie version of *M*A*S*H*. Alex Hawkins, flanker, always entertaining when he came to practice inebriated, later a TV football commentator, a not-care-about-pain special-teams kamikaze who was devoid of fear (he and I were considered the leaders of the special teams, but I was smarter than Hawkins because I *was* often filled with fear). Hawkins was the type of guy whom hard-nosed coaches love. "Sacrificing his body" is a phrase modern announcers would use, or "eager to run post patterns," or "willing to take a hit." How about Gail Cogdill? A record-setting pass catcher with the Detroit Lions, but just a sub on this team.

But let me tell you about a real backup. Our backup quarterback was none other than Earl Morrall, this year (1968) voted the most valuable player in the NFL. A substitute on the Colts was good enough to be selected as the best player in the whole world of football! Morrall, of course, would start against the Jets in Super Bowl III in place of John Unitas, who was suffering from tendinitis in his right throwing elbow. None of us believed Unitas would see any action, so when he did it was yet another surprise in a dark day that would be filled with too many.

No one believed we would need Unitas that afternoon. In Super Bowls I and II, the NFL Green Bay Packers had laughed their way to easy victories over the AFL Kansas City Chiefs (35–10), and Oakland Raiders (33–14). Laugh was the right word. The Packers literally laughed themselves silly prior to Super Bowl II while watching films of the Oakland Raiders.

Most teams subscribe to the adage of letting sleeping dogs lie, but even here the Jets did us a favor. Joe Namath not only refused to let us be complacent, but went out of his way to stir us up. He said Earl Morrall, the NFL most valuable player, was not as good a quarterback as Oakland's Daryle Lamonica, known as the "Mad Bomber," or Babe Parilli, the Jets' backup. Now he may have been right where Lamonica was concerned, but usually such remarks are better left unsaid.

More interestingly, Joe was quoted in papers coast-to-coast as having said that the eighteen-and-a-half-point-under-dog Jets would *beat* the Colts. He "guaranteed" it, and the guarantee has become part of sports legend. Maybe it is better not to tamper with such stories (what child wants to hear that Babe Ruth didn't call his shot on that famous World Series home run off Charlie Root and the Cubs?), but I'll do it anyway: Joe made no such guarantee. The night in question he was drinking in the same bar as Lou Michaels (what else would two athletes preparing for the Super Bowl be doing?), and they had an argument. Joe made a series of statements, I have them on firsthand account, each prefaced with an if, for example, "*if* Verlon Biggs has a good day and can get to Earl Morrall," and "*if* Johnny Sample does a great job on Willie Richardson," and "*if* Jim Hudson can stifle John Mackey," *then* he would guarantee the victory. Of course, this was a far cry from a direct prediction that the Jets would win. I think one of the "if"s was keeping ferocious Bubba Smith out of the Jets' backfield, where he would try to tear Broadway Joe's head off, a highly unrealistic goal whose fulfillment was the responsibility of offensive tackle Dave Herman. We felt Bubba Smith versus Dave Herman meant a big advantage for our side.

Often a team will use the boasting of an opponent to fire

itself up. A coach will go out of his way to post disparaging remarks made by opposition players onto the locker-room bulletin board, where presumably they will have greater inspirational effect than would a Knute Rockne half-time speech. Namath's comments provided no such stimulus for us. We were the savage, street-wise Baltimore Colts, and he was the new, unproved kid on the block, almost a pip-squeak, he and his team, and real tough guys don't lower themselves to be rattled by adolescents. We would let our record speak for itself, and indeed at 15–1 it was one of the greatest in football history:

Baltimore	27	San Francisco	10
Baltimore	28	Atlanta	20
Baltimore	41	Pittsburgh	7
Baltimore	28	Chicago	7
Baltimore	42	San Francisco	14
Baltimore	20	Cleveland	30
Baltimore	27	Los Angeles	10
Baltimore	26	N.Y. Giants	0
Baltimore	27	Detroit	10
Baltimore	27	St. Louis	0
Baltimore	21	Minnesota	9
Baltimore	44	Atlanta	0
Baltimore	16	Green Bay	3
Baltimore	28	Los Angeles	24
Baltimore	24	Minnesota	14
Baltimore	34	Cleveland	0

In a seven-game period, from the first Los Angeles contest through the Green Bay match, our defense gave up *three* touchdowns. Total. Not three touchdowns rushing, or three passing. Three. "The Colts," said Jimmy the Greek, "have the greatest defensive team in football history."

We were coming into the Super Bowl with terrific momentum. Our final regular-season game, the 28–24 win over the Rams in the Los Angeles Coliseum, was against a team we respected much more than the Jets. The Rams finished the sea-

son at 10–3–1 (two of the losses to the Colts), and would have
made the playoffs easily if they'd been in a different division
from ours (no wild-card teams at this time). These were the
Rams of Roman Gabriel, Jack Snow, Bernie Casey, Deacon
Jones, Lamar Lundy, Jack Pardee, Merlin Olsen, Dick Bass,
Maxie Baughan, and Myron Pottios.

Offensively I'd had my finest day at this point in my career
as a pro against the Rams: a 46-yard kickoff return, a 61-yard
touchdown catch from Earl Morrall, and a 9-yard touchdown
catch on a swing pass from Unitas. Other individual highlights
in a season where I saw spot duty as a running back, fullback,
defensive back, and special-teams player, were a 102-yard kickoff return in Detroit, an 86-yard kickoff return in San Francisco,
and an NFL-leading kickoff-return average of more than 35
yards.

In the Western Conference championship game we opened
a 21–0 lead on the Vikings in the third quarter and coasted in at
24–14. The Vikings, another team we didn't believe the Jets belonged on the same field with, featured Alan Page, Carl Eller,
Jim Marshall, Joe Kapp, Bill Brown, Ron Yary, and Paul
Krause. These were the Purple People Eaters when they were
young, just on the verge of being good enough to appear in four
Super Bowls. Most professional players never made a single
one.

The Sunday after taking apart the Vikings, we played what
one sportswriter called "perfect football" in defeating the
Browns in their own park, 34–0, the first time Cleveland had
been shut out in 143 games. The remarkable thing about this
score is that Cleveland had a truly great team, with such players
as Paul Warfield, Bill Nelsen, Tommy McDonald, Leroy Kelly,
Ernie Green, Bill Glass, Erich Barnes, Gary Collins, Gene Hick-
erson, Walter Johnson, Bob Matheson, and Monte Clark. We
were sky-high for Cleveland, playing with barely controlled fe-
rocity. I was half-crazed myself. On a punt I blocked one of the
Browns, almost went down on my back, and because he was
getting away from me, God forbid, I twisted around and blocked
him again, with the back of my shoulder and the *back of my
head.*

We flew into Fort Lauderdale the day after New Year's, a
Thursday, most of us happy to be in warm, sunny Florida after

that last game in bone-chilling Municipal Stadium with its wicked Lake Erie wind. Our headquarters was the Statler Hilton, right on the beach, just a mile away from where the Jets were housed, at the Galt Ocean Mile Hotel.

My roommate at the Statler Hilton was Cornelius Johnson, called "Corny," offensive guard, six feet two and 255, graduated from Virginia Union; he could have been mistaken for Lou Ferrigno's "the Hulk" except Corny was bigger and had more muscles. Nobody said a lot to rile Corny. He was the strongest player on the Colts, except maybe for Glenn Ressler (nobody knew how strong he was), looked it with his arms as thick as tree trunks, and it was a mistake to think you could outrun him. Fierce as he looked, however, a chief habit of Corny's was giggling, something not many people wanted to get close enough to him to learn.

The first two days in Florida were for taking it easy. The serious drills wouldn't begin until later, and the time off couldn't have been more welcome. Both we and the Jets had played football for twenty straight Sundays, including exhibition games, a brutal schedule for one of the most violent and physically demanding games mankind has yet to devise. I doubted that there was a player on either team who wasn't hurt, including the kickers. The two days off gave precious time for bruised bodies to rest.

It's hard to explain to nonathlete friends of mine just how violent professional football is, and I doubt if many fans, watching on television or sitting in the stands, have much of a conception either. Many of them may have played high-school football, and a few made it as far as the college game, but even those spectators do not, cannot, realize how rugged the sport is at the professional level. Down on the field you can hear it—the crack of helmets sounding like artillery rounds, the fearful, elemental grunts of the big men in the trenches, the brittle sound of a bone snapping, or, worse, the terrible shriek when a knee and maybe a career is lost—grown men growling like ferocious bears and sobbing as little children might, and you need to hear the noise to understand even a little bit. But even that is not enough.

Most fans can't comprehend how agile, talented, and

strong these athletes are. They have nothing in their experiences against which to compare it. A friend of mine who has known many gifted athletes told me of how he once sat at the U.S. Open in Forest Hills and watched Pancho Gonzales play tennis. Next to my friend was a father and his little boy. The boy asked, worship for his father in his eyes, "Dad, how would you do against Mr. Gonzales?" Solemnly, the father thought it over. He was probably a weekend player at his country club, maybe one of the better ones in his particular set. He wanted to be truthful with his boy. "Well, son," he said, "Mr. Gonzales would probably beat me three-six, three-six."

My friend snorted when he told the story. "I wanted to tell that guy, 'Three-six, three-six, you've got to be joking. You'd be lucky if Gonzales didn't knock your eye out with his first serve.' "

Pro-football players tend to hang around other pro-football players, and with reason. They feel other people generally do not understand them or their business, and after a while they give up trying to explain. Imagine this conversation, one similar to many I've heard:

> Player: Got to see the dentist. Hit Earl Campbell yesterday and four teeth disappeared somewhere straight up into my head.
>
> Friend: I know what you mean. We had this big sucker in junior high. Must've flunked a couple grades, 'cause he was bigger than everybody else. I used to hate to tackle that dude.
>
> Player: Yeah, I'll bet he was tough. The trouble was, Campbell was coming at me straight on, and . . .
>
> Friend: Well, you don't have to tell me. This tough guy came at me straight on one time, and I was looking for a place to hide. I know exactly how it feels.
>
> Player: Right.

Without an ounce of exaggeration, let me describe what would happen to, say, the average thirty-year-old who has competed in high-school football if he ran a single play in the NFL. Let's assume our imaginary man is in fairly decent condition, he jogs and works out a couple times a week, and doctors might say he is in pretty good shape. We'll call the man Homer.

When Homer trots onto the field he will immediately become disoriented by the riot of colors and the maddening, deafening noise of the crowd. A fan in the stands does not hear what the players do, standing as they are in a valley, in the bowl of the stadium. The sounds, coming from all sides, are awesome, overwhelming. Nothing in Homer's past has prepared him for this, surely no high-school game, and next he will notice the players. He is a maple sapling set down in a forest of redwoods, a Lilliputian in the land of the Brobdingnagians. In the huddle, the quarterback rattles off numbers, directions, colors, formations, and Homer's brain is as confused as his body.

Homer is lined up now. He is the running back in an I-back formation. Over the butts of his teammates he sees mountains, for that is what these defensive players are, and the mountains have the cruel, cold eyes of animals, darting back and forth, heads stationary, big cat eyes, or bear eyes, peering through face masks, hard, hateful, suspicious, hungry beasts who truly believe Homer wants to steal their food.

The play is designed to go between guard and tackle. When the ball is snapped Homer hears noises that are unbelievable, sounds that might come from Dante's hell, animals eating one another, ripping and rending flesh, but these are human beings, and the snarls and roars are because they want to tear him apart. Homer doesn't doubt this. He can't. His mind won't let him.

The coach has told Homer to run through a hole between guard and tackle, but any running back who has ever played this game will tell you there is no such thing as a hole. There might be a narrow strip or shaft of light, never anything more than that, and Homer must head for it. The offensive and defensive lines are locked in titanic, World War I-style trench combat, but there is that tiny slit he might glide through. His linemen, huge, cursing men, have held their blocks, and he hears the angry screaming of the maniacs against whom he is being protected.

Homer is going full speed, the coach has insisted on that,

and suddenly, looming (that is the right word) up ahead, blotting out the sun and the clouds and the sky, forget that slit of light, is a linebacker. We'll call him Lawrence Taylor, but he could have many names. Lawrence Taylor is six feet four and 240 pounds, and dislikes running backs. He is pathological about running backs. Homer sees Taylor's foot move, like a bull pawing the ground, and he can't believe, it's almost as if it were a dream, that this giant has been in a crouch. But he has been. Now he emits a whoop, eerie, terrifying, joyful (can Taylor really enjoy this?), and rises to the height of a colossus, his arms stretching out like the wingspan of a 747.

Homer is hit first by the helmet, an instant later by the shoulder pads, right in the pit of the stomach, and words don't exist to describe the pain and the shock, especially the shock, and his stomach retches and he wants to die. But it's not over. It has barely begun.

First a muscle tears, feeling like a sharp stick being pushed all the way through the body, front to back, a stick of lightning loose in the innards, nuclear-meltdown-hot in the stomach, the brain shouting the message, "Body under attack. Alert. Body under attack," but the message is useless; what good is this information, there is absolutely, utterly, no defense.

Yet the agony has only *begun*. Lawrence Taylor has been taught to use his legs, keep them moving, and Lawrence Taylor is a very good student. He will try to drive right *through* Homer. Now ligaments, muscles, and cartilages are being torn and ripped; Homer can hear and feel them rending and tearing, but he can't see, the world is dark for him, as if he were sinking deeper and deeper into a lagoon, his mind dizzy, whirling in a suction pool, down and down.

But Homer is being lifted *up*. Taylor, driving through, is also hoisting, and Homer is hanging there, a target, tackling dummy dangling off the hard turf. Taylor's teammates come. Pow! A helmet, the force of a sledgehammer behind it, pounds into the dummy's rib cage. Pow! Pow! From front and back in the classic sandwich come the hits, one in the small of the back, the other over the heart, delivered by big men who can kill with these blows, the only mercy being that Homer can no longer feel, no longer know that his body resembles a bizarre Tinkertoy. POW! This last blow is a forearm to the head, a wild, ax-wielding, free swing-chop which lumberjacks use to fell trees.

No longer is Homer at his apex in the air. He is coming down, Lawrence Taylor still holding him as he might a broken rag doll, the hands of other teammates ripping at his face mask, fingers clawing at eyes no longer seeing, the worst about to happen, here it is!

Homer's back is driven into the turf, as if a pile driver has planted him there. God didn't make the heart and central-nervous system to withstand this, and half-a-wink-of-an-eye later comes the fury of 240 pounds of Lawrence Taylor onto Homer's chest, an explosion of such bomb-bursting force that a crater has been created, a hole too shallow for the purpose, but literally what Homer now needs has been started.

Similarly true reconstructions could be provided to anyone who believes a down of pro football might be invigorating. Is it necessary to describe, for example, the mayhem someone like Mean Joe Green would wreak on a part-timer looking for a lark by trying to stop his pass rush? Or trying to launch a blitz against, say, an angry three-hundred-pound tackle like Joe Jacoby of the Redskins? Or running a post pattern over the middle against Ronnie Lott? The receiver might as well try to catch the ball, because he'll be hit regardless. I chose the fictitious Homer to be a running back, because for fourteen years, over three decades, I played that position in the NFL, and *everything* that happened to Homer, except his demise, happened to me.

Although it seemed a madhouse at the time, there was a touch of country fair to Super Bowl III, a relaxed and even laid-back environment that would be unheard-of now. Sportswriters and even fans had easy access to the players, something that could hardly occur at present, with management being extra-cautious about security requirements. Who the players talk with is carefully monitored now, and even a whiff of something resembling a scandal (talking to a friend who has a second cousin who has a neighbor who has a third cousin who is a bookmaker) can dry the throats of the NFL brass. They have a good thing going and don't want to take chances. Who can blame them? But who can blame players who occasionally complain of being spied upon?

But it wasn't that way, as I've said, during Super Bowl III. A lot of things were changing. This was the next-to-last year of the AFL. The merger would be in effect for the 1970 regular season, and for the first time teams like the Jets and the Vikings could compete against each other in something other than the Super Bowl. This wasn't the best arrangement for football players, who previously could sell their talents to the highest bidder. Now, once again, there would be just one bidder, the NFL, and the situation was not really different from, say, a worker in an industry where there is only one company. Of course, it was specifically because players earned higher pay with the existence of the AFL that the merger had gone through. The AFL had been willing to pay for talent precisely so that the NFL would scream uncle. It wasn't one company (say the New York Jets) trying to take business away from a competitor (the New York Giants) to produce a better product, to *compete,* but to force a merger, create a monopoly so there would be *less* competition.

Our first two days in Florida were spent getting used to the new environment. Workouts were in sweatsuits—helmets, but no shoulder pads or hitting allowed—and lasted an hour and forty-five minutes. There were wind sprints (my time in the forty has always been between 4.5 and 4.6), but mainly the purpose of the drills was to maintain timing, a certain easy edge, not to get completely away from the sport.

Head Coach Don Shula had an interesting way of approaching the "big" game, not that much different from that of Chuck Noll and Tom Landry, for whom I would later play. Shula thought as little as possible should change. If you did something consistently during the regular season, it was inadvisable to alter the routine. I'm not talking here just about plays, but about everyday life, including practice sessions. For the big game Shula wasn't going to introduce some monstrous practice regimen, or go the opposite way and figure we'd be looser if the sessions were less strenuous. What you got from Shula was that to which you'd become accustomed.

Shula was a different sort from the coach of the Jets, Weeb Ewbank. Ewbank was sixty-one, short, round, easygoing, and possessed a brilliant football mind. Shula, thirty-eight, was strong and forceful. He attracted a tremendous reputation as a defensive coach with the Detroit Lions, beginning in 1960. The

Lions were one of the great defensive teams in history, led by the likes of Alex Karras, Lem Barney, and Joe Schmidt, not to mention the inimitable Night Train Lane. Don's record at Baltimore heading into Super Bowl III was an outstanding 65–18–3.

There is a lot of loose talk about what a dynasty consists of in sports, and if a team goes all the way even in a single season, you are likely to hear the word applied. But I think the Colts really were. We had not had a losing season since 1957; our record was 116–53, a .686 winning percentage. "The Green Bay Packers," said *The New York Times,* "in the time of Vince Lombardi, were said to be a dynasty. These dynasties in professional sports seldom last a decade. The Baltimore Colts are a dynasty and their Super Bowl appearance is the climax to one that has endured beyond a decade."

Don Shula is a "yell" type coach, as opposed to Tom Landry, whom you won't find standing in a player's face and screaming. I saw Shula administer some brutal verbal beatings, loudly and with great vehemence, but seldom did he use curse words. On one occasion Colt middle linebacker Mike Curtis, during a practice session, put a terrific hit on a wide receiver, and you'd have thought Shula had gone crazy. Curtis was in the wrong here (why was he punishing his own teammate?), and Shula, shaking the bleachers with his roars, let him know. Bubba Smith was another one Shula yelled at, perhaps more than any other player, because Bubba was a poor practice player. Bubba was not alone in this category. I've seen other athletes of extraordinary ability who, probably because they were so gifted, did not perform at their peak during practice.

I've been asked if it isn't rather dangerous for a coach to yell at individuals like Mike Curtis and Bubba Smith. The answer is no. A player knows he can forget his career if he ever attacks a head coach. It's just something you don't do. Plenty of times players will fight with assistant coaches, but the head man is untouchable.

Perhaps Shula's greatest talent, and he has many, is his ability to judge a player on what he can become, not on what he is. I was a *basketball* player at the University of Illinois, never played a down in college football, and Shula drafted me. He saw what I *could become.* Another example is linebacker Ted Hendricks, called "the Mad Stork," drafted by Shula out of the Uni-

versity of Miami to a chorus of guffaws by many in the football
intelligentsia. Hendricks was too thin. He looked like a stork.
He'd be snapped in two. "Experts" said this bean pole could
never play in the NFL. But Shula saw what others could not.

As the Super Bowl drills became more serious, the form of
Don Shula loomed larger and larger. During practices he circu-
lated among the athletes, got down in the trenches with them,
so to speak, inserted himself right in the middle of everything
that was going on. What a contrast this was to my later years
under Tom Landry. The two, almost equally successful (after
all these years they are only one or two career wins apart), are a
study in contrasts. Landry stood apart from his players, aloof,
distant, and from afar watched his various teams go through
their assigned drills. Assistant coaches played the top sergeant
role which Shula, but not Landry, could so easily assume. But
you didn't hear Landry screaming. It just wasn't part of the
man. When one drill was over he would blow his whistle and the
players would begin another, or if it was time—and you always
knew it was—you would gather around Landry and he would
give a talk. But he wasn't screaming. He wasn't raising his voice.

For Super Bowl III I had several roles, including special
teams, backup running back, and backup defensive back. But
chiefly up to this time I'd been considered an offensive back.

The only player in the Jets-Colts game with previous
Super Bowl experience was our center, Bill Curry, now a thir-
teen-year veteran, who started for the Packers against Kansas
City in Super Bowl I. Everyone was interested in what the ven-
erable Curry had to say, not the least being the Colts themselves. What Curry mainly talked about was Vince Lombardi:
"He coached through fear. Most of the Packers were afraid of
him, of his scoldings and sarcasm. It's a form of motivation that
works for some people. But it didn't work for me."

Curry told us about how he so feared watching game films
and Lombardi pointing out his mistakes, that the dread started
before the game was even finished. He said he came "close to
being a mental case." I found it interesting that Lombardi's al-
ready-legendary practices, compared almost to Bataan death
marches or the forced labor of peons in salt mines, were thought
by Curry not to be as difficult as Shula's. "The Colts work

harder," Curry stated flatly, "have more contact in practices, than the Packers."

Shula's acquiring of Curry was typical of the coach's shrewd methods of acquiring key personnel. After Super Bowl I, according to Curry, because he'd twisted an ankle and thus inflamed Lombardi by having to come out of the game, he was left off Green Bay's exempt list in the expansion draft and New Orleans selected him. Whereupon Shula traded reserve quarterback Gary Cuozzo to the Saints for Curry and *two draft* choices. One of these was Bubba Smith! Therefore, for a quarterback who never made it big in the NFL—Cuozzo—Shula acquired two top starters, Curry and Bubba.

Which, if I may, brings me back to Bubba Smith. Just by himself he could make you think you couldn't lose. And he was a mountain, one of the most scary-looking people I have ever known. I remember one time when he came off the field. It had been raining and he was sweating. His body heat mixed with the water and sweat *popping* off his body reminded me of a monster emerged out of a lagoon.

Gone from our team was Jim Parker, an all-time great offensive tackle who had been with the Colts during my rookie year. The words *gigantic, mammoth,* and *monster* only begin to describe Parker. Physically, his head was the largest I had ever seen, and right in the middle of his forehead was a huge dent. For days I studied that dent. I decided it could only have come from hitting people with his head.

But Jim Parker was interesting, and not in the stereotyped way people too often think of football players, especially linemen. For example, Parker feared flying. I recall one time when he was in the restroom of a plane. He was as big as the restroom. The plane took one of those little dips, the kind that make your stomach fall a little, and the door came off the hinges and almost flew through the side of the aircraft as Parker charged out looking for an escape. This giant, feared by many of the toughest people in football, had a number of his own fears: snakes, for instance, which is why prankster Tom Matte kept one in his locker. Trouble was, Parker believed earthworms were snakes, and you didn't need a king cobra or a boa constrictor to shake him up.

We got the game plan for Super Bowl III on Monday, January 6, six days before the contest. For the offense this consisted of a single typed sheet of paper, a fact I think would surprise the average pro-football fan, who has fantasized a game plan to be some ultraexotic document never to be seen by ordinary mortals (later in the book I will reproduce an actual 1980 Cowboys game plan). Some fans even think a game plan might be as intricate and top secret as a cloak-and-dagger CIA file. Come to think of it, the fan may not be far from wrong. I've never seen a top-secret CIA file, but I wouldn't be surprised if it were as prosaic as an NFL game plan. Yet, simple and uninspiring as the secret-agency file or the football-game plan appears on the surface, a great deal of thought, research, and planning went into producing it. And it could be a disaster should the game plan leak to the enemy.

But not necessarily. Even if a defense could stand in the offensive huddle, hear the play being called, and understand what that play is, it would be no guarantee the play would be stopped. Many times audibles (changing the call at the line of scrimmage) are employed, and even if no audible is used, the offensive player, a running back, say, may change course in midstream—perhaps because of great reaction time—and confound everybody. How many times have you seen a running back head up the middle, then veer outside and go for long yardage?

In any event, the defense often does know what is coming. Smart defensive players look into a back's eyes. Often, if he is not a great back, he will be sneaking a glance at where the play is intended to be run. This is only natural—this attempt to get a lay of the land before it has to be traveled—but it can also be disastrous. The great backs, O.J. or Franco, stare straight ahead, and just naturally their peripheral vision allows them to see off to the side where they will be going. Other players, without the peripheral vision of a Simpson or a Harris, learn to trick defensive players. They may be sneaking a glance in one direction while having every intention of running in the other.

Actually, a tremendous amount of work goes into preparing a game plan, especially the one for the Super Bowl, and consists entirely of what you intend to do to your opponent. Its final form has been prepared by the coaches, but the scouts have had input, and perhaps anyone else who has knowledge of the team you're up against. A game plan is designed to attack individuals (supposed weak links on the opposition), or the entire team, or both. Cowboy game plans always attack both, but it was something else for the Colts and Shula in preparing for Super Bowl III and the Jets.

The Jets were a mystery to us; rather, their 3-4 (3 down linemen, 4 linebackers) defense was a mystery. No team in the NFL used it, and we had never faced it before. It wasn't that we scoffed at the 3-4. We just didn't know much about it. Had we known that to a large degree it was the wave of the future, we'd have been infinitely better prepared, but as it was, we weren't aware of why the defense stunted, or even how. I suppose we were similar to the first team in history who faced the T-formation, after a lifetime of competing against the single wing. That team might have been superior to its opponent, but the slick, modern, streamlined T placed it at a big disadvantage, like a man with a bow and arrow against a man with a rifle.

The Baltimore game plan assumed the Jets were outmanned, and they were, but it wasn't as if they were a Pop Warner team. They were professional athletes, and some of them—Namath, Matt Snell, Don Maynard, George Sauer, Emerson Boozer, Johnny Sample, Verlon Biggs—would have been stars in the NFL. But since the Jets were outmanned, we figured we would use what had worked for us in the past and allowed us to run up that 15-1 record, many of the victories against teams we considered superior to the Jets, and our nod to the mystery of the 3-4 was to use plays AFL teams had employed successfully. Of course we didn't believe even this was necessary; we'd simply take the field and outhit them, block more crisply, rattle their teeth with our tackling, use our superior athletic skills to provide them numerous looks at our backs. There would be satisfaction in teaching Joe Namath humility, but that was no big motivating factor. A mother cat might swat her kitten to teach a lesson, but takes no joy in the action.

In midweek before Super Bowl III the length and *intensity* of our practices increased. We were getting ready now. These meat-and-potato practices are unlike any that high-school teams have. High-school teams in practice go close to full tilt. The pros operate at perhaps 75 percent. What is there to prove in practice by going all-out and getting hurt? If you are good enough to get into the NFL, certainly courage is not often in question, nor is desire. And in the multimillion-dollar world of pro football, the players are too valuable to risk having them injured in practice. There is plenty of opportunity when the game begins to get yourself hurt, and the truth is no one ever played in the NFL without getting injured, many seriously, permanently, for life. Don Shula had been absolutely right by blowing up at Mike Curtis.

We had to generate our own intensity, but it wasn't difficult. If you couldn't get yourself up for this game, the *world* championship, nothing in life was going to excite you. I was amazed once to hear a boxer explain his loss in a championship fight to Muhammad Ali by saying he "couldn't get up" for the bout. I couldn't understand what he was talking about. Couldn't get up? Why was he a boxer? If he couldn't get up for Muhammad Ali, with the world title on the line, what did trigger his adrenal glands? I knew the Colts were up for the game. If a player hadn't been, he would have had to listen to living legend John Unitas, or human mountain Bubba Smith, or slavemaster Don Shula.

Money was important. A lot more important than it is now, where elite ballplayers make more in a season than the average citizen is paid in a lifetime. Losing World Series or Super Bowl money, as large an amount as that is, does not spell financial hardship for a Dave Winfield or a Dan Fouts.

My rookie-year pay was $15,000, with a $1,000 signing bonus, but I didn't make that much. My pay was immediately cut in half, to $7,500, when I was assigned to the taxi squad, and it didn't reach the $15,000 level—based on receiving a paycheck semimonthly—until I was activated at midseason. My salary in my second year—the Super Bowl year—was again $15,000, but when I was made a backup on offense as well as defense, I went to Carroll Rosenbloom and asked for more money. This was quite a scene, the black kid from Freeport, Illinois, talking money with one of the shrewdest capitalists in America. Rosenbloom lifted my pay to $18,000 a year.

Each player on the winning team from Super Bowl III would receive $15,000. This was more, for *one game,* than I'd been paid for my *entire first season.* And I needed the money, I had a family to support. It was the same with other Colts. Very few were making what even then would be considered big salaries. John Unitas, at $100,000 a year (he'd be making $1,000,000-plus today), was our highest paid. It amazes me still, and if I were inclined to dwell on the matter (I'm not, though many retired athletes do), I could curse the fates that had me born too early. Think of this: Pete Rose makes more money in a year than Joe DiMaggio was paid in his career; John Elway's *signing bonus* was larger than the *combined lifetime football pay* of Jim Brown, Sammy Baugh, Lou Groza, and Red Grange.

Enough about money for now. Clearly, $15,000 meant a great deal to me and all the other Colts. I've been asked if the outcome of the game would have been different had it been winner take all. Would we have been less confident? Better prepared? Winner take all would have been something, and surely not anything a mother would have wanted her children watching (someone like Mike Curtis would have more resembled a hungry lion defending its last scrap of food against a marauder than a human being—come to think of it, he wasn't *much* different from that anyway), but I do not think the outcome would have changed.

It is not that we let ourselves get out of shape, that we took it easy, or took the Jets too lightly. We were playing for the championship of the world, we were on edge, and we played as hard as we could. Only hindsight would have allowed us to know that our offense wouldn't function against the 3-4. The thought of losing was just not in our mind—as I'm sure it seldom was with Muhammad Ali in his prime—and I'm still not certain that is an unhealthy attitude. We were ready to play our best. We didn't let up on training, allowing ourselves to become physically less than at our peak. To imagine the Jets as a team that could defeat us would have required deceiving ourselves, which perhaps is what a solid favorite should do. But is this even possible? How could Muhammad Ali, time after time, persuade himself that his next opponent was a threat, when over and over again these individuals proved not to be? I don't know.

A healthy dose of fear never hurt any person or team, and maybe we should have convinced ourselves there was reason to fear, but I don't think it would have made any difference.

In this Super Bowl, the 3-4 defense, not the Jets, would prove to be our real nemesis.

2
Super Bowl III

I was up just after five A.M. on January 12, Super Bowl morning, thinking about the game and what lay ahead. My wife, Linda, had long since replaced Cornelius Johnson as my roommate, and she was up with me, just as the night before we'd been together for a quiet dinner and a few hours of television. Linda was more nervous than I was that morning. After the game she would be just as exhausted.

Usually players take taxis or drive their own cars to the stadium for home games, but this was at the neutral site, the Orange Bowl, and the Colts traveled by team bus. It was a strangely quiet group of football players. No loud talk, as was the norm for regular season games. We all knew this was something special, though how special no one could have realized until years later. Some of the very greatest players in the game have never participated in a Super Bowl.

The locker room was quiet too. Tense. I thought I'd never felt such tension. Each player is different, and should be left alone. I saw Billy Ray Smith throw up. Nothing unusual there. He always threw up before a game. We'd have worried if he hadn't thrown up.

Mike Curtis sat alone. Even if you wanted to bother Mike, you could see that to do so would be crazy. He was withdrawing inside himself, into a world I imagine is the color red, and you

could actually watch him grow bigger as he sat boiling in a rag-
ing, self-induced fury. Take long enough and you could see his
game face being etched, angry, fierce, bones ready to burst
through skin, the throb of blood vessels visible on forearms and
neck.

John Unitas and Earl Morrall seemed calmer than most of
the others. In the locker room they tossed footballs back and
forth, just as if they were already outside, warming up, putting
zip on the ball, God help anyone who got in the way. These men
have arms like howitzers, can knock a man down at twenty
yards with a thrown football.

Other players banged their fists on teammates' shoulder
pads, crack, crack, *crack,* while still others hit themselves hard
on the head with open and shut fists. Ways of warming up, getting loose. Ways to be sure the first hit in the actual game was
not delivered to a body too tight to take it.

Mainly I was awed. By the game itself, the stakes, and the
fact that *I* was in it. Many people still thought of me as a basketball player. That was fine. I allayed some of my nervousness
(some of these players, my *teammates,* had been childhood
idols of mine) by convincing myself the game didn't depend on
anything I did. I was a backup running back and fullback,
backup defensive back, and would play special teams. I knew
what I had to do, and just hoped everyone else felt the same
way. This was a pretty cocky attitude, and naïve also, since I
would be returning kickoffs and in a position to win the game
with a sensational run, or lose it with an ignominious fumble.
But it's how I felt. Maybe it's what kept me partially sane before the biggest game I had ever played.

When we first took to the field of the Orange Bowl some
ninety minutes before the three P.M. kickoff, I was once again
surprised (we had, of course, worked out on the field) by how
deep and thick the grass was. And I could smell the sea in the
air, snappy, pungent, salt and wind that reminded of old sailing
stories. I kept filling my lungs with the air, feeling it clear my
chest and nose and head. It felt wonderful. It would be even
more wonderful in a few hours when we were champions of the
world.

My best friend on the Colts at this time was Corny Johnson, and I managed to get over close to him on the field. In the

locker room I'd heard veterans talk about what they intended to do with their Super Bowl money. I thought it could be a diversion for me also. With my friend Corny, of course. I didn't talk about such things with John Unitas.

"What are you going to do with your money?" I asked.

"Build an addition on our house." Corny had a home in Virginia.

"That all?"

"It'll help with the baby."

He was always talking about adopting babies. Lots of them. I thought he'd make a good father. Later he did adopt a son. I haven't kept in touch with Corny, but I'm sure my impressions were correct: Corny and his wife would be great with kids.

"What are you gonna do, Pres?"

"I don't know. Maybe take Linda to Hermiston."

"Second honeymoon?"

"First. You should know that." Linda and I had been married during the season. Corny had been best man.

"You really like it out there."

"Big trees. Big mountains. Narrow roads running between. You'd like it too. It will be fun. After this game."

Linda's folks lived in Hermiston, Oregon, which is near Pendleton, site of a famous rodeo and birthplace of Bob Lilly. Despite travels as an athlete, I really hadn't seen much of America, but I knew there weren't many better places than this. It would be good to visit there. Maybe live there.

"What about when you come back?"

"I might not."

"Cut it out."

"Finish school, I guess. I'm going to finish."

I had twelve credits to complete. My ambition was to be a teacher and a coach, and thus I had majored in physical education, with minors in biology and recreation. I knew nothing would stop me from getting those last twelve credits, that the University of Illinois hadn't seen the last of me. As I jogged away from Corny, however, I knew all the schooling in the world—at least for coaching—could never be as valuable as what I was learning with the Colts. I've mentioned Don Shula. Three other Colt coaches were Chuck Noll (soon to gain fame with the Steelers); Bill Arnsbarger, considered perhaps the top defensive genius of all time, later head coach of the Giants, the man who molded the great Dolphin defenses and was now in charge at Louisiana State University; and Don McCafferty, who replaced Shula and quietly won a Super Bowl. Many potential coaches would give a lot to get the kind of experience I was being paid to obtain.

The stands were fairly well filled before we went into the locker room for the final moments before the kickoff, and it was even quieter in the Colt locker room this time. There wasn't much for the players to say to one another, and no need for false bravado or holler guys to get people whipped up. We were a seasoned professional army, efficient and businesslike, trained to a perfect pitch, and now there was a job to be done, not well, but brilliantly, the way we'd done it 34–0 against Cleveland two weeks before.

I think the reference to an army is very apt. Most coaches, I believe, would take it as a compliment. The good coaches, I'm convinced, would have been fine generals, and it would not surprise me to learn that Shula was a great student of Patton and MacArthur, or Landry of Robert E. Lee, or Lombardi of Napoleon or some other military strategist. I know for a fact that Woody Hayes of Ohio State possessed both detailed and voluminous knowledge of Civil War history. Top coaches train their teams much like the way armies are trained (including many of the petty and make-work jobs GIs have learned to bear), and the tactics employed (deception, all-out charges, probes for weak points) are like those used in battle. The terminology is even similar: blitz, bomb, containment, sweep, and so on. Coaches are often authoritarian types, in love with the concepts of precision and discipline, and so are generals.

The locker room now was really still, almost like a church sanctuary, except for the occasional scruff of a cleat. I know I was going over in my mind what I would have to do, going over it for the thousandth time, and I assume others were too. Specifically I was thinking about returning kickoffs. *You have to catch the ball first,* I reminded myself. *You have to catch the ball. Be in position to run the instant you have the ball, but first catch it.*

It was such a little thing, but on such matters can the out-

come of games be determined. There have been many speed
rockets in the game, real burners, but if they think ahead to
scoring a touchdown or making a spectacular run, and don't
catch the ball first, what contribution have they made? It is a
lesson I learned in training camp of my rookie year, and never
forgot it. I came off the practice field one day and spotted a
flicker of light coming from a meeting room where the movies
of games were shown. I looked inside and saw Raymond Berry,
the short-on-talent-but-not-on-performance All-Pro receiver,
hunched over the projector. On his head was a miner's helmet
with one of those little lights, which he was using to read plays.
Berry might have been there forever, so frozen in time did he
seem, and the impression was that he would never leave. This
marvelous receiver was one of several players I encountered in
my career whom I tried to emulate. This day he was scribbling
notes, like "WBIH," to himself on scraps of paper. They reminded me of radio station call letters, and I asked him what
they meant. "Watch ball into hands," he said. It was simple, but
if you remembered it during a game, it meant the difference between catching a ball and dropping it.

Two important matters remained before we went onto the
floor of the Orange Bowl for the game. The first was a talk from
Don Shula. He stood in front of us, spiffy in his tasteful attire
(he'd look good on the post-game victory show), his demeanor
deadly serious. No yelling now. No dramatics. No "win one for
the Gipper" speech (I never heard one of these in fourteen years
of pro football). No last-minute trick play, so secret it could not
be revealed until moments before kickoff. Shula was just a general—before the biggest battle of all—and he told us what we
had to do to win.

"You're a better team than the Jets." I remember these
were his first words. "But you have to prove it." The rest of
Shula's talk was reminding us what we'd learned in practice,
what was necessary for victory. Do this, he said. Do that. Don't
do this. It was really quite basic. If we did everything he had
taught us, he said, we would win, nothing had been left to
chance in this game. We believed him. But we just weren't,
couldn't have been, prepared for that 3-4.

Shula's talk completed, the players grew restless again. We
were bulls penned up too long. We wanted to go out and romp.

Or maybe some were thoroughbreds, Willie Richardson, say, or
John Mackey, and it was time to race. I understand why a
"Gipper" speech wouldn't work in the NFL. Assuming the players would respond to it, the result could very well be the opposite of what was intended. You don't want players *too* revved
up. They can become prone to mistakes. A defensive lineman,
blood in his eyes, ready to annihilate the quarterback for the
Gipper, or whomever, would be an easy mark for a trap block. A
back could easily overrun an opening. The adrenaline pumping
in a quarterback could make his passes sizzling, uncatchable
bullets. What is needed, among many, many other things, is
controlled fury. Wild men running through walls to get to the
field might have worked in Rockne's day, though I suspect the
stories are exaggerated, but not now, when the offenses and defenses are so fine-tuned and sophisticated. Clear heads are
needed.

One last time the room grew quiet. Even the atheists, so
called (it wasn't hard to get this epithet), bowed their heads for
the Lord's Prayer. Every team I have been on has said the "Our
Father" as a last act before going out to play.

I've been asked if I've been on an NFL team that prayed to
the Lord to win. The answer is no. On the face of it that seems
silly to me. What if the other team is also praying to win? What
we pray for is to do our best, that no one is seriously injured,
and as thanks for having the opportunity to play in such a
game.

Anyway, this last prayer is often quite moving. Great athletes, some of them subjects of tremendous adulation, for a moment at least, acknowledge a power far larger than their own.

There was a moment, a fraction of an instant, just after the
Amen, when there was no sound at all, not even breathing, and
then there came forth a noise that might have started in the
deep bowels of hell, crashing loud, elemental, a mixture of exal-
tation and fury in a terrifying, jarring cacophony—maybe the
Romans heard this when Attila attacked—that must have
shook the Orange Bowl itself, perhaps rattling buildings outside
and even boats out in the bay. Most human ears have not heard
sounds so forceful and fearful as the initial roar of a professional
football team the instant before it heads through the tunnel to
the field.

I ran, as wild as the rest, for there was really nothing else to do. A person would be trampled if he tried to stand still. Oddly, the last thing I remember seeing as we headed out to the sunshine of the Orange Bowl was a message hung on the locker-room wall, probably by one of our assistant coaches. It read: CAN JOE NAMATH DO WHAT HE SAYS?

Namath had wondered why we had signs such as this. He said we were in trouble if we needed reminders to get us fired up, and he wondered if they showed that we had doubts about our invincibility. I think the opposite was true. The reminders should have worried *him*. They were intended to keep us from being overconfident, to instill a little fear, and make us more dangerous when we attacked him. Either way, the message, in my opinion, had little effect.

We had to wait for the introductions before beginning. Our defense, rightly I thought, was introduced, and so was the Jets' offense. That would be the battle. I couldn't believe the Jets would even score against us. We could play forever, or until Lou Michaels kicked a field goal, but they wouldn't score. Bubba and Mike and Braase would push them back into the ocean. The Cleveland Browns, *in Cleveland,* with Leroy Kelly and Paul Warfield, had scored zero in the NFL Championship game. I remember what Norm Van Brocklin, coach of the Atlanta Falcons and former great quarterback, said when asked what he thought of Joe Namath. "I'll tell you what I think about Namath on Sunday night," Van Brocklin said, "after he has played his first pro game."

The introductions helped fire us up more. As each name was called, the roar from the sold-out crowd heightened even further our already soaring emotions. A crowd can indeed whip a team up. It's nonsense when a player says he's not affected by fan reaction.

I had mixed feelings about the coin toss. I'd be returning the kickoff if we won the toss, and in a way I wanted to get it over with, become part of the game from the start in a big way. I knew also that the team wanted to go on offense immediately, march right down the field and put points on the scoreboard, give the Jets a quick dose of the NFL and what they could expect all afternoon. On the other hand, I thought it might be better if we lost the toss and had to kick. I would be on the kickoff team, of course, but not in the critical role as returner. It would give me an opportunity to become familiarized with the feel, the ambience, of the action before having too much pressure. I couldn't make up my mind what *I* wanted, though obviously it didn't matter. The coin flip determined that the Jets would receive.

Standing just to the right of Lou Michaels, waiting for the whistle to blow, my blood seemed to be flowing at the speed of light. Everything raced in speeded-up motion. The adrenaline pumped gallons, it seemed, and I've never wanted something to start more.

My job was to go for the ball carrier, and I had to remind myself. Incredible. But my entire career I've had to remind myself. You can forget, with seventy-five thousand people screaming, and I've seen it happen to a lot of players. *Go for the ball carrier. Go as fast as you can.* I'd had an excellent year on special teams (the next year I was made special-teams captain), and this was no time to mar it.

The whistle blew, Michaels approached the football, and I went as fast as I could. First I had to locate the direction of the ball, then the pumped-up Jets who would try to put me down and keep me there, and finally the spot to where the runner would be going. If I took a good hit it might be the best thing that could happen, getting me "in the game" and all, but the idea is to avoid this. The worst part was still ahead. Unlike a play from scrimmage, where the guys who can hurt you the most are up front on the line, often on the kickoff the big men are downfield, their job being to form a wedge. I had to get past that wedge to the ball carrier, or through it, and often felt like a medieval knight charging a phalanx.

I didn't make the tackle, nor was I knocked off my feet, but I did manage to create some indecision and helped change the runner's course. He barely made it outside the twenty, and the special team came off the field yelling encouragement to the defense.

Right away it seemed the game would go as expected. Bubba dominated the line of scrimmage, and our defensive backs played tight on the Jet receivers, almost wearing them as a shirt. I'd hardly gotten off the field when I was back on, as part of the punt-receiving team. My job was to position myself right behind our defensive line, guard against an inside fake (surely it was too early for that, but it was necessary to be alert), and hit the Jets' upback, driving him to the sidelines. The good clean crack of helmet and shoulder pad took away any tension or butterflies I had remaining.

We started on our twenty-two. The crowd noise was terrific, louder than a regular season game, which is saying something. It seemed to me the majority of fans were for the Jets, and I was probably right: More people had come from New York than Baltimore, and the Jets were underdogs. Later I felt I might have been wrong. In the five Super Bowls in which I played, my impression always was that the other team had more support. Of course, a Super Bowl crowd is mixed, and perhaps unless you're playing in front of partisans at home, you get the impression the fans are against you.

"Go, John!" I heard myself yelling. I had been feeling good, and now it was like I'd gone to heaven. On our very first offensive play Earl Morrall had thrown a tight-end screen to John Mackey, and our superstar receiver, catching the ball behind the line, glided and battered (he did both exquisitely well) his way for a nineteen-yard gain.

All the Colts were standing up, as close as we could get to the out-of-bounds line, shouting "Go get 'em" and "Take 'em apart" at the offense, but of course they couldn't hear. The crowd noise was deafening. I honestly don't think I was able to hear myself yell. I looked up in the stands to see if I could find Linda, learn how she was reacting to the spectacle, to the greatness of the Colts, but I wouldn't have found her in a million years. Later I would be glad I couldn't. I wouldn't want to look up and see her.

Down the field the offense drove, as if Shula were diagramming it on a blackboard. I could sense the beginning of fear in the Jets. They'd *talked* their way into believing they had a chance, but now they were beginning to think maybe all those sportswriters and experts had been correct.

Tom Matte and our fullback Jerry Hill, running beautifully to the weak side, moved the ball relentlessly to the Jet twenty. Then, on a first down, Morrall overthrew second-string tight end Tom Mitchell, the first discordant note in an otherwise perfect symphony, and on second down he overthrew

Jimmy Orr. Later, when viewing the films, I thought Orr could have caught this ball had he stretched out, but I wasn't the one running the pattern; something could have happened that I didn't see.

On third down the sweet music turned sour. Quick as cats the Jets were in on top of Morrall, he had to scramble for his life and was tripped up at the line of scrimmage, the twenty. This was an omen, a sign of our future, though I doubt if anyone knew it at the time. On nearly every play the New York 3-4 defense rushed a linebacker, but the trouble was we never knew which one was coming. It was a blitzing linebacker who forced the slow-footed Morrall to scramble.

Well, we'd settle for three. Not bad for our first possession.

Back then the goal posts were on the goal line, so Michaels's kick would be only twenty-seven yards, barely more than an extra point today. It was at an angle (the hashmarks were set further apart than they are today), but still the kick was a chip shot, a virtual gimme.

The veteran Michaels, booting from the left hashmark, missed the kick by *two feet* to the right.

The letdown on the sideline lasted only moments. Collectively we thought, *So what? Okay.* "Hold them, defense!" I heard someone yell. Right. Push them *back,* defense.

Late in the first quarter, George Sauer, Jr., caught a Namath sideline pass and was introduced to Lenny Lyles, the defensive back whose goal was "to be hard as the ground." Sauer fumbled and the ball was recovered by Ron Porter at the Jet twelve.

I don't think anyone, even the Jet fans, doubted we would score. And we should have. On third and four from the six Morrall passed to Tom Mitchell, who had outmaneuvered Jet cornerback Randy Beverly. *This,* we thought, *would surely be our first touchdown,* but Mitchell didn't get his body around in time and the ball hit his shoulder pad and went floating lazily, maddeningly, off into the warm Miami air. It settled into the arms of the surprised Randy Beverly, an instant before the goat, now a hero.

Two outstanding opportunities—the missed field goal, now the interception—had been blown, and this time the letdown was real. *What do we have to do?* I thought, which was the beginning of a despairing idea shared by teammates. Worse was the thought that this might be the beginning of a trend: a blown easy field goal, a muffed touchdown pass. There were plenty of other ways we could foul up, and the worry existed that we would find them.

Well, go defense. "Go defense!" roared two dozen voices from the sideline. The touchback started the Jets on their own twenty, and no way existed for them to go eighty yards against the greatest defense ever to play the game. I thought of the Michigan State University chant of a few years ago, "Kill, Bubba, kill!" and thought, *That's it, Bubba, kill!*

But Joe Namath wasn't going to run anything anywhere near Bubba, or to the left side of our defense, backed up by the fanatic, Mike Curtis. Instead, Namath called plays aimed at our *right* side, where resided Ordell Braase and Don Shinnick, both older and not so big. I always enjoy hearing TV sports commentators saying that the way to victory is to attack a team's *strength*. This is insanity. You should attack a team's weakness. Let me mention Muhammad Ali again. Let's say you had to win a fight against one of two people, Ali or Caspar Milquetoast. Would anyone in his right mind suggest that the one to go after is Ali?

Four straight times Namath ran Matt Snell at our *right* side, away from Bubba and Curtis, and the result was twenty-six yards and a first down on the Jet forty-six. It was a beautiful thing to watch, the Jet strategy, if you weren't a Colt fan or player. Namath, constantly calling audibles, was earning a good deal of respect.

Actually, it would be difficult to give Namath too much credit. He was proving on the field that there was much more to him than talk, and no one could deny he was colorful. Before the game, for ten thousand dollars, he had shaved his Fu Manchu mustache, though his sideburns were still long, in marked contrast to our two quarterbacks. Both Unitas and Morrall sported crew cuts and were conservative in their life-styles, carryovers from another time. Namath, hunchbacked, was one of the first to wear white shoes (Unitas's were black and high-topped), and in many ways he fit the image of the protest-oriented 1960s. He was Broadway Joe and Joe Willie, no crew-cut establishmentarian he, and in bars and to reporters he had thumbed his nose at the Colts. Now he was proving there was fire behind his smoke. Another sign in our locker room had read: EARL THE PEARL WILL MAKE JOE NAMATH EAT HIS WORDS. Although we didn't yet doubt this would ultimately prove true, those four carries by Snell made us realize this would be no cakewalk.

Imploring our defense with words they couldn't hear, shouting ourselves to near hoarseness, the crowd a wall of sound, cameras along the sidelines forever, we watched in loneliness and helplessness as the Jet drive continued.

Namath missed on a first-down pass from his forty-six, then picked up six on a short throw to Bill Mathis. On third and four we wanted Bubba to kill, surely Namath would pass, but he set up and released the ball so fast Bubba couldn't get to him, and Sauer, disorienting Lyles, caught it for fourteen yards and a first down. Another rapierlike strike to Sauer, and the Jets were at our twenty-three.

Shula's face was grim. Everyone on our sideline wore a grim face. There were shouts of "Go, defense!," but the sound was more one of hope than conviction. Not so much disbelief—we had to believe it—as frustration marked our mood on the sideline.

Emerson Boozer plowed for two yards. On second down Namath hit Snell for twelve more and a first and goal at the nine. This is one of the toughest positions for an offense to be in: down near the goal line there is not much room for pass patterns, and of course it is very difficult to run against a stacked-in defense. The Jets, I think everyone felt, just would not score against us from nine yards out, at least not a touchdown.

They scored easily, and in a fashion that was humiliating. Matt Snell ran for five on first down, and then scored on the next play from four yards out. Both plays went at the right side of our defense. The Jets, running away from our strength, had simply jammed the ball down our throats.

The standout in the drive, I thought, was not Joe Namath, but Matt Snell. This was the only touchdown New York scored all day (had the oddsmakers guaranteed the Jets would cross the goal line only once, the spread might have been thirty points), and Snell came up with the big plays, both running the ball and catching it. He sparkled all afternoon. He carried the ball 30 times for 121 yards, and caught four passes. Namath played well—17 for 28, 206 yards—but it was hardly his greatest day.

Down 7-0, I stood at the goal line and stared 60 yards upfield, waiting for the ball to be kicked my way. I thought about that 102-yard kickoff return in Detroit, and the 86-yarder against the 49ers, and dammit I was going to do it again. I was going to get into the wind, as they say, grow wings on my heels, run as no one else who has ever played football. In just a few seconds this game would be tied.

But this was not the way to think, far less to help the team, but rather a good recipe to fumble and dig us into an even deeper hole. I forced myself to slow down. The noise of the crowd, which would grow to ear-shattering proportions while the ball was in the air, and the importance of the game, had me in a near-frenzy anyway (here it was the second quarter, I couldn't believe an adrenaline high could last so long), and it wasn't easy to restore a semblance of reason to my mind. As high as I was, I could imagine myself running before the ball left the kicker's foot. It is never a mystery to me when a lineman jumps offside in a key situation. He is so eager, so intent, so fired up, the wonder is that it doesn't happen more often.

I talked to myself. Those touchdown runs had just happened. I'd gotten a few critical blocks and that was it. I could do it again, *now,* if I got those blocks, but that was out of my hands. *See the ball,* I told myself. *Get in position to catch it. Catch it.* Then, only then, was the time to run as if the hounds of hell were at my heels.

The kick was end-over-end and very, very high (the average fan has a pretty good idea of how far a ball can be kicked, but often doesn't realize to what great heights it reaches), and I caught it smoothly enough and headed up the middle, right behind my wedge. Hey, I thought, and it was okay now, I'd put on some outstanding moves during that 102-yarder, maybe they can be repeated. The idea was for wedge and runner to move simultaneously to the right, after drawing as many defenders as possible toward the center of the field, and maybe I could spring it all the way. The players in the wedge were very close to each other (I've seen them so near one another they are holding hands), and I was right up behind them.

I returned the kickoff twenty-eight yards and was disappointed. But no one else seemed to be. Once again there was fire and spirit on the sideline, and a few players whacked my back and rump and said, "Good going." We were down 7–0 and it didn't seem to mean a thing. We'd been down before, to better teams than the Jets, and had come back. I joined everyone else in yelling, "Go offense!"

Actually, the return hadn't been that shabby. It turned out, in fact, that I'd set one of those records that are absolutely guaranteed not to last very long. Twenty-eight yards was the longest a kickoff had ever been returned in a Super Bowl.

There was no rush to get back the touchdown, but then again, why wait? It seemed I'd been off the field only moments when Tom Matte was racing for fifty-eight yards on a single thrust and we were in business on the New York sixteen. I don't know whether Earl Morrall called the next play or whether it was Don Shula, but on first down Earl threw to flanker Willie Richardson, and Johnny Sample, who had played for the Colts, intercepted at the two.

Three glorious opportunities. Three muffs.

And it got worse. Indescribably worse. What happened in the last minute of the first half is a play I'll never understand, no matter how often I watch it on film. The answer is buried in Earl Morrall's brain, and he would have to be the person to recall.

We had the ball on the Jet forty-five. Morrall handed the ball to Tom Matte, who headed for the line. It was a play we'd used before against the Jets, and was intended to draw them toward Matte. We had run this same play earlier in the year for a touchdown against Atlanta. Matte's fake was excellent, and the Jets converged on him just as we'd hoped: After all, he was at this point the game's leading rusher (fifty-eight in one bite), and couldn't be ignored. Matte suddenly whirled and tossed the ball back to Morrall. It was the flea-flicker, and the Jets were taken by complete surprise. Meanwhile, Jimmy Orr, our primary (that word is important) receiver, had done an excellent job faking a block, and then drifted far behind Randy Beverly. I mean, far behind. No one was within twenty yards of Jimmy Orr. Orr was all alone, lonely, waving his arms to attract Morrall, though this should hardly have been necessary since Orr was the *primary* receiver, the *first* player to whom Morrall should have looked.

Morrall threw instead over the middle to fullback Jerry Hill, a secondary receiver, who also happened to be open, though not, unfortunately, by twenty yards. But Morrall underthrew (did not lead) Hill, and strong-side safety Jim Hudson intercepted at the twelve.

It was incredible. We should have been ahead 24–7, but trailed 0–7.

No one in the locker room at half time was really down. We were not playing that poorly. Except for that one New York drive, the Jet offense had showed us little. Our own offense, save for the three goal-line interceptions and the poor kick by Michaels, was on a forty-eight-point-per-game pace. We didn't think the Jets could score forty-eight points against us in a season.

Well, there was a half to go, and no one, except Corny Johnson, was even entertaining the possibility that we might lose.

The offense was at one end of the locker room, the defense at the other (Shula always spoke to the offense first), and Corny and I sat on a bench. We ached to see more action, but really weren't that big a part of the game. We could hear the crowd and the fierce hitting, and no one cared more about the outcome, but all we had to do was look at our relatively clean uniforms, compared, say, to Mike Curtis's, who looked like he'd just returned from the swamps and jungles of Vietnam, to feel a little embarrassed. Ask any player who has spent a lot of time on the sidelines: It's humiliating, almost a badge of shame, to have a clean uniform.

"What's gonna happen?" Corny asked me.

"There's no problem," I said.

"Damn. But that score. We're behind, and we're supposed to be trampling these people."

Just then defensive back Charlie Stukes came by. Charlie loved fun, could always be counted on to have a grin on his face. He was a tension-breaker, someone every team could use.

"What's gonna happen?" Corny asked Stukes.

Charlie shot a glance over at the offense. "Depends on them," he said. I don't think the highest paid analyst could have said it better.

Corny was worried. It turns out he was the most astute of

all of us. Offensive guard Glenn Ressler was within hailing distance.

"What's gonna happen?" Corny asked Ressler.

"We'll get them. They're not doing anything different."

Ressler was wrong. We just hadn't fully appreciated the 3-4 yet.

Corny was about to ask somebody else "What's gonna happen?" so I wandered over by the offense.

"Big holes," Tom Matte was saying. "I mean, there are big holes to go through. Shouldn't be any problems the second half. We just got to go at that big guy's knees."

The "big guy" was Verlon Biggs.

There was no panic in the locker room, no ranting by Shula. As we took the field in darkening Miami, the gray tropical light almost eerie, it seemed for a moment as if we'd stepped into another dimension, another time. Not many games are played in twilight. I wonder what Rod Serling would have made of the Colts and the weird experience we were about to have.

I waited for the kickoff, ready to break a long one, but just decent field position would have been enough. No more mistakes, everyone had vowed in the locker room. Take it to them from the word go. We would get down in the sty and outgrunt and outsweat them; it might not be pretty, but we weren't going to lose this football game.

The kick was angled away from me and I never touched the ball. A secondary return man brought it back to the twenty-five, and Morrall led a grim-faced offense out onto the field. It hadn't been necessary for the defense to tell them they were unhappy (what is this zero points in two quarters business?), that was simply something that was understood. The defense had allowed just seven points, you would have to nitpick to criticize that, and we were behind because of the offense's mistakes.

It didn't take long to make another one. On the very first play from scrimmage, running the ball—nothing fancy—Tom Matte fumbled and the Jets recovered at our thirty-three. Of course, they didn't go very far, but they didn't have to, and it was 10-0 after Jim Turner booted a thirty-two-yard field goal.

The thought that we might lose still had not occurred to me, nor I believe to any of the Colts. So far the Jets had been merely annoying; we'd been hanging ourselves. Again I looked for a good kickoff return to put us in business, and again the ball was kicked away from me. The Jets had seen those long returns on the films, and never did kick another ball in my direction. It was odd. You would think an underdog team would be the one taking chances, but throughout the game it was the Jets who played conservatively. Short passes and a grind-it-out running attack centered on Matt Snell.

Billy Ray Smith was talking to himself on the sideline. Mostly uncomplimentary remarks about the offense. Mike Curtis wasn't happy either. Both were upset by our absence of offensive productivity, but it wasn't serious. They were annoyed at the length of time that had expired without our taking charge.

I watched with open-mouthed amazement as Morrall threw three straight incompletions and we had to punt again. Now the 3-4 was making itself felt. Our offensive front did not know which linebacker was coming (one always was), and the Jets were pouring through, often untouched. Our line became confused in its assignments, not knowing whom to block, nor even whom to look for, and once again the defense had to be called upon.

Again Namath ran Matt Snell away from Bubba and Curtis for short gains, and he mixed in two 14-yard passes to George Sauer, who on the day caught eight for 133 yards. It was a good thing for the Jets he did. Don Maynard was shut out.

Jim Turner climaxed the drive with a thirty-yard field goal, and it was Jets 13, Colts 0. What was disturbing about this drive was the amount of time the Jets took off the clock. It was ball-control offense at its best, the sort of show you would have expected from the Colts, and my heart just sank every time the officials moved the chain.

The first time I knew something different was happening was when I was coming off the field after the kickoff and heard the noise. It was a yelp of surprise and joy, and then a roar that grew louder and louder, cascading over the stadium, drowning everything else, a noise that can probably be compared to the time when Don Larsen struck out Dale Mitchell, or when Lou Gehrig said farewell in Yankee Stadium, a sound you could touch and feel.

Johnny U. was taking the field, and when I saw him *I* wanted to cheer. Johnny Unitas, the Miracle Man. Baltimore rooters were ecstatic, but not more so than the Colt players. He was as much a legend to most of us as he was to the fans. We jumped up and down on the sideline, our voices restored, beating one another on the back, shaking fists, making the ground tremble with our stomps.

Johnny U. I'd been in junior high school when he engineered that unforgettable 1959 drive against the Giants that sent the championship into overtime. Who could forget it? Every football fan alive had seen Johnny Unitas manufacture a miracle comeback. Two minutes in his hands were two hours. I felt deep in my bones that we would ride the magic of his arm to victory. Our poor start was just a prologue, a happening destined by fate so that Unitas could be hero.

Actually, no one on the Colts, save perhaps Unitas, had the slightest idea he would play. His arm was in terrible shape. But it turned out that Don Shula had intended to allow Earl Morrall to play only one series of downs in the second half, and if the offense continued to sputter, to substitute with Unitas. Shula had given Morrall a second series only because the first never got started due to that Matte fumble.

Morrall had a bad day. The NFL's most valuable player had completed only six of seventeen passes for seventy-one yards, with three interceptions. It wouldn't matter, I thought. Morrall would be forgotten. This game would be remembered because of Johnny Unitas.

The crowd really went berserk. No one, including myself, seemed to remember that Unitas was operating with a crippled arm. I was afraid our offense wouldn't be able to hear the signals being called, so great was the noise. The offense itself was fired up, given a new lease on life. It was good that Unitas was out there, even if he couldn't lift his arm, much less use it to throw.

A running play and two misfired passes to Matte and Orr, caused as much by that 3-4 defense as by Unitas's tender arm, forced another punt, but didn't dampen our enthusiasm. The great quarterback would find a way. He always had, hadn't he?

What was discouraging was that the Jets were once again on the move when the third quarter ended, with Namath running the workhorse Snell away from our strength, and keeping us off-balance with pinpoint short passes. The third quarter concluded with the Jets driving. We had run only eight plays in the entire period.

Another Jim Turner field goal, this one nine yards, and the Jets led, 16–0. But almost the entire fourth quarter remained. Sixteen points was nothing to John Unitas. Still I don't believe there was a player on our team who thought we would lose.

Sure enough, with Unitas at the throttle we started to move. The Jets expected Unitas to throw, and maybe for that reason he didn't, or maybe it was that crippled arm, but for whatever reason he mainly stayed on the ground with Matte and Jerry Hill. We moved down to the Jet twenty-five. On first down Unitas overthrew Willie Richardson, and on second down a pass to the end zone was intercepted by Randy Beverly.

We still did not realize what was happening—that we were going to lose. The first drive under Unitas, I thought, was just getting him warmed up, and the second had gotten us close. On the third, I figured, we'd be unstoppable. I expected our defense, as much inspired by Unitas's unexpected appearance as the offense was, to stop the Jets, which they did, and we took over on our own twenty.

On fourth and ten from our twenty, Unitas gambled and hit Jimmy Orr for twenty yards. Again the bench and the fans were afire, and this time Johnny U. didn't disappoint. He reached deep inside himself, all the way back to the University of Louisville, or those rugged days on the sandlot, or maybe to 1959 and that Giants game, and pushed us down the field and into the end zone. The crowd was hysterical, so were we, and seldom in my career have I seen a player cheered as Unitas was when he came to the sideline. The extra point by Michaels, after Jerry Hill's one-yard touchdown run, made it 16–7. A touchdown and a field goal would do it.

The madhouse we'd been witnessing was nothing compared to what came next. We used an onside kick and Rick Volk recovered on the Jet forty-four! Back on the field came Johnny Unitas, and if there had been a roof on the Orange Bowl it would have been blown off. The atmosphere was wilder than a Beatles concert, pure pandemonium, middle-age America, not really much different from its children, going crazy over *their* hero—crew-cut, straight-arrow John.

We gained twenty yards on the first two plays. First a dart to Orr, then a strike to Richardson, and we were set up on the Jet twenty-four.

I looked across the field to the Jet sideline. The mood was part amazement, part funereal. Thunderstruck is a good way to describe the Jets. It occurred to them that they were caught in a whirlpool, that they were going to play Ralph Branca to our Bobby Thomson. The Jets seemed more stunned than angry, as if they had sped up the reel of the game so it could show the future, and what they saw was a patented Unitas-inspired comeback.

On first down from the twenty-four Johnny Sample tipped away a pass intended for Willie Richardson. The next two plays probably decided the game. Each time a blitzing linebacker—we never were able to figure out which one was coming—harassed Unitas into first underthrowing, and then overthrowing, a receiver. It was fourth and ten, and we could have gone for a thirty-one yard field goal from Michaels that would make it 16–10, but Shula elected instead to go for the touchdown, and Larry Grantham was able to bat down a throw intended for Jimmy Orr.

There were two minutes, twenty-one seconds remaining, but not until the two-minute warning had passed did I realize we would lose. Matt Snell carried the ball six straight times, once for a first down. The Jets, cautious to the end, ran him away from Bubba, just as they should have. I watched the clock and the Jet sideline. Each second that came off the clock made me sick, weak. Seeing the Jets jumping up and down, celebrating, as we should have been, made me want to scream in anger and frustration.

The Jets were world champions, though no Colt player and few fans, even today, would judge them the better team. But the scoreboard read 16–7 when the hands of the clock stood straight up.

Governor Nelson Rockefeller of New York sent a congratulatory telegram to the Jets, and so did Mayor John Lindsay. Lindsay's read: "On behalf of all the citizens of New York City, congratulations to the players and management of the New York Jets. All of us are proud of you. Your smashing triumph is the greatest upset in the history of professional football. We are

looking forward to welcoming you world champions back to
New York City."

Joe Namath was awarded a Dodge Charger by *Sport* magazine as the most valuable player of Super Bowl III.

The game's statistics were relatively even, hardly a cause
for consolation since, as Corny Johnson had put it, we were
supposed to "trample these people." We outgained the Jets
143-142 on the ground; they had a slight advantage passing,
206-181. But we suffered four interceptions to their zero, and
that, plus the mystifying (to us) 3-4 defense, which seemed ever
to allow one of their defenders in our backfield, were the reasons
we lost.

Our locker room after the game was morbid. I felt a burden
of sadness like a heavy weight. Flashing continuously through
my mind was the scene of the jubilant Jets racing off the field,
fingers held up in the "We're Number One" position, hugging
each other as they went. Clearly Namath was the hero, and
each Jet went out of his way to shake his hand and pound him
joyously on the back.

I hated those "Number One" fingers waving in the air.
During the regular season we had defeated opponents far superior to the Jets. We had better athletes than the Jets. We were a
better team.

All of us joined in the after-game team prayer. The atmosphere was more that of a mortuary than a locker room. Giant
men, heads and shoulders slumped, sunk deep in a terrible depression. Occasionally a deep moan. Less often the explosion of
a pent-up curse. I heard a thrown helmet explode like a bomb
when it crashed into the wall. No one talked. Each player had
retreated into his own private hell.

One player, Rick Volk, almost died. He was discovered
lying in a bathroom, body convulsed, vomit pouring from his
mouth. He was in the process of swallowing his tongue when the
team physician, Dr. Norman Freeman, was summoned. Dr.
Freeman probably saved Rick Volk's life by freeing his tongue
with the only instrument available, a ballpoint pen. The
stricken Volk was rushed to Holy Cross Hospital. When he
came to, his first words to his worried wife were, "Who won?"

I've never, before or since, seen a locker room clear out so
slowly. No one wanted to leave. It was almost as if we thought

that by our staying long enough, the Jets would give us another chance. We'd tear them apart with another chance. But there wasn't going to be one. We'd never have another opportunity like the one just lost. That realization was absolutely numbing.

Wives and girlfriends were allowed to ride the team bus back to the hotel. I sat next to Linda and she told me it would be all right. I didn't say that I believed it would never be all right. I was utterly exhausted, drained of energy, and I kept seeing the Jets running off the field waving those fingers. *How could it be?* I was sick at heart, sick to the marrow of my bones. I lay my head on Linda's shoulder and blessed sleep came.

Late that evening, along with most of the other Colts, I attended a party at owner Carroll Rosenbloom's home, twenty minutes from Fort Lauderdale, right on the beach. Linda came with me, though I was terrible company. Mr. Rosenbloom seemed surprisingly happy. He was a snazzy dresser, natty, always had his hat brim turned down so he would look younger. If he was mourning our defeat, it wasn't evident to me.

Rosenbloom had a big blue and white (the Colt colors) tent erected on his sprawling lawn, and there was a dance band and rivers of champagne. I met Burt Lancaster and Teddy Kennedy. Most of the other bigshots, I imagined, had gone to whatever party the Jets were throwing.

It was more a wake than a party. Some of the Colts were getting very drunk. It's called dulling the pain. I looked at the drinking, the desultory dancing, the joyless faces. "Is it okay if I go off by myself for a little while?" I said to Linda.

"Are you going to be all right?"

"I'll try to be."

"You should do what you have to."

I walked along the beach behind Mr. Rosenbloom's mansion. Losing the game hurt like a knife between the ribs, but it was feel-sorry-for-myself time also. I wondered what I was going to do. What could I do? I had no job, and no idea of how to support Linda and myself in the off-season. The trip to Hermiston was out. School, also, at least for a while. We needed furniture for our Baltimore apartment. Well, I could build that. I was good at building things.

Linda and I had tried not to count chickens before they were hatched, but it hadn't always been possible. We'd come close to counting on that winner's share of the Super Bowl money. *But what could I do?* I'd have to get a job that required my presence only during the off-season. It would be madness to stop playing football.

But my football future wasn't all that bright either. I wasn't playing enough. Something would have to be worked out in this area. *You're going to have to do the things needed to get ahead,* I told myself. I wanted to get ahead. Succeed. Really be somebody. Certainly I was the typically insecure athlete, but I believe also, unfortunately unlike others I've known, I saw the need to plan a *life,* not just the few years allotted me as a professional athlete.

"That you, Preston?"

I'd been walking the beach (right where Carroll Rosenbloom later died) for quite a while, maybe an hour, going back and forth through the sand, and hadn't noticed the man who approached. It was Eddie Rosenbloom, Carroll's older brother, known to the players as a nice guy. I liked him.

"It's me," I said.

"Your misery doesn't like company?"

"It feeds on itself. Makes it worse."

"What's your problem? It's more than the game."

"The game was enough."

"I suspect you're right. You won't soon forget it."

"Never."

"I suspect that's right too. But is there anything else?"

Why not? I thought. Why not talk it over with him? I told Eddie Rosenbloom what was bothering me, which were doubts about my future, my football career, everything that stretched out over the years in front of me. Talking out loud helped. I've since learned that talking out loud to someone about problems can by itself help to solve them. Simply verbalizing what bothers you helps bring to the fore the solution. What I needed first of all was a job. Oh, I needed a long-range plan also, but that wouldn't evolve in a night. At the moment, what was required was work.

"I think I can help you," Eddie Rosenbloom said.

He said he had a friend at the Institute of Computer Management, a subsidiary of Litton Industries, who might have a job for me. He told me to give his friend a call when I got back

to Baltimore. It turned out I was hired for the job, which I kept
for two off-seasons, scheduling meetings at high schools and
talking about computer programming. The work turned out to
be both satisfying and rewarding. The Age of the Computer, at
least as it is today for millions of Americans, had really not yet
arrived, and I was able to steer a number of young people into
worthwhile careers.

It turned out I'd missed some excitement while walking on
the beach. Bubba Smith had walked out onto the dance floor,
grabbed Tom Matte, lifted him over his head, and thrown him
into a group of empty tables on the Rosenbloom lawn. It
seemed Bubba was unhappy with Matte's fumble at the beginning of the third quarter, and also with his inability to score on
that fifty-eight-yard second-quarter dash. Bubba, in his overly
negative reaction to defeat, probably had forgotten Matte's
one-hundred-yards-plus rushing.

Later, Bubba heard that Carroll Rosenbloom had bet one
million dollars on the Jets, which if true was indeed a worrisome
aspect of the game. I don't know one way or another, but talk
continues that perhaps someone was gotten to in Super Bowl
III. The talk became so persistent that recently I ordered a film
of the game and spent long hours studying it.

Surely no one on our defense could have been involved.
The defense played excellently, allowing just one touchdown
against an offense that had plenty of weapons. The Jets did not
win the game against our defense. The sixteen points they
scored, which were few enough, can be attributed to a game
plan that avoided Bubba Smith and Mike Curtis and relied on a
tank named Matt Snell for ball control and short rapierlike
strikes from Namath to Sauer. The Colts had lost just one of
sixteen games before Super Bowl III. We would have been *undefeated* if we had held every previous opponent to sixteen
points or under.

There are very few players who *can* fix a game. The quarterback, maybe. But he is perhaps the only one. I watched Earl
Morrall closely on the game films. He had had a bad day, yet
that can happen to anyone. The only questionable play I saw
was not throwing to a wide-open Jimmy Orr on that flea-flicker
near the end of the second quarter. The first-quarter pass to
tight end Tom Mitchell, which should have been a touchdown,

was muffed because Mitchell did not get his body around fast enough.

No, I think we just got beat. We weren't prepared for the 3-4 defense, the Jets were better than we gave them credit for (though they were not our equals), and it's tough to defeat any pro team when you throw four interceptions. Certainly I couldn't find evidence of a fix while watching the game films. Were proof ever offered—Bubba doesn't seem to give any that is convincing—that Carroll Rosenbloom wagered one million dollars against his own team, it would be a matter requiring close and thorough examination. And if hanky-panky *were* involved, it would be nothing short of a national disaster of the first rank. Bubba said of the allegation, "Please, God, make it a lie!" To which I can only add an amen.

Corny, Clara, Linda, and I didn't wait for the crowd to clear out before exiting Carroll Rosenbloom's party. It looked as if it might run all night, and the atmosphere could never be mistaken for festive. I was sure Burt Lancaster and Ted Kennedy weren't staying around. The four of us caught a cab (hearse?) back to the hotel.

We left the next afternoon with most of the other Colts on a plane to Baltimore. We didn't expect to be greeted by bands and screaming fans (there was a huge celebration for the Jets in New York), and we weren't surprised. Linda and I went home to our apartment. I tried to get my mind off football and onto making furniture. And of course there was the new job for which I needed to interview.

I got two calls that first day back. The University of Illinois student newspaper wanted to interview me, and also my hometown paper, the *Freeport Journal Standard.*

Life wasn't so bad, I thought. I'd just taken part in the world's most important football game, and there were people who wanted to hear what I had to say. Life wasn't at all bad. Surely at the beginning the odds had been very long that anyone would care a whit about what I thought or was doing, much less that tens of millions of people would have watched me on television. Yes, I wanted to go a long way further, but it was just as important never to forget where I'd been.

3
Growing Up in Freeport

I wasn't nearly as good an athlete as my brother. Rufus, Jr., was a year and two days older than me, and was strong and could run like the wind. As a senior in high school—when I was a junior—he was six feet one and 185 to my six feet two and 193, but no one doubted who the star was. He had that rare combination of a sprinter's legs and a powerful upper body, like a man who pumps iron, and he was not only exceptionally fast (100 yards in 9.7) but tough. He could outrun opponents, or run over them. It didn't matter to Rufus. As an athlete he was filled with himself, bursting with good health and energy, and he had everything. Rufus was strong, handsome, intelligent.

He was a football star, of course, but he could compete at the highest levels in baseball and track also. At baseball he usually played shortstop. He could range far to both sides for ground balls, had the speed of a fast-ball pitcher on his throws, and knew how to use his great speed on the bases. Going from first to third on a single wasn't a problem for Rufus. He might come all the way home. He had the good, soft hands a "natural" is born with, able to corral and cradle the hardest ground ball effortlessly. Most important of all, he could hit. Long boomers, or line drives that just might take your head off, the kinds of hits that make a scout's eyes gleam. In track he was one of the fastest runners in the state, consistently going to the Illinois State championships. And he was even good at basketball, the one sport at which I might have been better than Rufus.

He had dedication along with ability. Rufus drove himself to stay in shape. Long before regular practices began he conducted his own two-a-days out in our backyard, which in many ways was a field. Perhaps sixty yards from our back door were the Illinois Central Railroad tracks, and Rufus would run on the ties, hour after hour, marvelous exercise not only for speed but for agility and quickness of foot. It was similar to running between tires, except you could go forever on the railroad ties.

In the back also were coal bins, and near and around them Rufus practiced his moves—cutting, slashing, high-stepping. I'd watch with other family members through a back window. At first we'd admire him, think of joining him, but as he went on and on, pushing himself, driving himself, we knew there was no way. His dedication bordered on the fanatic. His whole life was sports.

Rufus and I were friends, though not as close as I would have liked, and we fought a lot. I mean, real fights. They were over silly things—a sports-rule interpretation, who was responsible for breaking a bat, and so on—but the battles were very serious indeed. Rufus usually won, he was enormously strong and quick, and I received some terrific black eyes. When one of us fought someone else, the other would stand close by to ensure that nothing dirty happened. There was no way we would permit a serious injury to occur. Our own disagreements were forgotten if the other was in danger. We were blood brothers and in a crunch would stand up for each other.

One reason Rufus was so good so early was because he always played with youngsters four and five years older than himself. Rufus was too good for kids his own age, and because he loved competition and always strived to improve, he sought out an older group. It was no fun for Rufus to win against lesser competition. And the older group didn't go easy on him. I think that's one of the reasons Rufus was so tough and mean.

When he did condescend to play with kids our age, Rufus always wanted to be on a different team from me. It was a way of putting down his little brother, but in addition, I believe, he so loved competition that he wanted the sides to be fair. My athletic skills were considerable, though far from on a par with his, as he enjoyed proving.

The first time we really played on a team together was in Little League. He was the shortstop, my position was third base, and there was genuine cause to believe we might make it as far as the Little League World Series. Our team was called Struccto, after the toy-making firm where my mother worked, and in compiling a 17–1 record we did make it as far as the semi-finals in Chicago.

In 1962, my junior year at Freeport High School, Rufus's senior year, we were on occasion in the same backfield as the team's running backs (on defense I played linebacker, he was a cornerback and safetyman), and it was quite a team. Freeport High School was in the Big Eight Conference, with teams like LaSalle Peru, Elgin, Rockford East, and Rockford West; you hear about the tough teams in Ohio, Pennsylvania, Texas, and California, but I doubt if any conference was more rugged than ours. In any case, I might have been in the same backfield with my brother, but he was the one who rightly got the headlines.

Rufus was *great*. To point out that he was first-team all-state in a football-crazy state doesn't do him justice. How about this? Rufus was the most sought-after high-school senior in the nation! More than one hundred colleges, including perennial powerhouses USC, Notre Dame, Ohio State, Michigan, Oklahoma, and Texas, wanted him to attend their schools. He was Heisman Trophy material, the kind of player who fills stadiums. It took not even a slight leap of the imagination to picture him starring, four years hence, in pro ball. He was the superstar running back who comes along maybe once every five years.

Our high-school coach was 290-pound Nate Johnson, formerly of the Cleveland Browns, an intimidator. His practices were tough, bordering on brutal. I didn't like football that much in high school, and liked it less as time went by under Nate Johnson. Our uniforms were always half-dry, we didn't have proper padding, and the ground always seemed hard as stone. Combine this with Nate Johnson and his assistants always screaming, and the pressure Johnson put on me to be as good as Rufus, and you have someone who wasn't enamored of football.

The fanatic Rufus could take it, but I chafed. I couldn't let on to Rufus. He probably wouldn't have been sympathetic anyway. Many times I suffered blurred vision and didn't say anything. I often hurt so bad inside that the only relief was going off by myself and moaning.

I was happy when football season was over and basketball began. Of course, I idolized Rufus, basked in his tremendous football accomplishments (no team in the rugged Big Eight came close even to slowing him down), enjoyed watching famous coaches line up like so many beggars to vie for his favor, but now it was time for *my* sport.

Our coach, Ron Norman, was white (so was Nate Johnson, so was every teacher I ever had). He had played college basketball at Iowa State, knew his business, and had a son a year behind me who later went to Iowa on an athletic scholarship. The son became an opponent of mine when I went to the University of Illinois.

Basketball practice was tough but fun. Lots of wind sprints, fast-break drills, rebounding drills, blocking-out drills. All of this was done indoors, which appealed to me, but mostly I enjoyed a sport where it wasn't necessary constantly to absorb pain.

I have long, narrow feet (size 13 shoe) and hands (often my fingers have been compared to those of a concert pianist), and I always have had outstanding leaping ability. As a junior I could dunk two basketballs, one after the other, on a single jump, even though I was only six feet two, and of course my forte was rebounding and defense. Rockford Auburn had a six-feet-nine center named Keith Stelter, and he never won a single tip from me. Because of my long slender fingers, my father, whom all of us called Daddy, predicted I would grow to six feet six or six feet seven.

I played forward in my junior year, and Freeport High School was ranked as high as number three in the state. I was voted the team's MVP and honorable mention all-state. It really made me happy to outdo Rufus, but he treated the accomplishment with monumental disdain. Football was his game, and maybe baseball and track.

Baseball was the sport I think our father would have liked Rufus to have been most involved in, but Nate Johnson's influence was paramount. Johnson viewed everything as an extension of football, and insisted that Rufus go out for track in the spring. At track he could develop his already blazing speed.

My dad, from reports I've received that I consider incontrovertible, was a tremendous baseball player. People who knew him compare him to the immortal Josh Gibson as a power hitter, but Daddy never had the chance to prove them right or wrong. He grew up in western Mississippi, hardly an enlightened area where race relations were concerned, and in that part of the country, in the 1920s and 1930s, blacks didn't play baseball with whites. Of course, in the major leagues concentrated in the North, blacks didn't play either, but Mississippi was something else. Everything, I mean everything, was segregated, separate, and unequal. In the 1950s my father took the family back to Mississippi for visits, and all of us hated it. It wasn't just the COLORED ONLY signs over restrooms, water fountains, and lunch counters, but a palpable feeling of evil in the air, a sinister, backward atmosphere that numbed the mind and the heart. Even today I try to avoid Mississippi. It has probably changed some, but not enough from what I hear. Why subject yourself to that?

Anyway, my dad's hopes of baseball glory were shattered long before he left Mississippi. He had to quit school after fifth grade to help support his family. As soon as he could drive a truck he took up that line of work. It was as a teenager that his hip was seriously injured in a truck accident, and to this day he still can't get around very well. The hip injury effectively precluded any possibility of an athletic career.

But Daddy was tough. He was six feet tall, and built strong. His thumbs, I always think of his thumbs, are double the thickness of a normal man's. My dad heard from relatives living in Freeport, Illinois. They said things were better for black people in Freeport. They couldn't be worse. Mom and Dad scraped up every cent they could find and moved north, and because my father, no, because both my father and my mother were tough, they survived. I would say they prospered, at least in every area of life that counts.

Rufus Pearson, Sr., moved to Freeport in 1941, and got a job at the Gunite Foundry in Rockford, the second largest city in Illinois. He was a steelworker. For almost forty years he worked for Gunite, driving fifty miles round trip each day so that he could work with red-hot slag, sweat gallons, and come home each night with a weary body and a headache that pounded his brain like a hammer. Often he'd leave for work before dawn and it would be dark when he returned. Serious hip injury or no, I think Daddy probably had the best attendance record at the foundry.

He worked at Gunite for thirty-eight years, and they gave him a gold watch when he retired. But he never got a promotion. Not even to foreman. And he always did hard, manual labor.

I didn't realize how strong my father was until I was eight or nine years old. For some reason a man was harassing, taunting, threatening my younger brother, Ed, and me. I guess he was drunk. Daddy came on the scene and told him to stop, to leave us alone. He told him more than once, but the man kept after us. My father knocked him cold with one *slap*.

Relatives of mine, especially my uncle E. J. Pearson, a tremendous athlete himself in his younger days, kept relating tales of my dad's prowess as a baseball player. There was nobody in Mississippi who could touch him, Uncle E. J. said. And E. J. had been around. He said my dad was as talented as anyone in the country.

That's why I know Daddy had to love sports and be a sports fan. Yet, amazingly, he never saw me in an athletic contest until I was with the Baltimore Colts, and he never did get to watch Rufus, Jr. He had to know how well we were doing, our names were often in the papers and people talked, but he didn't see us play. *He was too tired.* The job he had to support us took everything out of him, exhausted and utterly drained him, to the point where he couldn't even come out and enjoy the feats his sons were accomplishing.

I think Rufus and I inherited a lot of our athletic ability from our dad. He neither encouraged nor discouraged us in sports, but some of our talent had to be in the genes. We didn't do it intentionally, but I think the *kind* of games we played as youngsters helped us: tag, hide-and-seek, pump-pump-pullaway (a form of tag, but when people are caught they go after others—in the end one player may be trying to avoid twenty kids trying to tag him), marbles, and kick-the-can. I was very good at marbles, but each of these games helped develop one or all of the qualities of strength, speed, stamina, and agility.

When my father and mother, the former Catherine Horton, came to Freeport in 1941, they already had two children: Pearlee, born in 1936, and Alice, born in 1938. Rufus would follow in 1944, then me in 1945, Ed in 1949, and Mary in 1951. Ed was a good athlete, but not what is called world class, and if Rufus had competition it came from Mary. She had great speed. But there really was no competition for young girls growing up in Freeport, and she didn't have the chance to see how good she could be. I do know that Mary played mostly with boys, and she could outrun them all.

My mom was quite different from my father. She was very religious—a regular, fervent, and long-time member of the Church of God in Christ (Daddy didn't become religious until a few years ago)—and woe to a child of hers who didn't want to attend services on Sunday. My mother had been a beautiful young woman, slim, light-skinned, graceful, with long, slender, elegant fingers. I'm sure my own extraordinarily long fingers are a legacy from her.

My parents' first home in Illinois was a tiny rented house on East Winslow Street in Freeport. Later they moved a few doors down the block to a larger place (it was still very small). This second house is where I grew up most. Daddy bought it eventually, and still lives there. In the early days the bathroom featured only a commode (no sink, tub, or shower), and we bathed in a washtub. Heat came from a coal-burning stove set between our small living room and dining room, and five of us children slept in a single bedroom. What is most easy to remember is the roar of the Illinois Central trains as they sped past just outside our back door, creating a terrific racket, actually shaking the house as they went, rattling beds and especially dishes and pans and everything else lying loose. After a while we got used to the trains. We forgot what a fearsome noise they made until some visitor would remind us.

Mom had to work, too. Her first job after arriving from Mississippi was as a maid at the Senate Hotel in Freeport, but later she got a job and stayed at Struccto, the toy manufacturer, as an assembly-line worker for nineteen years, until a bad heart forced her to retire. Her attendance also was as regular as clockwork, a trait given Rufus and me by both our parents. We actually *liked* school, and our attendance records were usually near perfect.

My mother also never saw me play until I was a pro. If anything, she worked longer hours than my father. It was always still night outside when she woke up to hang the wash in the backyard and get the evening meal organized so that it would be ready for easy preparation. Nor was it a picnic coming home to a large family of children. Like my father, though, she knew what was going on, both in school and athletics, and often would ask us to catch her up on our progress.

Daddy never asked us about sports. But he knew. I learned that when he wanted to know something, he'd go to a neighbor or friend. I guess it was a macho quality he had, but also I knew he was very shy. That helped keep him away from games and crowds, and I'm sure his not going to see us play was one of the reasons Mom stayed home.

Growing up, we had enough food, but leftovers were unknown in the Pearson home. Each child was very aware of what his portion should be, and ready to fight if others exceeded theirs. I especially loved the vegetables, and my mother's delicious peach-cobbler pie. Many of our vegetables came from the garden she maintained in the backyard.

As a young boy I had a paper route, and was very reliable about it. Occasionally, though, I'd be tired from a combination of school and athletics, and would complain that I was just too tired to do the job. Daddy would go with me, carrying the heavy load of papers, delivering them. He wasn't too tired. I still regret that because I was too young to realize what being tired really is, I added my own burdens onto his.

Daddy was unlicensed, but a good barber nonetheless, and in spare hours and on weekends he cut the hair of neighbors. Of course, he gave us haircuts also, but what I remember most about his barbering was the razor strop. When we got out of line he administered some fearful beatings with that strop, but he was always fair. Sometimes I wish he would have been more demonstrative with his love. But what did I want? I realize he showed his love in a million important ways, giving us a respect for education, hard work, and the importance of living up to responsibilities. Both he and Mom were real heroes.

Ours was a racially mixed neighborhood (now it is almost entirely black) with plenty of Italians and Irish. They and the blacks were working-class people, and very few of us, especially the blacks, ventured often into the west side of town. The NO COLOREDS ALLOWED signs were in our minds; they were not hung over lunch counters, but they were quite real.

A number of times Rufus and I did venture over to the west side. We could often count on a police car stopping us and asking our business. I wasn't afraid of the questions. In fact, I wasn't afraid if the officer started to get out of his vehicle. That was a signal to run, and there wasn't a policeman in Freeport— or maybe anywhere else—who could catch us.

In school I don't feel I was challenged enough, either at the primary or secondary level. I can only assume I wasn't assigned tougher classes because those who make the decisions didn't think I could handle them. Advanced math, for example. I wished I'd taken much more math. When I talk to high-school groups today, I urge students to shoot higher than administrators might think they should. If you're told you can't accomplish something, and you believe it, the prophecy becomes self-fulfilling.

My favorite teacher was fourth grade's Mrs. McCarthy, a stern, no-nonsense type who didn't want to hear about students not being able to accomplish. Mrs. McCarthy didn't have any problems with discipline. She demonstrated her commitment to the belief that sparing the rod spoils the child. Like my parents, however, Mrs. McCarthy was always fair, and she, too, was an excellent teacher.

My principal at J. W. Henney Elementary School, John Hartung, was probably the most interesting educator I ran into, and is still viewed with awe in Freeport. Principal Hartung is six feet six, which means he looked eight feet tall to grade-school kids, resembled Marshal Matt Dillon, and at one time or another had a run-in with each of the Pearson children. To my knowledge, Hartung never disciplined anyone physically, but of course he didn't have to resort to that. His stare would freeze you in your tracks, and his Man Mountain Dean stature discouraged even the most unruly student. My encounter with Hartung occurred when through a school window he spotted me on a playground swing, arcing myself almost to the the top of the bar and then leaping far out and down to the ground.

Principal Hartung approached like an avenging Fury. His eyes blazed with anger. "You don't care at all about the safety of others, do you?" he said.

"Stay away from me," I said. I was afraid of this tall man.

Hartung's stare withered me, and the chewing-out he delivered would have made Vince Lombardi proud. Friends of mine watched and listened, and tears started to stream down my face.

"Don't touch me," I said.

I feared he would lift me up over his head and heave me as he might a useless cardboard box. Scared and humiliated (why had he singled me out?), tears tracking down my cheeks, I listened as he continued to lambast me verbally.

"You touch me," I said, "and I'll tell my daddy."

I knew this was a hollow threat, even as I uttered it. Daddy wasn't going to side with me. He'd made it very clear to all his children that if we had complaints about teachers, we should bring them to him, not to try to handle them ourselves. He made it clear that he was going to start out siding with them, and our case had better be a very strong one or *he* would handle the problem and we'd wish we hadn't brought it to him. In any event, my threat to introduce my father into the proceedings didn't deter Principal Hartung in the least, and he kept talking until he felt what he had to say had gotten through.

I believe my dad had the right idea. In most disputes the teacher is right, and the education process is not furthered by disruptive kids who find a sympathetic ear at home. *If* we were being mistreated at school, that would be another story, but, as he said, we'd better have a pretty good case. My leaping off a high-flying swing was hardly a rational form of entertainment, and while Principal Hartung concentrated on injuries I could have inflicted on others, my dad would have thought also about the injuries it could have caused me *and* the unnecessary bills which would have burdened the family.

Neither Rufus nor I drank or took drugs in high school. There wasn't much of these around, anyway, and we were too caught up in sports to pay any attention. I don't think Rufus

ever had a date, and mine could be counted on one hand. We
attended few parties. I didn't go to the senior prom.

None of this was because I wasn't popular. In ninth grade,
my homeroom class, without my knowledge, nominated me for
class president, and I'm told I would have won. But I had my
name withdrawn from consideration. It seemed like politics, a
popularity contest, and somehow I thought it was wrong to go
around *trying* to be liked. "Hey, you know me, I'm Preston
Pearson, vote for me." The words would have stuck in my
throat.

Besides, athletics were important to me and Rufus, and
not just because we enjoyed them so much. Both of us wanted a
college education, and we knew the *only* way we'd get one was
through a sports scholarship. That was the goal we had set for
ourselves. I can still remember Rufus running against those
trains that traveled just outside our backyard, and practicing
his moves against coal piles he imagined were defensive linemen. Often I did more than a thousand sit-ups at a session. If
college were denied us, it wouldn't be from lack of effort.

An individual in very good shape can flex his stomach
muscles and the outline of six muscles will appear. Rufus and I
worked to exhaustion so that *eight* stomach muscles would be
visible.

It helped that there were a lot of talented athletes in our
neighborhood, and the sports atmosphere was very competitive.
Our football coach, Nate Johnson, never tired of telling us
about Willie Keys, perhaps five years older than me, from the
same neighborhood. Keys once played a football game with two
broken arms.

Weight lifting wasn't part of our training regimen in high
school, and I believe this helped. I don't think youngsters need
weight lifting, at least until their junior or senior years in high
school. It seems to me that childhood is lost too quickly when kids
start hefting weights. Of course, at the professional level it is
very important, especially where preventing injuries is concerned.
Rufus and I did a lot of bike racing, a terrific form of conditioning, and of course any other exercises to increase speed.

I was proud of my bike. Winters I would get up before it
was light and shovel snow off the sidewalks of neighbors. I saved
not only enough money for a bike, but for a desk I'd always

wanted. The desk is still in my dad's home, and I enjoy using it whenever I visit.

I had only one fight in high school, and it was Rufus's fault. A big guy a year younger than me, named Sudy Mazeke, had purportedly gotten into a scrap the night before and came out second best. The news was all over Freeport High School; everyone, including me, was talking about it, and the rugged Mazeke was enraged. He wanted to know who was spreading the lie. He'd take care of the individual, but good. Rufus went to Sudy Mazeke and said I was the one telling the vicious slander.

"I don't want to fight with you," I told Mazeke when he cornered me in a corridor between classes. Despite my age advantage, Mazeke was a lot bigger than me.

I kept talking, and it seemed to mollify him. Just when the matter was about to be concluded peaceably, Rufus piped in: "There's only one honorable thing for Sudy to do. You've spread this rumor around, and he's entitled to make you pay."

What kind of logic was this? I knew Rufus just wanted to get me in a fight; I could see the mischievous twinkle in his eyes. But I thought he should be able to find better justification than that. Unfortunately, Rufus's reasoning seemed ironclad to Mazeke.

I tried to explain to the husky Sudy that half the school had been talking about his alleged fight, and I thought once again that light was getting through to him. But then Rufus put his oar in the water again: "Only way to settle this," he judged, "is man to man."

A restroom cubicle was selected for the "battle of the century," as Rufus billed it, and it seemed half the school trooped down to the first floor to peer over the partition and get a look at the action. Maybe Sudy thought it was going to be one of those "Oh yeah" fights, where each combatant tries to outtalk the other, or perhaps he was psyching himself for mayhem, but for whatever reason he wasn't ready when I unloaded on him. My punch cut his lip, hurt him, but to his credit he tried to fight back. After several exchanges the battle just petered out, as these things do, and later I found out that the story about Sudy's earlier fight was true. I don't know what caused that one, but the reason for the dispute with me could be traced directly to Rufus.

Shortly after Rufus's senior-year football season ended was an exciting time at the Pearson house. Several of the Freeport High School coaches, as a reward for a good season, took Rufus and me out to eat. "You can have anything you want," one of them said. "How about a good steak?"

"Fine," we agreed.

"How would you like it?"

Neither of us had any idea of what the coach was talking about. Nor did he understand the puzzlement on our faces. We didn't know he expected us to answer "medium rare" or "medium" or whatever. We'd never had a steak in our lives.

It was especially exciting because our telephone never stopped ringing. Colleges from all over America were calling to tout the virtues of their institutions to Rufus. Rufus felt the same way I did, that there was only one school, the University of Illinois. It was the biggest and most important state college, and I think most youngsters from our area wanted to go there. We'd listened to Illinois basketball and football games on radio, seen them on television, couldn't imagine a higher calling than wearing the orange and blue of the Illini. But it would have been madness for Rufus not to listen to other offers, and he did. I got to visit several college campuses with him because of this.

The recruiters said they wanted to talk to both of us (I was only a junior, but there was no rules violation in accompanying Rufus), yet I knew it was my brother who interested them. He was the most sought-after high-school athlete in the country, as close to being a surefire future all-American as you could get. I was just thrilled to be along. I don't think youngsters at this time thought much about pro careers. I know we didn't. College ball and a college education was for us the pinnacle.

Rufus and I visited the University of Wisconsin. Except for that steak with our high-school coaches, it was the first time we tasted what could be called really good food. It was an experience I wish our parents could have shared. They deserved it much more than we did.

Plenty of coaches came by our little house. Al McGuire, former basketball coach at Marquette (his team won an NCAA championship) and now a TV sports commentator, said that when he was recruiting, he could learn more from the parents than from the athlete. If a youngster had good parents, said

McGuire, he'd turn out just fine. I imagine a lot of coaches were impressed by my folks.

Rufus chose Illinois and Coach Pete Elliott, himself a former star football player. There were many schools Rufus could have attended where he would have breezed through without the least academic effort, but he took Illinois, even though he had to attend a summer session at Southern Illinois University (SIU) in Carbondale after his graduation to take required courses that had been omitted from his high-school curriculum.

Rufus was a bright young man, and he did well at SIU that summer. When he returned to Freeport we thought it would be for just a short visit before he was off to Champaign-Urbana and the University of Illinois. But Rufus would *never* leave, except for the time he was committed to a mental institution.

No one really noticed that there was anything different about Rufus. Little things, but nothing that seemed serious. He just said he didn't like school, and didn't want to attend. What troubled me was that he'd lost some of his desire to train, to maintain the peak of physical excellence which had always been so important to him. He didn't try to outrun trains anymore, or drive himself to exhaustion working out against the coal piles. He was more quiet than usual. He got a job with the Parks Department. But mainly he became withdrawn.

In some ways Rufus and I became closer at this time. I think it was because for the first time we were equals. I was his size now, even a little bigger, and more mature. We talked together about serious matters, confided in each other. Only when I brought up the subject of the University of Illinois did he clam up on me. He'd talk about "some people" who "were not meant for college." When that failed to impress me, he'd lead the subject into other areas.

Daddy and Mom tried to talk to Rufus also, but they had less luck than I did. Pete Elliott would call from the University of Illinois to find out what was happening, but Rufus, if he knew, wasn't telling. This was just the start of Rufus's problems. He didn't exhibit, nor did we see, symptoms that later would become frightening.

During the summer between my junior and senior years of high school I was involved in a serious auto accident and confined to a hospital for seven days. I was working for the Green

Giant Company, raking vines into a conveyor prior to their having beans plucked off them by machine; riding from one job to another on a rainy, stormy day, the vehicle skidded off the road and into a tree. I suffered a concussion and internal bleeding, and probably shouldn't have gotten out of the hospital and gone practically straight onto the football field.

Football was a nightmare for me during my senior year. I was constantly suffering from double vision. A number of times I simply blacked out. There were other injuries. At this time I didn't like football, didn't like being hurt (I never got used to this), and hoped never to have to play the game again. Playing running back, and a variety of positions on defense, I received a number of college-football scholarship offers. But I decided I could wait on these. I planned to have a great senior year in basketball, and that would be my ticket to college.

Rufus never came to see me play ball in my senior year. His reason was different from those of my parents, but equally valid. His high-school glory days were over, and he saw no sense in reliving them. He said he was going on to something else; what was past was past. I feel the same way today. I seldom go to Dallas Cowboys games. That part of my life is over, and it takes all my energy to concentrate on what I'm doing now. I know also that it is sad to see retired ballplayers still trying to relive their days as an athlete. It is depressing to me, for example, to see Dave Edwards, the excellent former Cowboy strong-side linebacker, recalling his days on the field. Baseball star Mickey Mantle, also, talking about his prodigious home runs. Mantle, I think, has himself finally realized the problem, that those times were wonderful but they are gone forever.

The problem with Rufus, of course, was the "something else" to which he was headed.

I was all-state in basketball in my senior year. It was quite an accomplishment because my forte was not scoring, which is the aspect of the game that usually grabs the headlines. I played center at six feet two and was able to out-rebound players who were much taller. I was an excellent defensive player and shot-blocker. People said my hands were designed for basketball, that my leaping ability allowed me to play many inches taller than I was.

I didn't have any doubt I'd make it to college on a basketball scholarship, and for a brief time I thought of becoming a surgeon. What happened, a career in pro sports, never occurred to me. Going to college by itself was much more than I could have expected. But the idea of being a surgeon was implanted by my biology teacher, watching me carve up a frog in class, remarking about my delicate fingers and the precise incisions I could make. Later, pro coaches would talk in a different vein: "Good hands" they would call the fingers I inherited from my mother.

There were some thirty basketball-scholarship offers waiting for me when my senior year's play ended. Being all-state in basketball-crazy Illinois helped a lot. It was quite an honor. The great Dan Issel, incidentally, was on the same all-state team. The problem was that none of the scholarship offers were from the University of Illinois. Wisconsin wanted me, and Michigan, Bowling Green, and Iowa State. I know my entire life would have been different if I'd gone to Bowling Green. There I would have played with Nate "the Great" Thurmond and Howie Komives, and being on the same team with outstanding players would have made me better. I'm sure there would have been no football career had I gone to Bowling Green. I believe I could have made it in the NBA, and am sure about the ABA. I would have had to play guard, I simply didn't have the height for forward, and would have specialized on defense in the manner of K. C. Jones and, today, Dennis Johnson. It would have been different, playing facing the basket instead of with my back toward it.

I think basketball players have to be much more creative athletically than football players, and much of it is done in the air. Reaction time has to be quicker. I really do believe I could have made it in pro basketball, though because of my lack of height, my career accomplishments would not have equaled those in football.

I still had football-scholarship offers I could accept as the time came to decide on a school, though none of those were from the University of Illinois either. But I wasn't going to accept them.

As I've said, I'd had enough of blurred vision, blackouts,

and poundings taken on the field. And this was only high school. If someone had told me then I'd be back for fourteen years of beatings *in the pros,* I'd have written him off as a lunatic.

The goal was to go to Illinois. It may not be as important for young people today as it was then, but playing for the big state school was the biggest honor most high-school athletes could imagine. I wrote a letter to Harry Combes, basketball coach at U of I, enclosing newspaper clippings about myself and saying, basically, "Hey, take a look at me." Combes wrote back and set a date when I should visit him.

It was a big production, driving to Champaign-Urbana. My mother knew how important the trip was for me, and also realized the time was coming when I'd be leaving home for good; there were tears in her eyes when I took off. This was nothing like the production that took place, however, when I actually did leave for school.

I was scared. I'd seen black athletes in Freeport who were two or three years older than me and who could have gone to college on sports scholarships but didn't. I heard them talk to one another as the moment of decision approached. "I'm not going unless you go," each would say. "Well, I'm not going unless you do." It was sad, and none of them went, but I understand why they didn't. They feared venturing out into the unfamiliar. Better to stay in Freeport, where they knew they could survive, than face a world for which they felt they weren't prepared. Also, there was a tremendous fear of failure. What if they went up to the big school and didn't make it? It would be terrible to come home and face their peers with the knowledge in everyone's head that they weren't good enough, for one reason or another. And how could anyone know in advance if he were good enough? We had nothing by which to judge.

But the apprehension was enormous, and of course more a product of my imagination than reality. No one really was going to laugh at me if I failed. In truth, just making the effort was admirable.

Obviously I wasn't thinking this way at the time. In my mind was the fear that I'd finally gone too far, reached my level of incompetence, as they say today. The worst would come later, when I returned to Freeport a failure, all my friends there to snicker and laugh and taunt. But I'd made up my mind to give it a shot. The older guys who hadn't tried at all didn't seem to be doing very well.

In my mind on the drive to Champaign-Urbana, every athlete I'd meet would be ten feet tall, strong as Hercules, and quick as a cat. I kept thinking it was folly even to consider challenging these titans.

It's true. Sometimes we make gods out of people who are only humans. When you meet them, test yourself against them, you begin to think, *why not me?* Frightened as I was of going up against the big state school, it was minor compared to the time, four years later, when I first stepped onto the practice field to work out with the Baltimore Colts.

I met Harry Combes in his office. I expected he'd put a basketball in my hands and tell me to show him what I could do, but it was nothing like that. Instead we sat and talked, and I got the impression that he was examining me as he might a horse. *What kind of teeth does he have? How strong are those legs? Those hands certainly are interesting.*

Combes, of course, had checked me out before inviting me to visit. He'd called my high-school coach, and other coaches in our conference. While he watched me and talked to me he was wondering if I was too short, and trying to decide whether my skills would improve with time. I could tell he thought it was a plus that I was in the upper third of my class academically.

He took me over to the Assembly Hall, and if his purpose was to impress me, he succeeded. The Assembly Hall could hold more than half of Freeport! I stood on the hardwood and imagined what it would be like to play in such a place. I wanted so much for Combes to tell me right then that I could come to Illinois, play basketball, and get an education. He'd talked about how important school was. This was something I felt I already knew. Play Big Ten basketball and get a college degree. I just might have an easier life than my parents.

But Combes didn't make a commitment. He said I would hear from him. He did make sure I got an excellent meal before I headed back to Freeport. I loved it. Later I learned this was common practice with black athletes in whom a school was interested: Give them a good meal. I was hardly unique in not having had experience with excellent food. Other perquisites were offered white athletes the school was trying to impress.

I heard from Coach Combes a few weeks later by mail. The University of Illinois was willing to offer me a partial athletic scholarship: books, room, and board. I would have to pay my own tuition. Combes said I should show up for registration and someone would be available to get me settled.

I had numerous full-scholarship offers, but there was never a hesitation about where I was going to attend school. With summer jobs I could earn the money for tuition. I'd find work at school for walking-around money.

The summer before I entered college I worked for the Parks Department. With Parks I cut grass, chopped down trees, policed recreation areas; the next summer I worked with the Highway Department repairing roads, learning to use a jackhammer, and scraping dead animals off the pavement and disposing of them. It was hard physical labor mostly assigned to black workers (whites seemed to get more cerebral jobs), but it helped to keep me in good physical shape. Evenings I trained as hard as I ever had in school. If the worst happened and I did have to return to Freeport, it wouldn't be because I wasn't in good condition.

I hoped Rufus would reconsider and go to school with me, but he was more adamant than ever. More withdrawn. I now know he was getting worse, but none of us could tell at the time.

Mom didn't see me off at the train station when I left for Champaign-Urbana carrying a single suitcase. It was very early in the morning when Daddy drove me there, half a mile from our home, and the scene simply would have been too emotional. I knew Mom was very proud of me, but also very sad that I was leaving.

I was seated in a coach when the train went by the back of our house. Mom was in the backyard, a solitary, lonesome figure, and she couldn't have known where I sat, but she was staring at the window I was sitting behind, and her head moved, eyes on me, as the train sped past.

4

The University of Illinois Basket- ball Player

    The college game I'll remember longest is the one we lost by the most points. The score was a horrendous 120–82. It happened in my senior year, and it would be untrue to say the defeat plunged us into deep depression. Sure, we had wanted to win, hoped it would be possible, gotten ourselves sky-high for the contest, but what did we really expect going up against 16–0 UCLA and seven-feet-two Lew Alcindor. UCLA would soon be considered the greatest college basketball team of all time, a distinction many would argue holds true even today. The reason I'll remember the game always has nothing to do with the score.

    The date was January 31, 1967, the site was Chicago Stadium, the event was billed as the biggest basketball weekend in the Windy City's history. Appearing at Chicago Stadium were Texas Western, defending NCAA champions, Brigham Young University, Loyola of Chicago (1963 champions), Notre Dame, Illinois, and UCLA. The coming NCAA Championship was already being billed as "No Chance Against Alcindor," so even a

terrific snowstorm couldn't keep Chicago fans from packing the
building to see the sophomore said to be the superior of Bill
Russell and Wilt Chamberlain.

We weren't in the best shape for UCLA, anyway. About a
month before, one of the largest athletic slush-fund scandals in
history had struck at Illinois, and the punishment meted out
was the most severe I've ever heard of, before or since: Our head
football coach, Pete Elliott, head basketball coach, Harry
Combes, and assistant basketball coach, Howard Braun, were
all fired, and twelve players (seven football, five basketball)
were booted off their respective teams. A total of twenty-one
thousand dollars was said to be involved (I imagine it was much
more), and what shocked the Big Ten athletic directors who
handed out the sentences was the fact that the coaches had
made the payments themselves. Payments from overzealous
alumni were old hat, but this involved the coaches themselves.

The University of Illinois administration professed pro-
found shock at the punishment's severity. The school, the university president, David Henry, pointed out, had turned itself
in, and much worse violators than Illinois had received wrist-
slap treatment in comparison. "What about Michigan State and
Bubba Smith?" some Illinois boosters wanted to know. The
payments to Illinois players, said to be one hundred to four hundred dollars at a time, were nothing compared to the Buick Ri-
viera that Bubba drove. This instance, said Big Ten
Commissioner Bill Reed, had been "thoroughly investigated,"
and it turned out that a Texas car dealer so admired Bubba that
he gave him the car on a "drive now, pay later" basis, meaning
he could retire the debt after he turned pro. This was nonsense,
of course, but Michigan State was never punished. Later,
Bubba admitted that he received some fifty thousand dollars
after his senior season at MSU (supposedly more than the entire
Illinois slush fund), but nothing was done about this either.

Certainly the punishment dished out to Illinois was harsh
in comparison to what other schools received. Woody Hayes got
a "reprimand" for a "personal loan fund" he administered, and
schools such as Michigan State and Indiana were let go with a
year or two of probation. I think Illinois got hit extra hard because records of the payments were recorded and turned over to
the commissioner. The evidence was right there in black and

white. In other cases there was verbal evidence, charges, and countercharges, but nothing so cut-and-dried as a written record. Illinois was so obviously, blatantly guilty, the matter could not be sugar-coated over.

One immediate result was that we took the floor against UCLA that night in Chicago Stadium without Head Coach Harry Combes, Assistant Howard Braun, and three of our starters: six-feet-eight Rich Jones (later played in the ABA), six-feet-eight Steve Kuberski (later with the Boston Celtics), and six-feet-ten Ron Dunlap. With these three in the lineup we had been ranked as high as number three in the country.

Before the game, Dave Scholz, our six-feet-seven-and-a-half-inch sophomore center, didn't help matters by talking about Alcindor: "The man's not perfect. I have a definite plan."

I groaned when I heard the remark, and didn't know then what I know now. You don't rile an opposing player, especially one of Lew Alcindor's ability. It is madness. I remember the rookie who claimed the Detroit Lions great defensive tackle Alex Karras was "overrated," and spent an entire game absorbing a fearsome beating. Other instances are too numerous to list. Leave the Lew Alcindors of the world alone and hope they sleepwalk through the game.

Anyway, Scholz's plan was to play far away from the basket, in the corner, "forcing" Alcindor to come out and guard him. Of course, the giant did no such thing. He ignored Scholz entirely, contenting himself with hanging around the basket to reject shots and grab rebounds.

Scholz's plan on defense was to play Lew one-on-one. The result of this was equally predictable. Alcindor scored forty-five points, mostly on dunks and layups, before the UCLA coach, John Wooden, mercifully removed him. The future Kareem likely could have scored one hundred this night, but there really wasn't any need for them.

But no one should be too hard on Dave Scholz. No matter what kind of defense we might have played, it would have done no good. Had we packed in the defense against Alcindor, Mike Warren (now a star of *Hill Street Blues*), Lucius Allen, and Lynn Shackleford would have killed us from outside. Warren, whom I guarded, and Shackleford were two of the best outside shooters I've ever seen, and the lightning-quick Allen was no slouch either. Warren, from the top of the key, could put them in blindfolded, and Shackleford's rainbow jumper, which looked foolish it went so high in the air, was monotonous in its accuracy. A Shackleford shot would come straight down out of the air and into the basket, then bounce so high on the floor you'd think it was going through again from the bottom.

It was a massacre. The eager Scholz was utterly unable to control Alcindor, but worse still, UCLA outmanned us at most other positions too. Nevertheless, out of such resounding thumpings came moments to remember, which brings me back to mine. In the second half I was guarding Mike Warren out at the point, getting tired of the smile on his face that each moment grew broader, and especially wearied of the ease with which Alcindor was scoring. The best Dave "I Have A Definite Plan" Scholz seemed able to do was to keep Lew four feet away from the basket, which meant all he had to do was turn around and jump a tad to dunk, or turn around (not jump) and lay it in.

Well, just this once, I saw the ball go into Lew, standing four feet from the basket, and out of anger and frustration I left Mike Warren alone and made a furious dash from the point to the basket. I took off, just past the free-throw line, in the highest leap I've ever made, luckily timing it perfectly as Alcindor turned to his right to lay the ball up. I caught the shot just before it hit the backboard, slamming the ball into the board and then far out beyond everyone. The puzzled look on Alcindor's face was like none I've ever seen. I don't think he ever had another shot blocked in his glorious three-year college career, and even as a pro no more than a handful. What puzzled him most was my size, six feet two to his seven feet two, and according to him the memory is still traumatic. He probably just wants to make me feel good—and he succeeds.

What good is a memory if only you have it? But every time I see Kareem he feigns a heart attack. The memory of that night in Chicago doesn't hurt him any, and it makes me glow. A good trivia question: Who was the only player ever to block a Lew Alcindor shot in college?

I think we could have given UCLA a good run for it with Jones, Kuberski, and Dunlap, especially enjoying somewhat of a home-court advantage, but the result would only have been shaving some points off the final margin. In Alcindor's three years at UCLA his team lost only one game, to Houston and Elvin Hayes by one point in the Astrodome, and Lew was playing with an injured eye. UCLA crushed Houston in an NCAA tournament rematch.

I wasn't getting any slush from that fund that resulted in the loss of our coach and three of our best players. I didn't even know it existed, nor that my teammates were receiving money. I do remember a statement made by the Ohio State head basketball coach, Fred Taylor: "For one thing, I'd like to see the kids who take excess money get rapped for a change. You can't tell me kids don't know what they're permitted to receive. A kid has to be pretty naïve not to know he's doing something wrong. I didn't cheat to get Jerry Lucas, and I'm certainly not going to for some hamburger. The salvation of the whole intercollegiate program rests with school control. We're always under severe scrutiny at Ohio State by our own faculty—and because of the league rules."

Leaving aside Taylor's calling athletes "hamburger," which says more about him than his players, his call for stiffer penalties against youngsters barely out of high school seems to me to be out of line. Five players on the Illinois basketball team were suspended from athletic competition, a heavy blow to those involved. And were these young people really to blame?

Basketball was, and I assume still is, a substantial moneymaker for the University of Illinois. Large numbers of people paid hefty prices to see us play. They didn't come to watch Fred Taylor coach, or because they wanted to donate money to the school's general funds. They paid to see the athletes. In exchange the players received a college education, admittedly very valuable, but the money the athletes produced for the school was far greater than the cost of putting them through four years. The players, in effect, were highly productive workers for the school.

Two of those said to have received money from the slush fund were graduated all-America football players Jim Grabowski and Dick Butkus. These two led Illinois to the Rose Bowl, a bonanza for the school and the Big Ten. Football is even more profitable for Illinois than basketball is.

I can't speak for Butkus or Grabowski, or for Jerry Lucas, who might not have needed money, but I can for myself. A lot of times at school I was literally hungry. Although I was receiving board and room, to get the board part of it I had to be in the cafeteria by six P.M., which often was impossible because of the length of practice. Breakfast was at a very early hour and a considerable distance from my dorm room, and often because I was up late studying I missed the morning meal. Lunch, on many occasions, was the only meal I had all day. Getting money from home was simply out of the question, as it was for many athletes.

What would I have done if someone shook my hand and left a hundred dollars in it? I'd have kept the money. And Fred Taylor is not correct when he says, "You can't tell me kids don't know what they're permitted to receive." *I* didn't know. Neither did Steve Spanich, one of the five suspended from our team. "We didn't know anything about a slush fund," Spanich said. "We were told the money we got was legal. We were given jobs by sponsors assigned to us, and we felt the payment we got was for the work we did."

I wasn't alone in knowing little but what I'd observed from the prism of a small-town working-class family. To say you'd like to see kids get rapped seems worse than insensitive. If I were in the same position as my parents, I would tell my son that under present circumstances he should take what is offered him.

The issue admittedly is a delicate one. But the fact is that a youngster receiving money is more likely to be kept on the team than a player who is not, or, in the case of the pros, someone who gets paid more than a teammate is more valuable. The powers-that-be, whether a college athletic department or a pro team's ownership, are more likely to keep the athlete in whom they have the most invested.

Should college athletes be paid? My answer is yes and no. Yes, because since the athlete is making money for the school, he should reap the benefit of his labor. Herschel Walker comes to mind. He probably made $500,000 or more for the University of Georgia every game he played. Why should the school, exclusively, reap this windfall?

But my answer is also no, and comes from my experience representing athletes. Very rare indeed is the college player, and only slightly less rare is the pro, who can handle goodly sums of money. I know I had no conception of how to handle sizable sums of money when I was in college, nor do most college students.

What to do? In basketball, and increasingly in football with the USFL, players are leaving college early to compete professionally. Millions of dollars are there for the grabbing, and it would seem insanity to continue on in college. Yet that is what is needed.

Take Marcus Dupree. He was nineteen years old when he signed with the New Orleans Breakers for six million dollars. The key is *nineteen years old*. Forget that he's from a small town in Mississippi and already has had trouble in college. He is *nineteen*. There is no way he is equipped to handle six million dollars, much less play pro football. He can't comprehend the magnitude of what he has gotten into, and I do not envy him a bit. He is a kid going into a man's game. I don't care how well he did at Oklahoma. The pro game is completely different and he is not prepared for it mentally or physically. Mentally he lacks the maturity the pro game demands, the intense desire required. Physically, no matter what a great specimen he may be, he is still a youngster up against men; his body is not ready for the beating it is going to take. Marcus Dupree could very easily suffer a career-ending injury before his pro career should ever have begun.

One asks where it will stop. Moses Malone and Darryl Dawkins were taken out of high school and thrown into the pros. There is less danger in basketball than in football, but I still think it is a mistake to let this happen. It is so easy, with great amounts of money involved, to come into contact with the wrong people. I'm sure it would break readers' hearts if they knew some of the athletes I do, great names in the sport, struggling now to keep body and soul together. I think of Thomas Henderson and Duane Thomas, trying to pawn or sell their Super Bowl rings, but there are many besides these two.

Brigham Young quarterback Steve Young recently signed a $40-million deal with the USFL Los Angeles Express, although he was not the outstanding football player of his year (Mike Rozier won the Heisman). Young received this guarantee without ever having played a single down of pro football, and it really can't be foretold what kind of performer he'll turn out to be. Proved veteran stars like Walter Payton, Earl Campbell, Tony Dorsett, Ken Anderson, and Joe Montana could rightly claim, if Steve Young is worth $40 million, their value is at least $160 million; but the point is that great sums of money are being thrown at young athletes who are not capable of handling it.

That was never my problem, particularly when I arrived in Champaign-Urbana from Freeport for my freshman year. No one was at the station to greet me, and I took a taxi to Weston Hall, the dorm I was to stay in, because I didn't know how else to get there. I arrived with two hundred dollars, which was going to be my bankroll for the entire year unless I found part-time work, and I hated parting with even a few dollars of it for that cab. I think when the news of the slush fund scandal broke, what upset me the most was the feeling that maybe the coaches didn't think I was valuable enough to the team to deserve help. It certainly wasn't because I didn't need help. As it turned out I did work part-time jobs, but these were made more difficult because of the hours I had to spend practicing and traveling. I'm grateful I didn't get involved in that slush-fund mess, but I certainly can't whip myself up into anger over those who did.

I was filled with awe on my first night on campus. I went around gawking like a tourist, craning my neck to see the tall buildings. This was the autumn of 1963, I was eighteen years old, and everything seemed very large compared to my frame of reference—Freeport.

That night I didn't sleep well. The room was quite small, even for one person, and I knew it wouldn't get any better. My roommate, a white upperclassman, hadn't arrived yet. I didn't sleep well because it seemed cold in that room. Actually, the temperature was just right. Generally, poor black families, such as mine, keep the heat turned very high because they cannot afford warm clothes and thick blankets. The high temperatures maintained in these black homes probably contribute to a number of health problems.

I'd made up my mind to do really well this first semester, and indeed my grades were the highest I received in my four years at Illinois. My prime motivation was fear. It would just have been too horrible to return to what I imagined would be the taunts of childhood friends if I didn't make the grade. That was the strongest motivation, but also powerful was the realization that if I failed I'd be throwing away all the hard years I'd spent getting there. I wanted that education. The sheepskin. That was what motivated me.

College was good for me. I had to learn to get by on my own, though of course not in such a harsh environment as faces many young people. For one thing, I had to learn to do my own wash, hardly a complicated task, but nonetheless one I'd never done. Mom always assigned us to the ironing, which I hated, but never to the washing.

What Mom and Daddy did give me was a sense of responsibility. They were never late for work. I was never late for class. I didn't have an alarm clock, but somehow always got there. Besides, I continued to *like* school. The physical-education courses, needed if I were to achieve my goal of becoming a high-school coach, were not difficult for me. Other subjects offered the challenge I often felt had been missing at Freeport.

Weston Hall was mostly white, and I didn't make any close friends. My roommate and I stayed out of each other's way; we were civil and amicable enough, but nothing more. He smoked a pipe and wore wool jackets, and though he might not have had brain one I figured he was an intellectual. He probably thought I was a dumb jock. In any case, I studied as hard as I could, determined to get good grades, and stayed to myself. The hardest part was a lack of self-discipline. In high school there were mandatory study halls. At Illinois there was much greater freedom.

Freshman basketball practice started November 1, and I was filled with the same fear I'd known before and would in the future. Maybe I wasn't good enough, perhaps this was all a bad joke and I was going to be exposed as inadequate. The worry had been there in high school, though not so seriously because that competition was known to me and I felt I could excel against it. But this was the big time, at least the biggest time I'd ever known: the mighty Big Ten, conference of every Illinois school kid's dreams, and only the best were invited here.

At this time freshmen couldn't play varsity ball. We had a schedule of our own. The rule has since been changed, chiefly I suspect because basketball players were becoming better so much faster that some frosh teams could defeat the varsity. I remember Wilt Chamberlain as a freshman and the thrill everyone experienced when his squad defeated the Kansas varsity. I think the freshman team of Oscar Robertson at Cincinnati accomplished the same thing. I doubt if UCLA was superior to Lew Alcindor and his frosh classmates.

My fears of not being able to compete at this exalted level dissipated with the first practice. I was good enough. And I was smart enough in school too. I could tell that from the reaction of professors. It was a great feeling, the realization that I really might make it.

I was a starter on the freshman team from the first day. I was worried that because I wasn't a great scorer I might be overlooked, but that fear was dismissed early. I started at both forward and guard, depending on which position the other team's top scorer played. My job was to hold him in check. It was felt I had the quickness and size to stay with most guards, and the strength and leaping ability to compete against much taller forwards.

My second semester experiences were more memorable because of the fraternity I pledged than because of my activities in basketball. It came about when an acquaintance named Hard Rock, a tough little guy who was on the wrestling team, invited me to check out his fraternity, Kappa Alpha Psi. I'd like to think he wanted me for my personality and good character, but I suspect being an athlete had something to do with it. Weighing even more heavily, perhaps, as I was unfortunate enough to learn, was the fact that people weren't exactly beating down the doors to get admitted. Nothing in my life prepared me for pledging Kappa Alpha Psi.

The fraternity was mostly black, as were two others on campus, and two sororities. I've always associated hazing and Hell Week with white kids, but Kappa Alpha Psi was in a league all its own. I've played in pro football games that were less punishing than KAP's Hell Week. While mostly white fraternities at Illinois contented themselves with forcing hapless pledges to swallow goldfish, crowd into telephone booths, or find their way home naked through the woods, Kappa Alpha Psi tried to raise brutality to new heights. It wasn't so bad being forced to act like you had no brains, or to pretend you enjoyed being treated like

a slave, or even having your head shaved so the only hair remaining formed a giant K. The really bad part was the physical
abuse.

Stark-naked pledges were led into a completely dark room.
No light at all. Right behind me was Joe Payton, a 235-pound
football player, and he had a bad feeling about this. His feeling
was confirmed. Suddenly candles were lit all around us, and fraternity members began beating us with rolled newspapers. They
hit hard. These were not playful swats being dealt out, but hard,
rough, hurting blows.

Robert Johnson, now president of Black Entertainment
Television, was a Kappa Alpha Psi pledge. In the basement of
the fraternity house he was knocked down and suffered a
wicked gash on his hand. A skin graft, coming from his right
thigh, had to be made to repair the damage.

Another time, stark naked, we were beaten with wet towels
tied into knots, slapped around, and struck with paddles. I could
see that husky Joe Payton was close to bursting into a frenzy
of retaliation, and he likely could have counted on me to join
him.

The worst was when the "Beast of Beta" showed up. He
was a high-up fraternity member from another school, and his
job was to see that pledges weren't being treated with kid
gloves. I figured there was no danger he would suspect this. I
was wrong.

Beast of Beta decided we weren't shaping up. The pledges
had been forced to learn to recite the Greek alphabet, an exercise I imagine had some merit, but Beast of Beta added a twist.
He ordered us to hold a lit match upside down between our fingers, and we weren't supposed to let it go until we'd gone
through the Greek alphabet. It is of course extremely painful to
hold a burning match, but some of us tried to do it until the reci-
tation was complete. Others, more sensibly, dropped the match
to the floor and started over.

What might really have made sense would have been to
say, "No more, this is silly and degrading, maybe even dangerous, and I don't need this fraternity that badly." But we were
macho, wanted to prove we were tough, and no one had the
nerve to be the first one to say, "Forget it." Also, there was psychological pressure. We were told numerous famous blacks be-

longed to Kappa Alpha Psi—Walter Fauntroy, the civil rights leader and congressman, was one—and that this illustrious company would serve us well in future years. Every time I was ready to tell Beast of Beta, or whomever else was harassing us, to take a leap, I thought of Walter Fauntroy or some other worthy, and held my tongue.

Gale Sayers, Harvey Martin, and Butch Johnson were other members of Kappa Alpha Psi. None of these attended Illinois, and I don't know if their experiences were different from mine. It is hard to imagine Harvey Martin taking such abuse, but then again I can't believe I let myself soak it up the way I did.

The worst was when Beast of Beta lined up a group of us and told us to put our hands out, palms up. He then took a half-inch-thick paddle and started beating on our hands. He kept it up. And up. The pain was excruciating, and after a while our entire bodies shook. I looked at Joe Payton and thought he was a hairbreadth away from homicide. A small fellow named Jimmy was in tears and nearly hysterical, but few of us could really identify with him. The least little thing caused him to whine, and it was almost embarrassing sometimes to watch him grovel and plead for mercy. Interestingly enough, when Jimmy became a full-fledged member of the fraternity, he devised methods to make life miserable for pledges that would have made Beast of Beta blush.

For a time I was dean of pledges of Kappa Alpha Psi, and I know life improved considerably under my reign. The fraternity "pranks" often can seem a harmless manifestation of college life, and they can be this, but too often there is a malevolent undercurrent of cruelty and sadism. I've seen the same thing in professional football. Good, hard hits are one thing; attempts to injure are another.

In the middle of my second semester I was able to move from Weston Hall to the Kappa Alpha Psi fraternity house, and I must say I was happier there. I disliked Hell Week nearly as much as the pledges, and remember specifically one torture Jimmy devised. A pledge was plastered with flour and molasses and forced to lie on the floor. Jimmy heated a spoon red-hot over the stove and then applied it to the pledge's back. The hideous result need not be described. I think my protests and the protests of others helped stop some of the more gross abuses, but Hell Week remained a true hell.

Many of the students in the fraternity house were from places like St. Louis and Chicago, much larger cities than Freeport, but from working-class and black neighborhoods like my own. I had not had a great deal in common with most residents of Weston Hall—our backgrounds were very different—but at Kappa Alpha Psi there were people in whom I could confide. Incredibly, if you could blot out Hell Week and hazing, the brothers were very decent sorts.

There was a lot of pride in our old, broken-down fraternity house, which was home for me during my remaining years at Illinois. We had an excellent mix of athletes and scholars (some members were both), and I know at least two of the brothers are now MDs.

The first semester before I moved into Kappa Alpha Psi was marked by the assassination of President John F. Kennedy. Of course, I remember what I was doing: walking from a class to Weston Hall. For some reason I didn't understand, I was terribly touched by his death. I know my father thought he was an honorable man, and I guess my impression was the same, though why it moved me so much I can't really say. Fresh from Freeport, I was hardly political, and had formed few opinions in this area. I guess a lot of black people thought they had lost a friend. Interestingly, this terrible event was my first impression of Dallas, Texas, my current home and scene of my most important years as a football player.

I worked at the Highway Department during the summer between my freshman and sophomore years, doing hard manual labor, and although I certainly didn't blow money (this was near-minimum-wage work), I wasn't as careful as I was the previous summer. I didn't think I had to be. During my first visit with Harry Combes, the one after he sent me the letter to visit the campus, he'd told me I would receive a full scholarship my second year if I made the freshman team. Not only had I made the team, I was a starter.

"I don't remember making any such promise," he said, when I stopped by his office before registering for classes.

"Well, I do," I said. I told him the time and the circumstances.

"I don't recall that," he repeated.

"I think you should live up to your promise." I was very shy, and these words did not come easily.

"I can't remember any promise. There wasn't one. And it's just impossible, anyway. There aren't any more scholarships available."

This was probably true. Illinois had enjoyed a banner recruiting year, and the freshmen crop, before the slush-fund scandal hit, would be the heart of the team that took us as high as number three in the nation.

"I don't know what I'm going to do," I said.

"I don't either." He had a smile on his face. How does one read a smile? I judged it to mean, *Well, I put one over on you. You weren't very bright, were you?*

My initial reaction was intense, and in retrospect almost surely healthy. I decided I would show Harry Combes he had made a mistake. I'd make the varsity team, become a starter. He clearly didn't care if this too-short, six-feet-two leaper even stayed in school, much less went out for basketball again: He had his hotshot freshmen, and these were the ones upon whom the future would be built. Well, I'd work harder than ever before, make his team despite what he thought.

I had to find work. I didn't even have the two hundred dollars I'd started my freshman year with, and there were necessary expenses just to keep myself whole. I got a job washing dishes in the fraternity kitchen, and another selling programs at the football games. I knew I was just scraping by, but it was worth it if the result was a degree and the opportunity to coach.

Illinois had quite a football team my sophomore year, and watching them kept me from becoming completely stale where the game was concerned. This was the Illinois of Dick Butkus and Jim Grabowski, later standouts with the Bears and the Packers respectively, the Big Ten's representative in the Rose Bowl. It was said of Butkus, a fearsome man: "If you stay on the field, he'll get you."

I really believe Coach Combes thought I was not very bright, but the way things turned out I think the opposite was true. I was and still am very angry with the university, and never attend any of the functions to which I'm invited. More important, I've refused the school's numerous requests to assist

in recruiting. As my years in pro football marched on, and my
Super Bowl appearances mounted, I became well known to
many youngsters, and particularly in my area of Illinois. The
school asked me to recruit Ira Matthews for them, an athlete
good enough to play later with the Los Angeles Raiders, and numerous other youngsters, but I've always refused to do so. I
suppose Illinois should be grateful I didn't talk with recruits,
because I would have told them to stay away from the school.

I've been told I hold a grudge too long, that Harry Combes
is long gone from Illinois, that bygones should be bygones. But I
try to keep *my* promises, and in many ways Harry Combes *was*
Illinois. He was their representative, and in truth had the ultimate say about whether an athlete continued in school and got
an education. I suppose I could have gone over his head, but I
was too inexperienced even to think of that. Besides, I doubt it
would have helped. Harry Combes's influence on campus was
significant, and in all likelihood the matter would have been
kicked back to him. Without an agent, attorney, or union, athletes can be pretty helpless. Under the circumstances I believe I
did the right thing—not making waves and giving extra effort to
contribute to the team. If I'd been able to cause a flap, it would
not have received the publicity that would have prompted the
Colts to draft me.

A fraternity brother was often in the kitchen while I
worked, flirting with one of the women cooks. Finally she just
got angry with him. "Why can't you be like Preston?" she said,
nodding in the direction where I was washing dishes.

"Preston?" he laughed. "That's right. Be like Preston. Do
nothing. Be nothing. Say nothing."

I was angry at the time, but the more I thought about what
the fraternity brother said, the more it seemed he had a point. I
seldom spoke up, not just because I was shy, but because I
wasn't sure I had anything to say. And what was I? Certainly
not as impressive as those Kappa Alpha Psi grads whom I heard
constant reminders about. What was I doing? Not anything
great. Playing basketball and going to college. I decided I was
angry because there was truth in what I heard, especially the
part about saying nothing.

It was almost a year later, as a junior, when I got up the
nerve to do something about it. I'd walked hand-in-hand with a

girlfriend into Huff Gymnasium, prior to a practice, and was confronted by Assistant Coach Howard Braun. His face was red and his eyes blazed. I thought that very little on earth could make someone this angry.

"I don't want to ever see anything like this again," he hissed, eyes darting back and forth between me and the girl.

At first I didn't know why he was angry. Then I realized: He didn't want a female in a hallowed male area. "Listen," I said, "I'll do most everything you tell me on the basketball floor. But nowhere else. You don't own me anywhere else."

Coach Braun was just amazed. He wasn't used to people like me talking back. I didn't calm his anger any, but he must have seen my eyes and how furious I was. He didn't say another word.

I think this small but important triumph gave me the confidence to stand up for my rights. It didn't happen all at once, and I never became a blazing militant, but it did help teach me that if you don't want to be pushed around, you have to stand up straight and say so. This applies even more in the pros. Management is often quite willing to take advantage of you if you let it happen, or if you don't have the clout to alter the situation. I think this realization later influenced me to play a key role in the NFL Players Union, and also to represent players in negotiations.

There were plenty of parties at the Kappa Alpha Psi fraternity house. It was known for parties, and I attended my share. I think in some respects they were good for me. I was never a heavy drinker, but I enjoyed dancing and meeting girls, and the parties helped improve me socially, something that could never have happened in Freeport.

Some of the best basketball I ever played happened after a party, and I've often wondered about the strategy of the vast majority of coaches who dictate a spartan off-field regimen for athletes. I'm thinking specifically of Coach Tom Landry of the Cowboys because I played under him for so long, but his ideas are shared by most other coaches. In 1983, for example, after I'd retired, Coach Landry, undoubtably a tactical genius, initiated a plan shared by many teams prior to this (Pittsburgh and Baltimore, for instance) whereby players stayed together in a hotel the night before *home* games. The purpose of this, of course, is to keep the players' minds on the game (where else would their minds be?), but I think it is counterproductive. I also think it is merely an extension of the Cowboy strategy to hold training camp in Thousand Oaks, California, rather than in Texas. Surely the weather in Texas is conducive to getting players in shape (the Houston Oilers train in Texas—and no jokes, please, about the Oilers' record: They lose because of their personnel).

Forget the fact that training camp is too long, that football at the highest level requires a fine edge that can be dulled by the tedium of a season that is already too long. What matters particularly is that most Dallas Cowboy players live in Dallas, yet they are training in California. The athletes are always away from their friends and family and any business interests they have (and they are wise to have business interests, since most pro careers are brief as a flicker). Whatever advantages are gained by separating the player from his normal environment are outweighed by the worry he suffers because of the separation.

Coaches contend that they want the players concentrating on football. I ask, what else would they be concentrating on? If I know I'm going to be facing Dick Butkus on Sunday, I guarantee my mind is going to be on that subject. An athlete would have to be a fool to be thinking of something else. The pro-football player knows his career can end at any moment, with the horror of a shattered knee or the tragedy of permanent crippling, and he knows also that he must make the most of the short time allotted him in the limelight. There are always younger men coming along, often bigger and stronger (you hope not more hungry). Self-discipline is in the end more important than any imposed by a coach.

I'm not in any sense advocating that anarchy should prevail. I am saying that baby-sitting is not part of the job of a coach. I usually avoid questions about how to pick a Super Bowl winner, but I'll offer one idea here. I believe you'll find that most winners of Super Bowl games were the teams with fewer off-the-field rules (Tom Flores and the Oakland Raiders, for example, versus Dick Vermiel and the Eagles), the teams that offered the most freedom of expression.

One of my best friends at Illinois was Don Freeman, a six-feet-three forward who became the all-time Illini scoring champion. Freeman helped me a lot in college, in many respects taking the place of Rufus as an advisor and confidant. Like me, Don Freeman was very shy, but he was quite a leader. He led by example, through the standards he applied to his own game, the tenacity with which he played. He had enormous spirit and desire, and seeing that he could overcome his height disadvantage gave me hope. Freeman also encouraged me to maintain my grades, to keep my life straight, always to give 100 percent in whatever I did. Freeman later played for the Dallas Chapparals in the ABA and the Los Angeles Lakers in the NBA, and was a vice-president of RepublicBank in Dallas. Most important, he's still a good friend, and I could do worse than model myself after him. The E. F. Hutton commercial could apply to Don Freeman: When he talks, people listen.

In basketball I was usually assigned to guard the opposition's most potent scorer, unless he was a seven-feet-two center like Kareem, or some other young tower. I guarded Cazzie Russell, Jimmy Walker (Providence, later with the Pistons), Rick Mount of Purdue, Archie Clark and Lou Hudson of Minnesota, Pat Riley of Kentucky (now the coach of the Lakers). Cazzie Russell and Jimmy Walker were the toughest for me. Walker was frighteningly, awesomely quick, but Cazzie was more difficult because he could go both inside and outside. He was a deadly shooter from the perimeter, with his flick-of-the-wrist jumper, and he could also post up, muscle you under the basket. Cazzie, of course, was one of the great players ever in the game.

My on-court personality couldn't have clashed more with the way I was in daily life. I was very aggressive, I had to be because of my lack of height, and I was involved in a number of fights they still talk about in the Big Ten. I had no idea that the tough brand of defense I played against mostly much bigger men would catch the eye of an NFL coach and lead me into a career completely unexpected.

It was on a visit home during my junior year that the situation with Rufus reached a climax. My parents told me they were very worried about him. He was staying by himself in his room, only leaving to work at his job making batteries for airplanes, and often when my parents looked in on him he was wearing a T-shirt over his head. In addition, he reached a frightening level of verbal violence. His threats of inflicting bodily harm were accompanied by eyes that were inflamed with hate. The phrase "looks that could kill" applied to Rufus.

Once I saw him threatening to hurt my parents. Then he bolted out of the house, slamming the door so hard he rattled the walls. Mom was trembling. She asked me to call the police, to ask them to get him psychiatric help. She feared he would hurt someone.

I should have known there would be trouble when I mentioned possible violence, and the officer on the phone immediately said, "We'll take care of it." I tried to tell him more, but he'd heard all he needed to.

Mom and I went into the backyard and spotted Rufus several hundred yards away at the train station. He was just pacing back and forth, shoulders slumped, a lonely figure in need of help. We raced to the car to get him.

The police beat us there. It may have been the worst scene I have ever witnessed. The two officers had slammed Rufus against an automobile and were handcuffing him behind his back. They shoved him around as they might an animal. Mom was shaking her head with fear and horror. This wasn't at all what we'd intended. We'd wanted to help Rufus, not subject him to the nightmare of being treated as a criminal. All the cops had remembered was my saying "possible violence."

It got worse. Mom and I had to go to the police station to commit Rufus to a mental institution in Rockford. My father also was crushed by all of this. With Rufus I always think of the words of John Greenleaf Whittier: "It might have been."

Rufus stayed at the mental institution for a year. Mom visited him every week and Daddy went when he could, and the doctors always talked about how well adjusted and intelligent Rufus seemed. He was intelligent, but well adjusted he was not. The doctors said they knew something was wrong with him, but they didn't know what. To this day they don't know what.

When Rufus came home he was on medication. He still is. We don't know what's the matter with him. It breaks my heart.

Rufus took up smoking when he got home—three or four packs a day. The medication stopped the verbal violence, but it didn't make him whole again. He no longer worked out at all; his once-wonderful body began the too-early process of decay.

He tried to find work, but that year in the institution made it virtually impossible. Many employers have an unreasonable antipathy to hiring anyone afflicted with the taint of mental illness, no matter that the individual poses no danger and is perfectly qualified for the job. It was a long time before Daddy was able to find a job for Rufus. My brother was able to do the work, and I'm sure it benefited everyone that he was once again productive, but Rufus remained reserved, withdrawn, uncommunicative, a prisoner in a world only he inhabited.

Like most citizens, I view with suspicion the legal defense of temporary insanity, but I often think and wonder about the subject. What happened to Rufus is just so heartbreaking. Sometimes I believe that, given the wrong set of circumstances, anyone can become mentally unbalanced. My family and I would like to know what went wrong with Rufus, but chiefly we wish something could be done to restore him to what he was. I guess it is like when a tooth hurts. You don't go and ask the dentist why; why isn't important. You just want the remedy.

It was in the spring of my junior year—1966—at a Kappa Alpha Psi party that I met Linda Finley. I didn't give her a lot of thought at the time, nor did she lose any sleep thinking about me. She was just there, and I noticed her, a small, vivacious, attractive white girl at a party primarily attended by blacks. This was unusual enough, and what especially caught my attention was how comfortable she seemed. She was just having fun, black or white didn't matter to her (it's virtually impossible to fake this), and I thought this was a person worth getting to know better.

I ran into Linda later in the Student Union cafeteria, and this led to a couple of dates, nothing even resembling seriousness. When we went our separate ways for summer vacation, neither was really on the other's mind. I asked Linda if she thought I'd see her in the fall. "If you want to," she said, "you'll give me a call. If not, I just can't see any use thinking about it."

Neither could I. But the next semester I did make the call.

The years 1966 and 1967 were politically active ones on college campuses, what with the war in Vietnam, and the University of Illinois was no exception. I wasn't personally involved in the protests. I really wasn't sufficiently versed on the issues, but I did feel a kinship for those who opposed our country's involvement in the conflict. For one thing, they seemed to raise questions that weren't being answered. More important, they were opposed to war, a stance that has always appealed to me.

I remember reading about people saying the hippies and yippies would go away real fast if some football team was turned loose on them. I don't know about that. I knew many of the football players at Illinois, and later in the pros, and I never noticed any obvious displays of support for the Vietnam War. I think athletes were divided into as similar a percentage of supporters and opposers as was the public in general. Now the *coaches*—they were different. There were more coaches in support of the Vietnam War.

I gave Linda a call shortly after returning from summer vacation (which for me was working a full-time job), and we began dating on a regular basis. Linda was two years behind me in school, but much brighter, much more sophisticated. She was very skilled at math, accounting, and bookkeeping, and although she had not decided on a major when I met her, eventually became a CPA. Just five feet three and petite, she was open and sincere, and one of the most honest people I've ever known.

Linda's family was living outside Chicago when I met her. She didn't tell them about me until much later, which probably was best. Her father was a career military munitions inspector, and Linda was an army brat. I think this gave her a broader perspective than many of her peers. She had lived in Switzerland, West Germany, and Japan, and had seen and learned firsthand about things I hadn't even read about.

Linda knew much more about life than I did, but even she wasn't prepared for the reactions, mostly from white people, that we would encounter. Today an interracial couple can expect to experience people doing doubletakes, but in 1966 you were more likely to be met with glacial stares of hostility. It happened wherever we went, on campus and off. The hatred was very deep. A white woman with a black man is the combination that most terrifies racists. They may not like a black woman with a white man, but it doesn't drive them crazy.

This surprised me more than Linda. She'd seen more of the world, knew more about racial bigotry. There were times I didn't notice. Linda would have to tell me.

One time we drove to a fast-food restaurant and I went in to get some burgers. Four or five whites of college age or older were parked in a car next to ours, and when I came out Linda was tense, tight-lipped.

"What's wrong?" I asked, as I pulled into the street.

"Nothing."

"C'mon. Something's wrong."

"It's nothing, Preston."

"I know it's something."

It turned out she wanted me to get away from there before she told me. Of course, she'd been called a "nigger lover," nigger this and nigger that, the worst kind of racist rot, coming from real men, four or five of them against one little girl, and she didn't want me to know because of what I would have done to them. It wasn't so much the "nigger" that bothered me. I figure a "nigger" is someone low and dirty, and I'm neither of these. It's that they abused a defenseless person.

But it was bad. The sad, miserable truth I was learning is that many persons still can't get beyond color to what really counts, the character and moral worth of an individual.

It got so bad we drove out in the country one night, parked, and I said to Linda, "Everybody tells me this can't work. I agree with them."

I looked at her, and we both started to cry. We'd gone to dances together, ate out together, went to movies and parties, and just took walks. She always came to basketball games to cheer.

"We can't let other people tell us how to run our lives," Linda finally said.

I looked at her, this spunky little girl whose best quality was being herself, and I thought, *Well, she's right.* It was our life. It was what I'd told Howie Braun when he'd gotten mad because I'd brought a girl into the gym.

The hostility just brought us closer. What else could it do? We were in love with each other and, besides, what were the choices? If we broke up, the idea would be that maybe we really didn't love each other that much after all. No, the hostility worked to bring us closer. It was only natural that, being under attack, we would cling closer to each other.

Linda was very strong, a person who could make up her own mind, and I know her influence helped me in later years to stand up for my own interests. She would weigh the good and the bad of a situation quite carefully, and then make her decision based on what was right. I could do worse than to emulate her.

During several basketball games in my senior year I was told by Assistant Coach Howie Braun that I should play extra hard, that NFL scouts were in the stands to watch me. I never paid much attention to this. I was a *basketball* player. Why come to see me? I hadn't played football since high school, didn't particularly like the game, especially the ease with which a player could be injured. But Braun assured me it was true. He said Big Ten coaches had been talking about how aggressive I was, what good athletic ability I had, and that NFL coaches had taken heed. In any case, I never saw, much less talked to, an NFL scout.

A few friends said, "Hey, maybe the Bears will take a look at you." I doubted it. I had received a brochure telling me about the Dallas Cowboys in my junior year, but had heard nothing from them.

If there were scouts in the stands, they may indeed have been impressed with what they saw. As I've said, I had to be superaggressive because of my lack of height (and the fact that I was usually guarding the opposing team's star), and if fights mattered to a scout (and I learned they do), I got into my share of those.

In any case, I barely gave a thought to pro football, and certainly it was far from my mind when in early May 1967, the most important visitor of my life knocked on my fraternity-room door.

"Who's there?" I said. *It had better be important,* I thought. I had good reason not to want to be disturbed.

"Coach Key. I need to talk to you, Preston."

Coach Ronnie Key was an assistant with the football team. I had no idea what he wanted, and didn't think I wanted to hear.

"Can I come see you in a little while?" I said. *Go away,* I thought.

"You've been drafted by the Baltimore Colts. Coach Don Shula is on the telephone to our office. He wants to talk to you."

"What's that?" Linda whispered.

"I've been drafted by the Baltimore Colts," I told her. It hadn't sunk in.

"That's wonderful," she said.

"Let me in, Preston," Coach Key said. "I want to shake your hand."

I opened the door an inch and peeked through. It was Coach Key, all right. I looked at Linda, then back to the door.

"You okay, Preston?" Key sounded concerned.

"I'm fine," I said. I realized I'd just slammed the door in his face. "Ah, the room is a little messy."

"Won't bother me a bit. This is a big moment, son. Let me in."

Well, I can state categorically that it would have bothered him. Much, if not all, of his happiness would have gone poof if he'd known Linda was in the room with me.

"This is such good news," Linda said to me.

"What is?"

"That you've been drafted, you dummy. Get some decent clothes on and go with him."

I opened the door, just a crack, and peered out again. It really was Coach Key. This was hardly a man known for his humor. No way would he be involved in a fraternity prank, or some other wiseacre scheme. I shut the door again.

"I've been drafted by the Baltimore Colts!" I shouted, as loud as I could.

"I know," said Linda. She gave me a long hug.

"Stand behind the door," I told her, when I had my best clothes on. I couldn't think of anywhere else. My room wasn't much larger than a closet.

"He won't see me, Preston. You just go."

The Baltimore Colts! My honest and truly favorite team. Everyone has a favorite team, and the Colts were mine. I guess it was because of Johnny Unitas and John Mackey and Willie Richardson. Walking, no, flying across campus with Coach Key, I fantasized about what it would be like just having my name on the same roster as Johnny Unitas.

The Chicago Bears would have been okay, I decided. Gale

Sayers and Willie Galimore and Dick Butkus. But the Baltimore Colts! I didn't bother to tell myself to slow down. I knew I probably wouldn't make the team. I hadn't played football in four years, a lifetime in sports. But I'd go to training camp with them. I'd meet Johnny Unitas and John Mackey and Willie Richardson. And I'd give it everything I had. I wouldn't fail to make the team because of lack of effort.

I heard Coach Key tell me I'd been drafted as the Colts twelfth-round draft choice. No one from the football team had been drafted, and it was clear he thought I would have gone higher had I heeded his advice and that of Coach Pete Elliott. They had wanted me on the football team. I was cordial with them whenever they broached the idea, but told them truthfully that I just wasn't enamored of the sport.

Things were different now. It wasn't that I suddenly loved football. Put simply, I had nothing better to do, and in fact had been worried for a considerable period of time about what I would do when the school year ended. I knew I would be twelve hours short of my degree, because of the demands of basketball practice and the need to hold down various jobs to keep myself whole. My scholarship, partial though it was, would run out with the end of the spring term. I assumed, though no definite plans had been made, I would have to get a job and save enough money so I could finish those twelve hours. There was no sense even looking for a coaching job until that was accomplished.

But now life had changed for me. I had something in front of me for which to reach. When we arrived at the office to which Shula supposedly had called, I was already thinking about what great experience I'd acquire just going to training camp. And I was thinking about how hard I was going to work.

Coach Shula was really on the telephone. To say I was wide-eyed and thinking *Oh wow!* sounds corny, but that is indeed what I was thinking. The great Don Shula was calling me, and the entire University of Illinois football staff was huddled around, smiling and patting me on the back.

"Preston?"

"Yes, sir."

"Preston, we've drafted you on the twelfth round."

"Yes, sir."

"We have a contract there for you to sign."

"Yes, sir."

Coach Shula kept telling me things, and I kept saying, "Yes, sir." He could have told me anything, and that would have been my reply. I heard him say, although it really didn't sink in until later, that the Colts wanted to use me as a defensive back, at least this was their thinking now, and what kinds of workouts I should do before training camp, and where I should go for help.

"I'll see you later in the summer," were his last words.

"Yes, sir," I said.

I hung up the phone and a man I'd been barely aware of began talking to me, explaining things I didn't understand. Suddenly I realized it was former football great L. G. DuPree. Long Gone DuPree, a spectacular player in his prime. He had a contract he wanted me to sign, and something else too: a $1,000 signing bonus.

The contract called for $15,000 the first season, *if* I made the team. There was never any doubt I would sign it, and I probably did the right thing. As a Number 12 draft pick I was hardly the player the Colts were building their franchise around, and the offer was probably a take-it-or-leave-it proposition. I took it, right there, on the spot.

It was one of the most purely happy moments of my life, though of course I know now that this was only because my experience in the business world was zero. But the feeling was one I'll never forget. I had a $1,000 check. Not only more money by far than I'd ever had, but more than my father, or his father, had ever had. A thousand dollars. In my hand. And L. G. DuPree patting me on the back. And dreams of untold glory to come.

I knew nothing. I do know that youngsters, like I was in 1967, need good, sound, solid business advice. I had no more business signing a complicated contract than if I had been trying to fly a spaceship. And I had no business with $1,000 in my hand either.

I took the money home a few days later, Daddy helped me open a checking account, and then he cosigned a note with me for a new Bonneville. I still remember the look in his eyes. He knew buying that car was a mistake, but he was going to let me make it. It could have been worse—the Colts could have given me a $30,000 signing bonus to blow—and Daddy, realizing it was hopeless to try and talk me out of it, hoped I would learn something for the future.

But that didn't occur until later. The $1,000 was gone in an eye's blink, and the Bonneville, predictably, ended up being repossessed. In this instance the Colts were not unfair with me where money was concerned. What was wrong, if I may use the analogy, was putting a loaded gun in the hands of a child. Like many other young athletes, I was not prepared to manage money.

It was great that one night, though. I couldn't cash the check, of course (I didn't even know how to endorse it), but Linda and I pooled some nickles and dimes and went out to enjoy some good hamburgers and talk about the future.

5
A Rookie with the Baltimore Colts

It was hot. Hot the way Westminster, Maryland, in early July is hot—humid, suffocating, inhuman, a bright sun scorching everything to brown, a burning, blistering, brutal sun no one stands in long, except rookie football players. Some seventy-five of us had been summoned to the Colts early-season camp, and not one was prepared for what awaited. A rookie pro-football training camp is some hellish exercise you might read about, but never do you expect to experience it firsthand.

I thought I was in good shape. I'd pushed myself beyond what I imagined possible since learning of being drafted. The vow I'd made to be in condition had been kept. Almost every waking moment, except when I was working at my abbreviated summer job, had been devoted to getting into shape. I'd thought I was ready for whatever would be thrown at me. I was dead wrong.

The mistake everyone made, including myself, was believing that somehow we'd start out slow and work into the difficult regimen. Wrong. It's just the opposite. You *start out* with the murderous routines and it gets "easier," if that word can be used to describe a form of torture. On the first day you start out hitting *right away*. In high school and college this comes later, but not in the NFL. You put on pads and *hit*. The number of players over the years who didn't understand this, and thus lost careers, must be in the thousands.

I'll never forget the wind sprints that first day, and the grass drills. The wind sprints were fifty yards each, running all out (if you're slow, or "dog" it, you're likely to be cut), but it was the *number* of them that made you dizzy and weak. You kept doing them, over and over, pushing yourself to go faster than the poor devil next to you, and the coaches, not at all tired, kept ordering more.

The grass drills also were endless. You'd run in place until told to fall flat on your chest, then bounce up from that to run in place again until told to hit the ground. On and on this went, the sun burning a hole in your head, salt from sweat dripping into your eyes and blinding you.

And the hitting. Let me describe the Pittsburgh Steeler "nutcracker," the most infamous drill of all, though the Colts had their own variation. In the nutcracker a player stood in the center of a circle, and when another player's name was called he'd charge at the man in the middle, the only thought in mind being to destroy the other guy. Hardly had the tanklike collision ended (sometimes it hadn't) when another player's name was called, and he came bellowing and roaring after that same teammate in the center. This absolutely unfortunate soul never had the slightest idea where the next charge would come from, whether from behind, right, left, or straight on. He could only stand there and try to fend off as best he could.

Then there was the drill with the two blocking dummies. They would be set a few feet apart, and a player had to run between them. An offensive lineman blocked for him, and a defensive man tried to bury him in the dirt, but he had to run between the two dummies. This drill produced some terrific crashes, especially when the tackler avoided the blocker.

We were hitting the first day, with full pads on. The inside of my helmet rubbed all the skin off my forehead, and the chafing was terrifically painful. But there was so much pain it was actually hard to know which area to concentrate on. A number of players quit the first day. I could see it coming, just looking in their eyes: *What in hell am I doing out here,* the eyes said, and they would throw down their helmets and stalk off cursing, or some would try to sneak off, hoping to be able to get away without being seen, and others would simply collapse in a heap, not able to move a muscle, vomit drooling from their lips, sometimes leg muscles contracting wildly, involuntarily.

And this was from the morning session. Of course, we started immediately on two-a-days, each scheduled, I'm sure, for when the temperature would be hottest. When we staggered away from the "morning" session, which ended in the afternoon, it was hard to imagine going through it again in just a few hours. No one was hungry. The coaches had told us to eat, but such an extreme of weariness saps the appetite. A number of players preferred to catch some sleep, a grievous error.

Life in pro football had been changing when I came to the Colts, and the change accelerated. A good example is conditioning. The veterans of the 1950s and 1960s, generally, started to get in shape a month or so before the season began. This usually isn't possible anymore. The competition is too fierce. I would start getting ready for the new season two weeks after the Super Bowl. The Cowboys, especially, were most helpful. The team would prescribe an *individualized* conditioning program, tailored to each player's needs. I lifted weights daily, ran wind sprints, did distance running. The Cowboys even had their own training facility, open year-round, in North Dallas. Of course, the younger players didn't need the conditioning programs as much as the older ones, but the fact is that players with pot guts and short wind, common previously, couldn't cut it anymore.

I ate because the coaches suggested it, and I was pretty much doing what I was told, not a bad attitude for a rookie to adopt. Later I learned to force myself to eat. The strength was desperately needed.

Yet another pitfall awaited those smart enough to eat: the nearly overwhelming desire to take a nap—to blot out the pain and exhaustion with sleep. The coaches advised us to use this time to learn the playbook, which was virtually the first thing given us when we arrived. It was the wise player who followed this advice. The coaches, especially Don Shula, had no intention of patiently waiting for a young player to learn his assignments. It was know it yesterday or get out. It helped me, I believe, that once again I listened to what I was told. I was learning plays rather than resting.

The afternoon session of the first day was, if anything, worse. Maybe it was worse because we were told to expect more of the same, and anticipating the agony increased the pain. I don't believe high school or even college athletes have any frame of reference to understand what I'm describing. The calisthenics, workouts, and drills are murderous.

No matter how much I'd tried to get in shape, I couldn't have prepared myself adequately for getting beat on, play after play, by 270-pound fanatics who knew the coaches were looking for "physical" people. Immediately I learned I wasn't trained for football, not at this level. In football, with the possible exception of a kicker, the player is going to get beat up, badly. I mean he's going to be pummeled and mugged and hurt. All parts of the football player's body must be strong. He must learn to dish out punishment, and to take it (better yet, to fend it off). The blow can come to any part of the body, so all need to be strong. Football players have much stronger upper bodies, for example, than do basketball players. In basketball you can probably get by without an exceptionally powerful upper body. And the legs needed for the sports are also different. The football player needs the leg strength to take hits, the basketball player for jumping and grace. A football player needs to do a lot of weight lifting, and I greatly increased my time spent at this, though chopping down trees or lifting rocks in a quarry might accomplish the same result. A basketball player often is better off jumping rope. The legs of most basketball players would not stand up long under a pro-football pounding.

Surprisingly, after that first day of misery I thought I would make the Colts. I thought I was a better athlete than most of the players in camp, and I knew I had the drive and willpower. They had picked up some tricks that only a lifelong player of the game would know, but these weren't so difficult to learn. Yes, I thought, the first day had been good. I'd shown I was a hitter and possessed superior skills, raw as they were.

During the ten days of rookie training camp I stayed in a Baltimore hotel. We had the choice of eating meals either with the team or alone, and I usually ate with the group. I couldn't really afford anything else, and I also wanted to immerse myself fully in the football atmosphere. Later, with the Cowboys, no choice was given: You had to eat with the team.

There were cuts every day, and players just deciding they'd had enough and leaving camp. What players dreaded (that is the right word) most was a knock on the door. They assumed it was "Turk," or the "Axe Man," as the assistant coach was known, the man whose opening line never varied: "Coach Shula wants to see you, and he wants you to bring your playbook." That meant the individual was gone, off the team, a terrible blow to someone who really might not have another occupation. Knocking on doors at training camp was a no-no; it was better to identify yourself by shouting. A knock on the door could induce heart failure.

I very much feared being cut. Although *I* thought I was doing well, it was impossible to know what the coaches thought. I didn't know what I would do if I were dropped. Return to Freeport, I guessed, get a job, and work to save money to return to school. Making the Baltimore Colts seemed a much better alternative.

Linda's father had been transferred by the military to Oregon, and the family, Linda included, now lived in Hermiston. Linda planned to go to school in Oregon, and as a couple we'd adopted a wait-and-see attitude about our future. We were writing often, and if I made the Colts the plan was that she might join me in Baltimore. Her parents had been told about our feelings toward each other (I hadn't met them), and to say they lacked enthusiasm is a big understatement. Linda's father was flat-out opposed, but her mother tried hard to understand. Linda thought it was the background each came from: Her mother's parents were from Finland and Sweden, while her father had grown up in Tennessee and Kentucky.

There was no doubt about how Linda and I felt. We missed each other, and being almost a continent apart just seemed to increase our love. *If,* I thought, *I could first get myself into a position to support a family.* Right now I had nothing. I didn't get a penny of that fifteen-thousand-dollar contract unless I made the team.

The veterans showed up at camp ten days after the rook-

ies, at which time everyone moved into dormitory quarters in
Reisterstown. I was amazed that Johnny Unitas was only three
lockers away from me. I sat there that first day openmouthed,
and watched him. This was the Johnny U. I'd watched so often
on TV, and his standing so close seemed like something out of a
dream.

He and I had the worst shoes on the team, I noted proudly.
Mine were those I'd used in high school, with the big, long, old-
fashioned cleats. His were older still. I thought they must have
been the pair he'd worn almost a decade before in the great
sudden-death overtime championship game against the Giants,
featuring the most memorable moment in Colt history, when
Alan Ameche from Wisconsin took the hand-off from Johnny U.
and ran over Sam Huff and the rest of the Giants for the world
title. Unitas's shoes were black and high-topped, something
from another era (as he was), but his shoulder pads were even
more surprising. They looked to be out of the 1930s, the kind
Bronco Nagurski and Red Grange wore, and appeared to be
ready to crumble into dust. I couldn't believe they gave him any
protection at all.

Just after the veterans arrived we were having a run-
through drill, offense against defense, without pads, and I got
my first intimation that the coaches were noticing me. Wide receiver Ray Perkins (now head coach at Alabama) caught a pass
over the middle, and I came rushing up from strong safety, handling him pretty roughly. It hadn't been intentional, I was
merely so concentrated on what I was doing that I forgot, and
Coach Shula gave me a stern lecture (nothing nearly as bad as
the one given to Mike Curtis, which I described earlier). I could
see in Shula's eyes as he raged that he wasn't as angry as he
pretended to be. I even thought he was a little pleased. He was
looking for desire and aggressiveness and had seen it.

Chuck Noll, later to achieve lasting fame with the Steelers,
was the Colt defensive-back coach, and I knew he also had noticed.

The first real test, however, came in our initial exhibition
game, and I know I had a good one. Playing strong safety, I intercepted a pass and made several good jarring tackles. I made a
few mistakes, but they were "good" mistakes, caused by aggres-

siveness and mainly a lack of familiarity with the game. I just hadn't played enough football. At least that's the way I hoped the Colt coaches would look at it.

The knock on the door came the next night. I looked at roommates Cornelius Johnson and Charlie Stukes and figured the bell was tolling for me. For a moment I hoped it was a practical joker, of which there were plenty, but the knock on the door was going too far even for most of these. I went to the door, knees shaking, and opened it.

"Coach Shula wants to see you," the Turk said.

Good-bye, pro football, I thought. I followed the big assistant coach down the corridor. It occurred to me that Johnson and Stukes hadn't looked at me. It's never easy to look at a condemned man. For a moment I thought I had hope—Turk hadn't asked for my playbook! But the hope died as quickly as it came. Turk had simply forgotten, that's all.

Coach Shula was behind his desk, smiling. Smiling! Is this the way it was done?

"Preston," he said, "I have good news for you."

"You do?"

"We're going to give you a chance to learn."

"Great." I had no idea what he was talking about.

"We're going to put you on the taxi squad."

I stared at Shula. I didn't know what to say. The taxi squad meant I had made the team, and would do everything the team did except play in games. I would have to work just as hard as everyone else, know just as much, attend all the team meetings, but I would not play. But I could be "activated," as they put it, on a moment's notice. I waited for Coach Shula to go on.

"I don't want you to breathe a word of this to anyone," Shula said.

"Yes, sir." Later I learned why. There were players Shula knew he would cut, but he didn't want *them* to know it. If they were aware that *I* was guaranteed a position on the team, particularly if they knew *others* had the same promise, simple arithmetic would tell them they were out.

"I have more good news, Preston."

"What's that?" I was not sure how good the first piece of news was. I'd made the team—which was wonderful—but I wouldn't be playing, which wasn't so wonderful, and I knew as a taxi-squad member I'd only receive half-pay: $7,500 of the $15,000.

"We want to sign you for another year."

"You mean, for next year too?"

"Yes. At fifteen hundred dollars more than this year."

"I don't know what to say."

"It's to protect both of us. You have a contract for two years. We know we can call on your services for those two years."

I had no idea what I was doing. No experience at all in this area. Coach Shula said the contract would protect both the Colts and me, and I believed Shula. Would this great man mislead one of his players? I couldn't accept the idea. Frankly, it scarcely entered my mind.

"We have the contract right here, Preston. You can sign it now, if you like. As you can see, it calls for a fifteen-hundred-dollar raise."

I signed it on the spot. Handed it back to Shula.

"Obviously," he said, "you shouldn't say anything about this either."

"Yes, sir." Well, I was going to tell one person—Linda. I'd have to think it over, and so would she, but maybe this change in my status was enough for us to consider getting together.

I did think it over. I've thought about it ever since, every time I hear some management spokesman say "the club" doesn't want to deal with agents, player representatives, or attorneys. Of course they don't. They'd much rather deal with a financially unqualified athlete who has no idea what this game is about. The chips are all on their side of the table.

The contract Coach Shula gave me didn't protect "both of us," though that is what he had said. I wasn't protected at all. The Colts could drop me from the taxi squad and not owe a dime. But the contract did protect them. I couldn't negotiate with another team if somehow I had a good rookie year, nor could I insist on a reasonable raise if I surpassed expectations. I was tied to the Colts, but they weren't tied to me.

For me, actually, it was not the worst imaginable deal. It did provide a *feeling* of security, and being told I was on the taxi squad took off a lot of pressure. It was no longer necessary to kill myself to make the team, and I could relax just a shade and *learn.* That, although I was not aware of it at the time, was very important. All I needed to make a career in this league was a chance to learn.

Incidentally, being on the taxi squad I made a point of learning what the phrase meant. It seems that in the heyday of George Halas and Curly Lambeau, players were kept around in case injuries necessitated their being reactivated, and to help pay their keep they were expected to drive to the airport, like a taxi driver, and pick up visiting businessmen, newly acquired players, important sportswriters.

At the time I was grateful for what Shula did; but his action points out just one of many injustices, still prevalent in pro football, that need to be corrected. Players who management knows have no chance of making the team are kept on in training camp to serve as cannon fodder. Warm bodies are needed. Some poor guy has to be there for Bubba Smith to tackle, so Bubba can get in shape, and that someone can't be Johnny Unitas. Unitas is too valuable; an injury cannot be risked. Thus, people with no chance at all are kept on to suffer through the brutalities of camp, their hopes growing each day, because bodies are needed to get the regulars into condition. These unfortunates take a terrible pounding for nothing, and it is amazing to me how even the press, supposedly knowledgeable about the subject, gets taken by what seems a transparent ploy.

For example, sportswriters love to praise those teams which invite, or allow, the largest number of free agents into training camp. Somehow this is seen as "democratic," opening up the roster to everyone, giving even the humblest Walter Mitty a chance at fame and fortune in the glamorous NFL. But the truth is that this individual has no chance of making the grade in the NFL, and management knows it. The individual is being used.

I talked over my new contract with Linda, and after I got an apartment in Baltimore we decided to try living together. It was going to be tough on $7,500 a year, but preferable to being almost three thousand miles apart. I was at practice when she flew into Baltimore, and when she gave the cab driver the address she wanted, he insisted she had to be wrong.

"Why?" she asked.

"Well, it's just wrong."

"Tell me why."

"Trust me, lady, you've made a mistake."

Linda finally got the cab driver to say, "Well, lady, that's where the blacks live," and she calmed him (or did she?) by saying, "I'm marrying one of the blacks." Anyway, she thought the story was wildly funny.

The hazing of rookies started shortly after the veterans arrived in camp, but it was different from what I'd known at Kappa Alpha Psi. The most important difference was that it had a purpose. A hotshot rookie out of college really didn't know anything, hadn't proved anything, and the hazing was a way of telling him so. He might have to run silly errands for some veteran, or give up his place in the food line, or sing his alma mater's fight song on demand, but the intention was to bring him down to earth. The difference between the college game and the pros is night and day, and reading headlines doesn't help the young player at all. He needs to learn sacrifice and how to take humiliation, to submerge his ego into a *team*, and the hazing, I believe, gets those lessons across.

I shy away from using the word, but on the best teams on which I played there was a real *love* for one another, and great pride in being one of just a few. The determination and skill and, yes, the sacrifice and humiliation required to make it in the NFL, forged a special bond among the players. In the last few years I think people have seen less of this (just as the hazing has virtually disappeared) and I believe the new players are missing something.

I enjoyed my first Rookie Show. We had to stand on a stage and do silly acts, but some of it was genuinely funny, and there was nothing really mean or cruel involved. Some rookies balked at the hazing, which was a mistake, and this was often interpreted, rightly or wrongly, as a sign that the individual thought himself more important than the team. Worse for that individual, he was doing something very dangerous. During a scrimmage, a key block could be missed at a critical time and the player could take a fearsome hit. It was hoped he got the message after just one of these.

The Colts of 1967 knew they were a good team, and you could tell by the way they carried themselves. They were bursting with healthy confidence. We were not a team that hoped to win, but one that expected to. I just wished I could be off the taxi squad and on the field for the actual games.

We gave a signal of things to come in our final exhibition game, crushing the Cowboys, 33-7, in Dallas. I watched the great Cowboy receiver Bob Hayes, former Olymic 100-meter gold medalist, the fastest man alive, and largely by himself he was changing the way football was played. It was simply impossible to cover Hayes one-on-one, and coaches had to devise zone defenses to cope with him. Today, of course, the zone is practiced almost universally in the NFL.

The regular season opener was played in Baltimore, and I stood in street clothes on the sidelines and watched my teammates nip the Atlanta Falcons, 38-31. Johnny Unitas threw for 401 yards, a Colt record, and the game wasn't nearly as close as the score. We were ahead 31-7 at the half. This game was the first time I'd seen the veterans really go all out, and the sound of the hitting echoed in my ears for a long time afterward. It drove home to me ever more clearly the kind of physical condition and strength I'd need just to survive. Hearing the noise was not just the roaring of the crowd, but the cracking of the big men out on the field. I wish every football fan could watch—or rather *hear*—at least one game from the sidelines.

Our second game was a 38-6 rout of the Eagles in Philadelphia, with Unitas passing the thirty-thousand-yard mark in career passing, the first NFL player to accomplish the feat. Taxi-squad members didn't travel to away games, but since it was a short drive from Baltimore to Philadelphia, some of the players made the trip on their own. Linda and I wanted to go but couldn't. Our old car just couldn't make it that far. We watched and cheered my teammates on television. Linda was as much a Colt fan as any of the players.

Next came a home game against the San Francisco 49ers, and a 41-7 laugher. The week before, the Eagles had managed only two field goals against us, and San Francisco didn't score until the fourth quarter. It was becoming clear that we were an awesome team on both offense and defense. Against the 49ers we had no turnovers and punted only once.

Nor did the Bears score a touchdown the following week in Chicago. We crushed them 24-3, and again I had to watch on

TV. It was almost enough, being a member of this team, but I still ached to be on the field doing my part. Realistically, my teammates couldn't be doing much better no matter what I did, but the desire to be out there was enormous. In truth, I hadn't played a game of football that counted since high school.

The Rams tied us the following week in Baltimore, 24–24, in a game Bubba Smith must have thought was an instant replay of one he had played in college. Bubba had been the star of Michigan State when Notre Dame decided to play for a 10–10 tie rather than go for a win, sitting on the ball and running out the clock in a contest that had been billed as the national championship. It happened again to Bubba. The Rams ran out the clock, refusing to gamble, much as Notre Dame had, and the Colt fans booed their caution. In the locker room afterward it was as if we had lost. No one talked much about it, but the thought had nonetheless been there that we might have been good enough to have been the first NFL team to go unbeaten and untied for an entire season.

Linda and I were married at the Baltimore County Courthouse the week after the Rams game. Corny Johnson was our best man, and he threw some funny, colored rice on us when it was done. We hadn't even been sure we'd be able to be married. Maryland was south of the Mason-Dixon Line and many residents actually considered it a southern state. Until just recently it had been illegal for a black and a white to be married in Maryland. But we didn't have any trouble. When we were getting the license a young black man and his white girl who said they were from New York asked me if they could borrow three dollars so they too could get a license. I said sure, even though I didn't have much more than that myself.

Linda's mother and father (her mother more quickly) eventually came to accept the marriage, and I grew to love and respect them. Her father still calls occasionally, just to talk, but it wasn't always so easy. He once told Linda she "wasn't his daughter" if she went ahead with her plans. It is good to see people change and grow.

My parents had no similar problems with Linda. Mom always called her "my daughter," and Daddy, wisely, considered that we were grown up and responsible for our own decisions.

Linda and I did have the following weekend alone in Baltimore, watching on television as the team played to a second straight tie, 20–20 with the Vikings, in Bloomington, Minnesota, giving us a 4–0–2 record for the first six games of the season. It seemed that almost every week John Unitas was breaking another record, and in this game, in which one of his patented late-fourth-quarter drives earned us the tie, it was for most career completions—2,131—breaking the mark of Y. A. Tittle. I was still in awe of Unitas, and not just because I was a rookie. You could tell many of the veterans felt the same way. I imagine that after a person accomplishes so much, his teammates, who are as much enamored of sports as any fan, begin to realize they are playing with a certain Hall of Famer, and accord him the utmost respect and deference. I imagine this holds true in any area of endeavor.

Don Shula didn't change the practice routine after the Minnesota game, but it required no special insight to tell he wasn't pleased with ties. No one wanted to find out how he would react to a loss, but even with this considerable incentive it took another fourth-quarter Johnny Unitas-led drive to defeat the tough Washington Redskins, 17–13. It was a duel between the number one and number two quarterbacks in the NFL, Unitas and Sonny Jurgensen, and Johnny U. won it, barely, 242 yards passing to 226.

Next week was the game we'd circled on our schedule before the season even began. The Super Bowl champion Green Bay Packers were coming to Baltimore, and the entire city was up for the game. The two teams were widely considered to be the best in football, and fans were talking about the game as "a war."

It was the first professional game in which I would play. Defensive back Jimmy Welch had been hurt, and early in the week Coach Shula told me I was being activated. I would have to be ready to play offense and defense, and would be in on all punt and kickoff plays. My first game as a professional would be against the mightiest of the mighty!

I called Linda to tell her the good news, and then my parents in Freeport. I talked with my brother Ed, nineteen, two years younger than myself, and his enthusiasm, if anything, was greater than my own. The game would be televised in Freeport. It would be the first time my parents had seen me play football.

Many players say they never want to see anyone hurt. But I wouldn't be telling the truth if I said I was greatly saddened by Jimmy Welch's injury. I knew very well that the only chance I had to play this rookie year was if someone were hurt. It bothered me, feeling that way, and I tried to imagine scenarios where no one suffered. An injury that didn't hurt, perhaps (what could this possibly be?), or some fortuitous stroke of fate where a player suddenly retired to go on to something better. But I knew it would only happen if someone were injured, and in the back of my mind I hoped it would occur (way in the back of my mind—the thought was too ugly to dwell on).

I'd seen the Packers so often on television, and had never even dreamed I would one day be facing them. Now I listened to the Colt coaches telling us about these legends. Over the years I would form my own thoughts, starting with Vince Lombardi.

I do know that Lombardi wasn't particularly upset if an important opposing player were injured. It was so much the better for winning. Nor do I think I would have responded well to Coach Lombardi. His methods of bringing out the best in a player included brutal harangues, insults, a mean-spirited way of urging the athlete to do better. That Lombardi was a great coach no one can doubt, and a number of his former players hold him in high regard. Others are not so filled with praise.

What a defense the Packers had! Defensive end Willie Davis, as nice a guy as you'll ever find off the field, was a terror when he put on his pads. Hog Hanner was aptly named. He looked like a hog on the field, his uniform always covered with dirt, and the rougher the game, the more Hanner liked it. Dave Robinson, 250 pounds of left linebacker, may have been the best ever to play that position. Then there was Mr. Ray Nitschke. The "Mr." is intentional. He was utterly ferocious, this former barroom bouncer, and one of the few middle linebackers who can be mentioned in the same breath with Sam Huff and Dick Butkus. The hardest I've ever been tackled (not hit, *tackled*) was by Ray Nitschke. I was with Pittsburgh at the time, and I didn't see him coming until the last instant. That brief flicker of an instant may have saved my life, allowing a precious microsecond to adjust to the impact. As it was, rolling on the field in agony, every bone seeming broken, I thought death might be more merciful.

In the Packer defensive backfield were Herb Adderly, all-pro, and the great Willie Wood. Wood was lightning quick, a marvelous leaper, smart, and enormously knowledgeable about the game. Wood could stand underneath the goal posts and occasionally bat away field goals that otherwise would have been good. I've always thought he would have been an outstanding head coach in the NFL, as would Lionel Taylor, Charley Taylor, and Willie Brown. All of these would have been excellent head coaches, and the undeniable reason they never got the chance was prejudice against blacks, especially as leaders of pro-football teams.

And what an offense the Packers had! Bart Starr was not as talented as Johnny Unitas, but he was a magnificent field general, cool under fire, and a wonderful, quiet leader. The center of the Packer offensive line—Jerry Kramer, Jim Ringo, Forrest Gregg—was the best team of three ever to play those positions. Just as a pitcher, catcher, and shortstop are the heart of a baseball team, so were Kramer, Ringo, and Gregg the hub of the Packer offense. Coaches today still measure the effectiveness of their sweeps against those led by the Packers' brilliant pulling guards, Kramer and Gregg.

Boyd Dowler and Max McGee were top targets for Bart Starr's passes, and tight end Marv Fleming was one of the game's most underrated receivers (except among fellow players). Fleming and I are two of just a handful of players to have a record of five Super Bowl rings (he received two with Green Bay, three with Miami).

Jim Taylor and Paul Hornung had been replaced at running back by Donny Anderson and Jim Grabowski. Anderson, supposedly in the mold of Hornung both on and off the field, and the rugged Grabowski, were touted as the finest young running back combo in the league.

More than sixty-thousand people packed Memorial Stadium for the showdown between the Super Bowl champions and the undefeated Colts. I was extremely nervous before the game, but the butterflies disappeared when we took the field for the pregame warm-up. It was very important for me to have a good game, not just because my career was on the line, but because Linda was in the stands and my folks were watching back home. I realized it would be the first time Linda had seen me in a game that counted.

I delivered a good enough block on the opening kickoff return, but I still consider my introduction to pro football to be the second play for which I was on the field. We were punting and I was playing left end. My job was to get to the punt receiver as rapidly as possible and make the tackle. I'd have plenty of assistance. At this time, interior linemen did not have to wait for the ball to be kicked.

Across the line from me was Herb Adderly. He had come up quite close and I'd seen his approach. It was loose, casual, like a man on a Sunday afternoon walk in the park. He had a gentle smile on his face. He looked like a nice guy, I decided. Besides, how tough could he be? He had no physical size advantage over me. I looked in his eyes (someone had told me this was a good idea), and they were peaceful, tranquil, serene. I almost felt sorry for him, for what I was about to do to him.

The ball was snapped and I took off, going almost full speed with my first step, intending to breeze right on by this dreamy old man. The first step was about all I was able to take. I saw a flash of elbow coming toward my face, "the bone" it is called by players, and then there was a horrible, teeth-jarring crash-splat, and I was literally bowled over backward, overturned, and when I came down I was flat on my back. Conventional wisdom is that you see stars when you are leveled, really walloped, and it's true. I couldn't have seen them with my eyes, there must have been some mix-up with my brain (which hadn't been working when it considered Adderly), but the stars spun and danced and bobbed, bright as a nova one instant, dead the next, bright once again. The mind that had betrayed me once now urged me to get up, *don't let Adderly see he hurt you* (as if he didn't know), and I got to my feet in sections and managed to stagger ineffectually down the field.

Welcome to pro football, Herb Adderly had told me, and I learned the lesson. I never made the mistake of underestimating someone again. The fact that it had been the all-pro Adderly spoke volumes about how green I really was. Yet I was also young, and it was that youth which allowed me to bounce back.

Actually, I had an impressive debut against the Packers, making a number of hard hits and not too many mistakes. Probably no one will remember, though, except my family, because the game itself was eminently memorable. There was no reason to concentrate on me.

The game was a tiring, brutal struggle. Jim Grabowski and Elijah Pitts were knocked out of the action early, and for our side Jerry Hill and Tom Matte were sidelined with injuries. It was a game, most of the way, that only aficionados would appreciate. No long runs or spectacular catches, no scoreboard lighting up with high numbers. Don Chandler kicked a field goal for Green Bay in the second quarter, and the teams entered the final stanza with the score 3–0. If you like hard tackling and superb defense, this was your type of game.

Early in the fourth quarter Bart Starr hit Donny Anderson with a thirty-one-yard touchdown strike and it was 10–0 for the Pack. Most NFL teams, even the top-level ones, would have little or no chance against the world champions in such a circumstance. The Packers were known for getting *better* as a game rolled along: Players had to be in the absolute peak of condition to play for the driven Lombardi. But there was a difference between the Colts and all other top-level teams: We had Johnny Unitas.

With a maniacal pro-Baltimore crowd screaming encouragement (Memorial Stadium was known as the world's largest outdoor insane asylum), the Colts got the ball on their own thirty-seven-yard line with exactly six minutes to go. With two minutes, nineteen seconds left, culminating a ten-play drive, Johnny Unitas hit Alex Hawkins for the score and it was 10–6 (Lou Michaels missed the extra point because of a mishandled snap). I was riding one of history's greatest adrenaline highs when I took the field for what everyone knew would be an onside kick. I wasn't even aware of my feet touching the ground; it seemed the deafening noise had swept me up and carried me to my position.

Rick Volk recovered the onside kick on the thirty-four! Volk had mishandled the center snap (he was replacing Bobby Boyd, injured earlier in this bruising game) on the missed Michaels extra point. That lost point meant we would have to go for a touchdown, no matter what.

But was there any doubt? Was there any doubt even when a run and two missed passes left us with fourth and five? When the Packers vicious pass rush forced Unitas to scramble for his life? Of course not. Johnny U. ran for six yards and a first down on the Green Bay twenty-three. On the next play he hit Willie Richardson with the game-winning touchdown, and Willie threw the ball high and far up into the stands.

In fifty-one seconds Johnny Unitas had thrown two touchdown passes against a team many still believe is history's greatest. My first pro game was one of the sweetest of all.

The crowd left Memorial Stadium limp and exhausted, and so did the players. The difference was that we had been beaten up. I ached everywhere it is possible to feel. Linda and I got back to our apartment and lay down, "just for a minute," because we needed to grocery shop for dinner.

"Some beginning," I said.

"Yes."

"I hope Daddy saw it."

"Um."

"And your folks."

"Um."

"And . . ." but it was hopeless. I looked over at Linda and she was sound asleep. She'd played the game as hard as any of the athletes, and now she was dead to the world. A minute later I was asleep too. The clock read the same when I woke up, and I still hurt, but it was twelve hours later.

I was getting to know many of my teammates, and these relationships grew closer when I came off the taxi squad. This was probably only natural. The one thing that had been missing for me, seeing action in the games, no longer posed a problem. There is the feeling, perhaps unjustified, that you're not a full-fledged member of the team if you aren't on the field contributing.

I was close to Alvin Haymond, Tony Lorick, Jerry Hill, Rick Volk, and especially with Charlie Stukes and my best man, Corny Johnson. John Mackey was a player, like Ray Berry, whom I chose as a role model. The press often talks about football players being role models for kids, but the players themselves often look up to fellow players. The trick is to choose wisely.

I couldn't have shown more good sense than I did in selecting John Mackey. He was highly intelligent, and already was staking out a position for himself in the business world. When I began to look at how I would spend the rest of my life, I remembered what I had observed of Mackey.

This great tight end was also admirable for the way he stood his ground against management. I doubt if he would ever have bought the "this protects both of us" line I'd swallowed from Coach Shula. Memories of Mackey have served me well as I've come to represent young players, every bit as raw as I ever was.

Another friend was Lenny Moore, for a long time the holder of the record for most touchdowns in a season. Lenny Moore often laughed about his great abilities, downplaying them, and he was marvelously witty and amusing. Anyone who thinks all football players are on an "I" trip should have known Lenny. He never talked about himself, except deprecatingly, good-naturedly, and he never took himself seriously. I now think he might have made a mistake, that his refusal to acknowledge his great abilities meant he never got paid what he was worth.

Lenny owned a bar called Lenny's, and it was a favorite after-practice hangout for players. The atmosphere was probably not the best for me. I had a wife and I would have been better off spending time with her. Still, Lenny's was a pleasant place to go for a hassle-free drink and some good conversation. Lenny couldn't have been a more cordial host.

There were cliques on the Colts, not where the playing of the game was concerned but in off-the-field matters. There were plenty of business opportunities to be shared, but these mainly came to white players who preferred to keep them to themselves. Many of the Colts were investing in stocks and bonds, and you could hear them talking about the latest inside tip they'd received, but come close and suddenly all was silent. I think the same atmosphere largely pervades today. While the pay of black and white athletes is roughly comparable, off-the-field opportunities are much fewer for blacks. The life facing a black athlete after his retirement is much more bleak than for a white.

After the Packer game we went on a real tear, as can be seen by a look at our season record:

Baltimore	38	Atlanta	31
Baltimore	38	Philadelphia	6
Baltimore	41	San Francisco	7
Baltimore	24	Chicago	3
Baltimore	24	Los Angeles	24
Baltimore	20	Minnesota	20
Baltimore	17	Washington	13
Baltimore	13	Green Bay	10
Baltimore	49	Atlanta	7
Baltimore	41	Detroit	7
Baltimore	26	San Francisco	9
Baltimore	23	Dallas	17
Baltimore	30	New Orleans	10
Baltimore	10	Los Angeles	34

Against Atlanta, Unitas completed thirteen of sixteen passes for 340 yards in the first half alone, resulting in a 35–0 lead. His twelve-straight completions were one short of an NFL record. Nevertheless, Unitas was anything but a one-man band. The defense was spectacular, led by Bubba and Mike Curtis. The latter, another of the many who are nice off the field and ferocious when on, once almost decapitated a fan who ran onto the playing surface to get a ball. Curtis's reasoning: "He shouldn't have been out there."

We were 8–0–2 after the 41–7 rout of the Lions, and people were talking everywhere now about the possibility of the Colts being the only team to go unbeaten for an entire NFL season. Remarkably, the Rams, at 7–1–2, were only a game behind us. Had we been in any of the other three divisions, we would already have clinched a playoff berth. The second-place club in the Century Division was St. Louis, 5–4–1; in the Capitol Division, Philadelphia, 5–5; and in the Central Division, Chicago, 5–5.

By shutting down the San Francisco 49ers the next Sunday, 26–9, in the Bay City, we held them without a touchdown, meaning we had given up only three TDs in the last five games. The Rams had beaten Detroit, however, 31–7, on Thanksgiving Day, and we still led them by only one game.

I was seeing action on about 25 percent of our plays (a good reason why the special teams are so important), and getting a reputation as aggressive and hell-for-leather. This surprised me as much as anyone. I had always been aggressive in athletics, as opposed to my demeanor off the field (or court), but I hadn't liked even the violence and pain of high-school football, which is infinitely magnified in the pros. I think it was because I felt I *had* to succeed. I really didn't know what I would do with my life if the football part of it ended. (I thought of giving pro basketball a try, but I'd never been a sensational scorer, the type that attracts NBA and ABA coaches.) Also, if I'd learned anything from my parents, it was to do my absolute best at whatever I tried.

But I was being noticed, and in a positive fashion. I hit hard and had a nose for the ball. Oddly, doubly odd because he was my coach, a person I hardly noticed was Chuck Noll. He didn't make much of an impression on me either way, I suppose, because he was quiet and just doing his job. As time would reveal, however, he was watching me very closely. Later I would have a great number of impressions of Chuck Noll.

The Colts went to 10–0–2 the next Sunday against Dallas, 23–17, a routine Johnny Unitas performance in which he drove us to the winning touchdown with only ninety seconds remaining. (Is it any wonder we were confident in the Super Bowl against the Jets when he entered the game with us losing?) Dandy Don Meredith quarterbacked the Cowboys this day, and we intercepted him four times. Ironically, the Cowboys, at 8–4, clinched the Capitol Division championship with their loss. We were still fighting for our lives against the Rams, but felt it would be over the following week, the second to last of the regular season. We were hosting the cellar-dwelling New Orleans Saints, while Los Angeles had to go to frozen Green Bay to play the defending Super Bowl champions.

New Orleans was easy. Our offense took the day off and we still won, 30–10. Every Baltimore touchdown was set up either by an interception or a fumble recovery. Unfortunately, the

Rams upset Green Bay, 27–24, to set up a do-or-die game the following Sunday in Los Angeles.

It had never happened before in pro football, and it never would again. We were 11-0-2 with one game remaining, but since the Rams were 10-1-2 and we had tied in the first encounter, we were faced with the certainty that a defeat would knock us out of the playoffs. What a difference from today, when an 8-8 club is a threat to be in the running for the Super Bowl. If we lost just one game out of fourteen, we were locked out.

I'd been pretty well battered in the New Orleans game, proving that it doesn't take a team with an outstanding record to beat you up. Any NFL team can hurt you badly. All have young, eager, kamikaze-like hitters. What follows are just *some* of the injuries I've suffered while playing pro football: left eye permanently damaged, calcium deposit on neck, calcium deposits on right arm and all ten fingers, bone chip in right hand, bone chip in left hand, fractured ribs, spinal-column damage, two broken fingers, one cracked finger, two hip pointers, right thigh operation leaving a scar like a bullet wound (a potentially fatal injury), torn ligament in left knee (nine-inch scar), turf toe (sounds funny but isn't) on both feet, calcium deposits on both ankles from virtually countless strains and sprains, right shoulder nerve damage, chipped left elbow bone, scores of groin pulls and charley horses, and twelve lost teeth.

I was considered lucky.

Before the showdown with the Rams, it seemed there was a fifty-fifty likelihood I would start in the defensive backfield. Lenny Lyles was injured, and the battle for his position was between me and Alvin Haymond. I couldn't have been more eager to be in there. Coach Shula ultimately chose Haymond, because of the two strikes I had against me—my basketball background and the fact that I was a rookie—but it was a close competition.

Lenny Lyles's wasn't the only injury we had. Several other key players were out, and in fact more than half the team was not up to par. The Colts had been hit by a flu bug, and a particularly cold week in Baltimore did nothing to alleviate its effects.

It was a fierce game in the Memorial Coliseum, and that 34-10 score, a Rams victory, in no way mirrored the action on the field or the relative strengths of the teams. This in no sense is meant to be an alibi. The Rams won, but I'd be doing an injustice to the record if I didn't explain why the outcome was so lopsided.

The Rams had one of the great defensive front fours of all time: Deacon Jones, Merlin Olsen, Roger Brown, and Roosevelt Grier. Brown (for Lamar Lundy) was the only change from a unit known as the Fearsome Foursome, but it was Deacon Jones (along with Roman Gabriel) who made the big differences in the game. Jones was the originator of the hurtful head slap, a painful, disorienting, stunning hit to the head just as the ball is snapped, and our tackle, Sam Ball, who was assigned to the Rams end, simply couldn't handle him. Unitas was sacked seven times as the Los Angeles front four seemed to be living in our backfield. Jack Pardee of the Rams had one of his better days at linebacker.

Roman Gabriel was to the Rams offense what Deacon Jones was to the defense. Gabriel hit eighteen of twenty-two passes, many of them to Jack Snow and Bernie Casey.

Along with the Rams at 11–1–2, we had the best record in the NFL, but there would be no playoffs. The other three playoff teams, besides the Rams, were Cleveland, 9–5; Dallas, 9–5; and Green Bay (ultimately the Super Bowl champion again), 9–4–1. No team, before or since, has ever had as good a record as we did and not gone to the playoffs. The plane ride back to Baltimore reminded me of funerals I'd attended. The worst part was the thought, the knowledge, that we were the better team. It was a feeling we would relive a year hence, except more painfully, after the Super Bowl upset by the Jets.

During the off-season between my rookie and sophomore years, Linda and I first visited my parents, and then hers in Hermiston. I loved Oregon, the mountains and clean white snow, the clear fresh air. We talked about settling down there some day.

I had a military obligation to fulfill (the Colts had gotten me into the Army Reserve), and while Linda stayed with her folks in Oregon, I spent six months at Fort Bliss in El Paso and Fort Huachuca in Arizona. I went into the service as a private, and when I got out six years later, that was still my rank.

I reported straight to training camp after the military stint, a veteran in the NFL now, and found a team champing at the bit to get the season started, to reach the pinnacle this time, a win in the Super Bowl. If losing big games builds character, all of us, when this season was over, would be paragons of virtue.

6
A Fair Chance to Start

Two main problems facing me at training camp for the 1969 season, my third in the NFL, were my contract (I didn't have one) and Coach Shula telling me I was being switched full time to running back. Regarding the contract, I sought out and listened to the advice of numerous players, most of whom weren't much better equipped in a business sense than I was. It puzzled me. Clearly Shula intended to keep me on the team (why else the change to running back?), but I had no contract and there wasn't any movement toward getting me one. Had the Colts just forgotten? Did they expect me to play for the $17,500 I'd made the previous year? I didn't know.

"Why don't you go straight to the head man?" defensive back Alvin Haymond said.

"Rosenbloom?"

"Sure. Tell him you don't have a contract. He's in charge of this lash-up, isn't he? It's his responsibility"

"I don't know if that's the thing to do."

"Sure it is. Go to the top. The money comes out of Rosenbloom's pocket. You should head for the source."

I looked closely at Haymond. I assumed he was leveling

with me, but it was hard to tell with him. Besides, every time I looked at Alvin I was reminded of myself. He had a big gap in his mouth, where two teeth had been knocked out, and I had even bigger gaps. I'd lost my four lower front teeth in my rookie year, going one-on-one with John Mackey. He'd caught a pass in a scrimmage, and I'd made the mistake of letting him turn upfield. Mackey's forte was running with the ball after he'd caught it, and I hit him right on his thighs, which were as broad as most men's backs, just as a knee was coming up. My mistake was trying to *tackle* him, which was what the coaches instructed. With someone like Mackey, you should try to hold him up, get in front of him, something, but not tackle him.

"You think Rosenbloom will see me?" I asked Haymond.

"Why not? You're a valuable man. You helped his team get to the Super Bowl last year."

"We got beat."

"Don't talk about that when you see him. The subject is that you deserve more money."

I realized Haymond was smarter than me. He had only two missing teeth. I'd lost my *upper* front four trying to block Bubba Smith on an end sweep, and again I was just following instructions. "Hit 'em in the numbers," the coaches tell you, which is absolutely wrong, at least with behemoths like Smith. They are *strongest* in their chest and shoulder areas. Also, I had to jump even to get Bubba "in the numbers." After this, my mouth looked like the entrance to the Holland Tunnel.

"Maybe I should hand him my eight lost teeth," I said to Haymond.

"He doesn't care about that. Mention those touchdown returns. The 102-yarder was a beaut. Tell him how tough it is to switch from defense to offense. An old dog learning new tricks."

"I'm not old."

"Whatever. Running back is a glamour position. Should pay a lot more than defensive back."

"I hadn't thought of that."

"And it's a harder position to learn."

"Right. I'll go see Rosenbloom."

And I did. Rather, I requested a meeting with him when he visited training camp, and we got together in a little-used room just off to the side of the weight room. "There's something that's bothering me," I said.

Rosenbloom was instantly concerned. He always tried to look much younger than he really was, dapper, debonair, but he wanted to play the role of concerned father, too, if he could. Right away I realized he was expecting something scandalous, trouble I'd gotten into, drugs, maybe getting mixed up with the wrong crowd.

"I'd like to help if I can," he said.

I told him I wanted a $4,000 raise, to $21,500 a year, and I gave him all the reasons why I deserved it, except for the eight teeth I'd donated to the Colts, which was the best reason. Immediately I could tell he wasn't interested in my problem, he didn't consider it his business, and he found it all a trifle amusing—$4,000 was such a *small amount* to him. He spent more than that on a party. I could see his eyes twinkle; it was funny that I was giving such an impassioned plea for $4,000. I was just getting warmed up, about to tell him I was *captain* of the special teams, for heaven's sake, but he'd heard enough and waved me to silence. He said, a trace of hesitation in his voice, I'd get the $21,500, and that was the end of the discussion.

I'll always remember his hesitation. Rosenbloom knew that with any kind of representation at all I would have gotten much more, but he wanted me to think I was driving a hard bargain. What he didn't know was that I might have quit football if I hadn't gotten the raise. The injuries and constant hurt did not make the game a joy for me. Also, this was my third year and I still wasn't considered a starter, where the bigger money was, and I knew the average pro-football career was less than five years.

Coach Shula changed me to running back for several reasons. The Colts were down to only two reliable running backs, Tom Matte and Timmy Brown (if one of these were injured we were in big trouble), and it seemed the position might be best for me. In my first two years I'd been used often as a guinea pig. I'd been sent over the middle to catch passes, playing the part of an opposing team receiver, and the defensive backs would try to hit me, a task they often found difficult. I was very elusive. In addition, I'd proven an effective blocker against linemen (forget the Bubba Smith episode) and linebackers.

But chiefly what Shula noticed were my hands, sensitive, strong and true, the "good hands" I'd had since childhood, hands that rarely dropped passes. And I would catch them over the middle, knowing I was going to be shaken to my toes by some freight train of a defensive back, and *hold onto* them, a talent that is rare indeed.

Plus the Colts really did need help at running back. Lenny Moore had retired and Tom Matte was slipping. It wasn't long before I thought I should be starting instead of Matte, a sentiment I know was shared by many of my teammates, but veterans of his stature are not so easily displaced.

Many of the plays, especially what became my bread and butter—coming out of the backfield to catch a pass—were no different from what I'd run in high school, and I had no trouble picking them up. The difficulty I had was with audibles. In high school when a quarterback called a play, that was it, you ran it no matter what the defense was. In the pros the play is often changed at the line of scrimmage, through an audible. I'd hear the numbers and colors pouring from the quarterback's mouth, and just couldn't understand them. I had a mental block.

In practices Shula would order Unitas to audible on almost every down, hoping through brute repetition to help me along, but time after time I'd become confused and mess up the play. Then one time I got it right, something just clicked, and I never again, ever, had a problem with changed signals at the line of scrimmage. It's still a mystery to me why it took so long to learn, why all of a sudden I was its master. I suspect this experience could apply to people, for example, who say, "I'm simply not mechanically inclined." Maybe this is because they don't give it a real chance. Perhaps they would be mechanically inclined if they worked at it, over and over, as Shula forced me to do.

I got my first nickname this third year: "Diablo." It came from defensive end Ron Hilton, who felt I resembled a demon or devil on special teams. This I couldn't understand either. I didn't like the hurt or the violence of pro football, yet I became Diablo charging under a punt or a kickoff.

Linda and I had moved into a larger apartment, still in the same section of Baltimore, for the 1969 season, and we were expecting our first child in December. When I came home happy with my $21,500 contract, more money than any Pearson had ever earned, she shared my joy, but there was also something reserved in her manner. She knew better than I the uncertainties of pro football, how quickly a career can be gone, and that what you lose in the present may never be acquired. A player's career can end before he ever negotiates that sought-after, lucrative contract. Waiting for next year can mean waiting forever.

The 1969 Colts were subtly different from the first two teams I'd been on. A great deal of talent remained, and the confidence a champion needs was there, yet there were small negative undercurrents that should have warned us all wasn't right. I saw a great deal of bickering, and cliques that got together after practice to complain. Mostly the trouble was generational, the old versus the new. The older guys thought they had earned the right to start; the younger ones felt the elders should be eased aside to allow superior talent to play. The Colts were in transition, and much of this was inevitable. When *do* you replace an aging star? Competition for starting positions can be healthy, but the rifts we experienced hardly contributed to the cohesiveness needed in a champion.

We went 6–0 in preseason, five of the victories over AFC teams, and the difficulties that would be so glaringly evident later on went virtually unnoticed. Our final preseason game was a 27–7 romp over the Cowboys in Dallas, with Roger Staubach starting at quarterback. *The New York Times* described his performance against us: "Roger Staubach presented the specter of the scrambling quarterback in the Cotton Bowl tonight to the shock and concern of his coach, Tom Landry, and the temporary delight of a crowd of 58,975.

"The 27-year-old rookie quarterback ran all over the field, and not by plot. But his team, the Dallas Cowboys, lost by 23–7 to the Baltimore Colts, adding substance to the premise that scrambling does not win."

Right. Scrambling didn't work because Ralph Neely couldn't handle Bubba Smith, though the news accounts failed to say this.

I imagine the writer for *The New York Times* might want to take back the comment about scrambling, but I still smile at the portrait painted of Tom Landry. The "shock" is more appropriate than the "concern." Later I got to see so much of

Landry, and shocked he must have been by the antics of Roger the Dodger. I didn't notice Landry this night, however. I was too busy enjoying being part of the rout of his Cowboys. We held them to 99 total yards, and Staubach to 6 of 21 passing. We intercepted 4 of his throws, almost as many as he completed.

I started the regular season opener against the Rams, gaining 43 yards on 11 carries and catching 3 passes for 42 more. That was the good part. The bad was that I lost a punt in the sun (the Rams recovered) and we lost the game, 27–20. It was only our third regular season loss in three years. That was the last time I was placed to receive a punt, which was fine with me.

But it was the following week that really woke us up to our problems. We went to Bloomington, Minnesota, and the Vikings killed us, 52–14. Joe Kapp threw *seven* touchdown passes, tying a record that still stands, and the Purple People Eaters (Larsen, Eller, Marshall, and Page) manhandled our offense. This was the Viking team that the same year would make it all the way to the Super Bowl, and Alan Page became the first and only defensive lineman ever to be named the league's most valuable player.

It took a fourth quarter Johnny Unitas-led drive to avert a third straight loss (the Colts hadn't lost two in a row at the beginning of a year since 1950). John Mackey caught the game-winner in the 21–14 victory against an Atlanta team we had crushed twice the year before.

The following week it took another comeback in the fourth quarter, led by you-know-who, to defeat the Eagles, 24–20. I hadn't started in any game since the opener against Los Angeles (Tom Matte was injured for that one), and had been told by Coach Shula that I might be used in the *defensive* backfield. I was what would be called a "valuable utility man" in baseball, but I wasn't happy with the role. I was the leader of the special teams, but it was obvious to me that this was a career-shortening job. I've seen clusters of players topple like bowling pins in this thankless assignment.

We were 3–2 after defeating the Saints, 30–10, in New Orleans, but still were not back to where we'd been. I'm sure our lackluster play contributed to my wondering whether I wanted to go on with pro football. I was enjoying myself, but a career on the special teams was hardly glamorous. Mostly, it was dangerous. I weighed the benefits of playing professional football against the terrific sacrifices it exacted.

Unitas tried for another miracle against the 49ers, bringing us back from a 24–7 deficit to 24–21, and passed up a chip-shot field goal in the last two seconds for a pass into the end zone that was batted away. In those days there was only sudden death for post-season games, and no one who knew Unitas, or for that matter Shula and the rest of the Colts, was surprised we went for the win.

I was bruised in the 49ers game, nothing any worse than what was commonplace, and again I wondered if all this were worth it. The most seriously I'd been injured occurred the previous year, against the Rams; when returning a kickoff I tried to split two tacklers and was hit hard in the back. The blow hurt right away, but after the game a big knot, a lump, arose on my lower back, right next to the spine, and the only way I could walk was bent over at a ninety-degree angle at the waist. I went to trainer Eddie Block and he told me to use ice.

Eddie Block was an older man, very short, and had been with the Colts a long time. He was a good trainer, though perhaps not as up-to-date as he should have been. He'd had at least one heart attack already, and many of the players found it difficult to discuss their conditions with him. He didn't like you to disagree with what he said.

I had several run-ins with Eddie Block. He had trouble believing me when I told him a certain area of my body hurt. He'd actually tell me I didn't hurt in those spots. One time when we were arguing he began to scream at me. His face grew red, then he started to cough, then to hack and wheeze. Other players came to him and made him sit down. I told him I'd do what he suggested, even though I didn't think it was right (and it was *my* body), and this appeared to calm him down. This also happened with other players. They had feared for Eddie's life when he began to scream at them.

The thing was, Eddie Block wasn't a doctor. He was a trainer, albeit a good one, yet he was the only person who examined me that day when I was bent over, with my face parallel to the ground. I remained that way for four or five days, with that knot the size of a baseball next to my spine, and felt that the ice treatment was like trying to treat cancer with an aspirin. The injury did go away—all of a sudden, as it turned out—but I still believe there was a chance I might have been permanently paralyzed.

Trainers like Eddie Block were terribly overworked. He had to tape forty or fifty players a day, and he put in twenty-hour workdays. One thing wrong with the system was that Block and the various NFL team doctors worked for *the club,* not the player. The club paid their salaries, or retainers, and their obligations were to the management. Of course, management wanted the players playing, not recovering from injuries, and this was hardly an arrangement designed to protect the athlete.

Nor did management want you to seek a second opinion, to go to another doctor to see if you really were fit to play. In any other area of life, business or personal, you are advised to get the widest range of advice, but not in pro football, where what is involved is your most precious possession, your health.

I didn't miss a single game those three years with Baltimore, and I agree that it is indeed necessary to "play hurt." No NFL team could field eleven players if they didn't play hurt. But just as undeniable is the fact that many teams, in their zeal to win, place victory above the individual player's welfare.

I've had a heart murmur since I was a child. I knew it, and every pro team I played for knew it. It was not deemed serious enough to keep me out of action, yet when I retired, after fourteen years, I had a nightmarish time trying to obtain my medical records. I needed them for an insurance policy I was purchasing, and I wonder if the reason they were so difficult to obtain was because another, independent doctor might have judged that I shouldn't have been anywhere near a football field.

During my third season I was more moody than is normal for me, and Don Shula, who is an outstanding coach precisely because he can spot such behavior, approached me one afternoon after regular practice. Jim Duncan and I were staying late to field kickoffs, and Shula just walked over to me.

"I've sensed a different kind of attitude in you," he said.

"I don't think I'm getting a fair chance to start."

"You're a young kid. You're learning. You've got a lot of time."

"I don't know. You brought in Timmy Brown. It seems like it may be four or five years before I get to start."

"You've got plenty of time, Preston."

"I've studied Matte and Brown. I think I can catch the ball as good as Matte, and run as well as Brown. I've worked hard to learn from them, but I think I've passed them."

"Well, maybe we can work some things out."

Corny Johnson and Charlie Stukes had seen me talking with Shula, and they wanted to know what it was about. "You told him *what*?" Corny said, when I repeated the conversation. "That you're better than *Matte*?" Looked at in a certain way it did sound a bit brash. Stukes said he didn't think I had it in me. "Here I thought you were shy," he said, "and you're telling Don Shula how to run his team."

But I did play more. Shula used me quite a bit, in both offensive backfield positions, and I played some defensive back too, along with special-teams duties. Actually, I had *four* positions, unusual in a sport that already was becoming extremely specialized.

We ran our 1969 record to 5-3 with a 14-6 win over the Packers, the only team ever to win a Super Bowl. We held Green Bay without a touchdown, and hoped maybe we were at last back on the track, but this was a different Packer team from the one that had dominated most of the 1960s. Perhaps the biggest difference was that Vince Lombardi had gone on to the Washington Redskins.

The 49ers dropped us to 5-4 the next Sunday, as John Brodie, imitating John Unitas, passed for the winning touchdown in the last two minutes. Just a minute before this, Unitas had put us ahead with a strike to Ray Perkins.

One thing that hadn't changed about the Colts was our penchant for thrilling games. In a sense we were the original Cardiac Kids. With less than five minutes to go against the Bears, we were down 21-14, and Shula called on John Unitas to come off the bench. We won, of course, 24-21, with the winning field goal being kicked with twelve seconds remaining.

After ten games we were 6-4, and would have been a good bet to be in the playoff contention had we been in a different division. But the Rams, our traditional nemesis, were a remarkable 10-0.

We were eliminated officially two weeks later (it had been unofficial for a long time) when Detroit tied us 17–17. The week before had been a 13–6 squeaker against Atlanta, and such a score against a weak team like the Falcons indicated we were less than playoff caliber.

Our second-to-last game of the season was a visit to Dallas and a 27–10 thumping by the Cowboys. Staubach had not yet replaced Craig Morton as the Dallas starting quarterback, and Morton teamed with Bullet Bob Hayes for 181 yards on just five receptions (36 yards per catch). We played a zone against Hayes, but obviously it was inadequate to the task. The great Mel Renfro, perhaps the finest defensive back ever to play the game (one of only five Cowboys in the "Ring of Honor" at Texas Stadium), intercepted two Unitas passes, and Bob Lilly was almost equally impressive at defensive tackle. I couldn't have known it, of course, but I was watching many of my future teammates on the great Cowboy teams of the mid- and late-1970s.

We ended the season in Los Angeles, scene of that horrible loss at the finish of 1967, playing a Rams team that was one of the favorites to reach the Super Bowl. If a game were ever played for pride, it was this one. Everybody on the Colts approached it as if the championship were at stake. It had been Baltimore's worst year since 1963, and the veterans, inspiring many of the newcomers, wanted something positive to remember during the off-season. The final score of 13–7 didn't indicate our dominance from the opening whistle, as we held Los Angeles to 53 yards rushing and just 106 passing. Unitas, "the Johnny U. of old," Associated Press called him, passed for 260 yards.

Something more important than any football game happened seven days after the victory over the Rams, and had we made the playoffs I wouldn't have been present to witness the event. Gregory Keith was born, with mother doing fine, on December 28. I was the one who felt sick and exhausted, and Linda and I joked about it. After I played a game, she was usually worn out—after she had a baby, I was the one most in need of rest and recuperation. Somehow it seemed a good sign.

I called my folks first. Mom told me to "say a prayer of thanks," something I'd already done.

I called Linda's folks and gave them the good news. Much of our troubles were behind us, and they reacted as any proud grandparents would.

Gregory Keith weighed eight pounds, was a healthy little guy, and whenever I held him, which was as often as Linda would let me, I wondered how his life would be. *Don't be a football player,* I thought, but right away I realized he should be whatever he wanted. We just had to take care of him, give him plenty of love, and make sure he knew all the choices. It also hit me—it really hadn't before—what a large responsibility he was. I was going to have to work harder as a father than I had as a football player, because there was no questioning which was more important.

I got my degree after the 1969 season. Linda (who also returned to school), Gregory Keith, and I moved to Champaign, Illinois, during the spring of 1970, and I got those letters behind my name. I know this was a prouder moment for my folks than any accomplishments I might have had in athletics.

Don Shula left the Colts to take the head coaching job with the Miami Dolphins, and Don McCafferty replaced him. I wondered, but not for long, how this would affect my status in Baltimore. I returned from classes one bright spring morning and McCafferty was on the phone. Such phone calls, despite possible popular misconceptions, are not trips down memory lane.

"Preston," McCafferty said, "we've traded you and Ocie Austin to Pittsburgh for Ray May."

That was it. I couldn't think of anything to say, and McCafferty wouldn't have wanted to hear it if I had. He was just doing his job. He figured I was grown up and would know how to adjust.

First I told Linda, then I tried to figure out if I was happy about the trade. Every player has an ego, usually a large one, and the first thing he does is look to see for whom he was traded. I was no different. *Ray May,* I said to myself. *That's not bad. Ray May is a helluva football player. The Steelers must like you if they'd trade Ray May.*

They were also getting Ocie Austin, but I didn't let that fact deflect my line of thought. Ray May really was an outstanding linebacker. The Colts were getting a top defender.

Right away I thought the move to Pittsburgh would be a good one for all of us. They'd had a terrible 1–13 record in 1969, Chuck Noll's first year as head coach, which meant they couldn't have an abundance of star players. Without even going over their roster I figured I'd have an excellent chance of starting, of getting the opportunity to prove what I could do—or couldn't.

I thought about the Pittsburgh Steelers. I remembered hearing a lot of talk about their rookie tackle, Mean Joe Greene, and how they had some other young players of potential. There was talk about how the Steelers intended to build their organization right, through the draft and with youth, which is what every team with a wretched record says, but there were knowledgeable people who took them seriously. There had even been praise for Chuck Noll, unheard of for a 1–13 coach.

Chuck Noll, I figured, was the answer. He had to be. It was too much of a coincidence that he was bringing me to Pittsburgh, after having coached me in my first two seasons at Baltimore. I must have impressed him, I told myself. Well, if he were serious about building a winner from scratch, that would be fun to be part of, better than the uncertain situation I faced in Baltimore. With Shula gone, I wasn't sure where I stood. I knew it was Shula who had first gambled on an untried basketball player.

I went to the library and read about the Steelers. Building from scratch is what it would be: In their long history in the NFL, the Steelers had *never* won a championship.

One thing did catch my eye. The great pass-catching artist Lionel Taylor was coach of receivers at Pittsburgh, and I thought there was no end to what I could learn from him. As events turned out, it was even more than I thought. Lionel Taylor would show me how the skills of a basketball player, hand/eye coordination, grace, and the gift of peripheral vision, could be transplanted to football and actually provide a big advantage over players who'd never played basketball.

Anyway, I looked forward to going to Pittsburgh. To starting. It would have been impossible to know that I was getting in almost at the beginning of one of the greatest dynasties in professional football.

7
Building the Steeler Dynasty

I used an agent to negotiate my first-year contract with Pittsburgh. The agent's name was Jerry Lichter, he was a Baltimore CPA, and he came on the recommendation of John Mackey. He listened to me give reasons why I thought I should receive a certain amount (I was likely to be a starter, was coming from a great team to a terrible team—which really needed help—and not only that, had been a leader as special-teams captain with the Colts), and then went to management and negotiated from my standpoint. The contract he got was for $27,500.

The point is, Lichter listened to me. The year before, Terry Cole, running back with the Colts, and I got the idea of letting Cole's agent represent both of us in a package deal. We thought we could do better than the aging running-back combination of Tom Matte and Timmy Brown (forget that a majority might disagree), and that with a united front, like baseball's Don Drysdale and Sandy Koufax, who negotiated jointly, we might get more favorable contracts.

"What do you think you're worth?" Terry Cole's agent asked me.

I told him.

"Well," he said, "I don't think you're worth that much."

This, I think, is the wrong way for an agent to deal with a player. He can certainly give reasons why he thinks the player might be out of line, using facts and figures, but at bottom his job is to try to negotiate what the player wants. Certainly it is not to say bluntly, "I don't think you're worth that much."

Anyway, I *was* worth that much. I'd told the agent I wanted $25,000 a year, and *on my own* I got $21,500, with a minimum of argument from Carroll Rosenbloom.

Chuck Noll had traded also with the Giants, getting Frenchy Fuqua and Henry Davis. Frenchy had to be the original space cadet. We became good friends, ran around together, generally enjoyed each other's company. But Frenchy was flaky. He had great athletic ability, which he relied on to prosper, and for a while was the most popular player in Pittsburgh. Eccentric doesn't describe his behavior. He always reported to camp with a pot belly, and often cavorted about in a purple cape, blue jumpsuit, bright, sloppy hat, and cane. He wanted to put water and goldfish into the plastic heels of his shoes.

The trouble was that a lot of the players were laughing *at* Frenchy, not with him. I felt sorry for him, decided I would try to help. It took place in the Steeler locker room.

"Frenchman," I said, "I'd like to say something to you."

"Go ahead."

"You know what some of the guys are saying, don't you?"

"No. What?"

"I think you should take a look at yourself. Figure out where you're going."

"I don't know what you're talking about."

"I know you're doing ads for a Volkswagen dealership. I hear you're not being paid."

"That's right."

"That's dumb, Frenchy. You should be paid."

"It helps promote my name."

"You're one of the best-known people in Pittsburgh. It works the other way around."

"It's good for my image."

"Bull it is."

"What are the guys saying?"

"It's bad, Frenchman. You don't want to hear."

"Tell me."

"Look at yourself, Frenchy."

"I want to know."

"They're not laughing because you say and do witty things. They're laughing because you're ludicrous."

"I don't believe you. You're jealous of me, Preston. You're jealous of how well I've done."

Frenchy and I remained friends, but I never volunteered advice to him again. Later, I seldom volunteered advice to new running backs and receivers as well. A lot of veterans were this way, and it wasn't because we feared we'd be helping people take our jobs. Many of the players in the late 1970s didn't ask for advice, and gave the impression they didn't need any. It seemed that the growing glamour and high salaries of the sport persuaded them that they already knew about all they needed to, and help was not welcome. Often I saw a rookie making a disastrous, but easily correctable, mistake, but I wouldn't go to him with advice. When a newcomer did ask for help, I always gave it as best I could, and so did other veterans, but this was a far-too-rare occurrence. I remembered how I'd shadowed Ray Berry when I was a rookie (Berry was another who wouldn't volunteer information, but would do anything to help if asked), and I believed the newer players could do the same.

The 1970 Steelers really were a team determined to build the right way, concentrating on the draft, and virtually every key player for their great championship teams was acquired while I was in Pittsburgh. It was something to watch it grow.

The year before I arrived, 1969, the first draft choice was Mean Joe Greene, six feet four and 275 pounds, from North Texas State. He promptly became rookie defensive player of the year, causing Chuck Noll to say: "We're gonna build a championship team in Pittsburgh, and Joe Greene will be the cornerstone."

That was a bold prediction based on the abilities of an unproven defensive tackle, but absolutely prophetic.

Other 1969 Steeler draft picks were Terry Hanratty, John Kolb, and L. C. Greenwood.

In 1970 the Steelers drafted Terry Bradshaw, Ron Shanklin, and Mel Blount.

In 1972: Franco Harris.

In 1973: Loren Toews.

And in 1974: Lynn Swann, Jack Lambert, John Stallworth, Jimmy Allen, Mike Webster, Tom Reamon, and Charles Davis.

Just a glance at the preceding and you see almost the entire nucleus of the great Steeler championship teams. Chuck Noll deserves a great deal of credit for the phenomenal Steeler resurgence, but so too, I think, does owner Art Rooney.

"Mr. Rooney," everybody called him, because he deserved respect, not because he demanded it. He was the best pro-football owner I worked for, or ever heard of—a kind, caring, totally reasonable man. Anyone with a problem could go to Mr. Rooney, and if he could help, he would. And he *listened*. He listened, for example, if a player thought he deserved more money, and he always seemed willing to compromise. He was flexible, unlike the Cowboys' owner, whose attitude often was: "We have a team structure—take the offer or leave it."

Art Rooney still lives in the same lower-middle-class north Pittsburgh area where he grew up, though of course with his money he could live anywhere, and he still has many of the same friends. He cares about the Steeler players, it almost could be called love, and so does his oldest son, Dan, who runs the day-to-day operation.

Mr. Rooney bought the franchise in 1933, purportedly from racetrack winnings, coincidentally in the year when Pennsylvania blue laws, prohibiting sports events on Sunday, were repealed. The Steelers were the Pirates until 1940, and in 1941 combined with Philadelphia as Phil-Pitt. In 1944 they joined with the Chicago Cardinals as Card-Pitt, and didn't win a single game. The Steelers still hadn't won a championship when I joined them in 1970.

Moving to Pittsburgh was much tougher on Linda than on me, which is usually the case in football marriages. The player realizes he probably will have to move on at some time. His wife often would prefer to stay put. Linda had grown fond of our Baltimore apartment—I'd made every stick of furniture it contained—and we had a newborn baby besides, but she offered no resistance when I was traded. It was probably an upward career move for me, and definitely a chance to break into a starting lineup. We rented a nice apartment near the airport and settled in for what we hoped would be a long, successful, and prosperous stay.

I was looking for good investments I might make. Perhaps it was still uncertainty about my football career, but I very much wanted something to turn to when I was finished. In Baltimore I'd been a member of the Thursday Night Club, a group of young men who got together to consider buying stocks, and I'd bought some land I still own in El Paso, Texas. I also made an unwise investment, recommended to me by John Williams, who had been a Colts number one draft pick. Along with others laying out the same amount, I put up three thousand dollars for an invention, a gadget that warned *before* power was about to go out in a major electrical installation. It had seemed like a terrific idea, but nothing came of it, and I lost the entire three thousand. I just wasn't getting proper advice.

But I was learning. I had two off-seasons of experience with a computer firm I'd been touted onto by Ed Rosenbloom. I was gaining confidence and contacts through speaking engagements, and I felt, given time, I wouldn't be confined to that dreadful limbo that awaits most retired pro-football players. One of the tricks was to avoid hustlers, who are as attracted to pro athletes as bears are to honey. The athletes make good salaries, their names have value, they usually think the glory ride will last forever, and they are absolutely no match for fast-talking wheeler-dealers with get-rich-quick schemes.

All eyes were on Terry Bradshaw my first year in Pittsburgh. He was first of the first, the first Steeler draft pick, the first player chosen in the *entire* selection process. Bradshaw was six feet three and 218 pounds with a howitzer for an arm and great college stats from Louisiana Tech. "He's the best rookie quarterback I've ever seen," said Art Rooney, of the blue-eyed, blond-haired quarterback.

A lot of fun has been poked at Terry Bradshaw over the years about his purported lack of intelligence. Thomas "Hollywood" Henderson said Terry couldn't spell "cat if you spotted him the 'c' and the 't.'" I knew Terry better than Henderson ever did, and I believe that what many people thought of as not being bright was really something else.

I first met Terry at a pre-preseason practice at Three

Rivers Stadium, and later the same night at the hotel where we were staying. He impressed me then as being young and immature, a kid from Louisiana who wasn't ready emotionally for a big city. Besides that he was shy, a small-town product who was both intimidated and awed by his surroundings. Most of all, as first of the first he was under terrific pressure to perform and produce, immediately. A great athlete he might be, but that gave him no inside track on how to handle this extremely difficult situation.

Bradshaw also, I believe, was awed and intimidated by the presence of Terry Hanratty, a cocksure, extremely likable quarterback from Butler, Pennsylvania (thus, much-loved in Pittsburgh), who had the added advantage of having played at Notre Dame. Hanratty had been the number two Steeler draft pick the year before Bradshaw, and many people in Pittsburgh were cheering for him. So were some of the players.

Terry Bradshaw didn't study much. He could probably get away with that at Louisiana Tech, where the system was not so complicated, but he didn't have a chance with that kind of approach in Pittsburgh. I don't think Terry's lack of study was caused by laziness. I believe he didn't learn the system as well as he could have because that gave him the opportunity in his own mind not to compare his performance to Hanratty's. If he failed, I think Bradshaw was telling himself, it wasn't because he lacked the ability, but that he couldn't pick up the system. Of course, Bradshaw's not knowing the system led to stories about his not having brains.

I remember a long drive we were on that had reached all the way to the opponent's twenty-yard line. Suddenly, eyes glazed and looking around, Bradshaw said, "What we got down here?" meaning what plays from the game plan can we use. The players in the huddle were thunderstruck. The heads of linemen came up, a wide receiver lifted his eyes skyward. *What kind of quarterback is this?* everyone was thinking. *He's supposed to be our leader, and he doesn't even know what the plays are.*

Bradshaw did finally come up with a play, not a particularly good one as I recall, but the impression of not being in command was much more lasting. Terry also seemed to have trouble putting his words together in the huddle. He spoke haltingly, uncertainly. And the words lacked authority. Again, I don't think this was because he was stupid, but because he hadn't worked hard enough to learn the system.

And Bradshaw looked worse in comparison to Terry Hanratty, who was always crisp and authoritative. Of course, Bradshaw was far more talented than Hanratty, a vastly superior athlete. The problem was he just didn't believe it himself.

Often there was confusion when Bradshaw was quarterback. His indecisiveness in huddles, the halting way he would stutter out a play, the fact that he let anyone and everyone talk (often at the same time)—these were not the qualities looked for in a leader. I couldn't imagine John Unitas even for an instant putting up with the babble that took place in Steeler huddles.

And Terry couldn't read defenses, his critics gleefully pointed out, another sign of "his lack of intelligence," but I never thought it was that. He didn't study defenses, so how could he read them? Many of these critics praised his running ability, and it was substantial and impressive, but Terry ran so much because he didn't know how to wait until a receiver was open.

I spent a number of nights at Terry's home, studying Chuck Noll's system and watching game films. I liked Terry's wife, Melissa, outgoing, honest, friendly. I think Melissa's ebullience was one of the reasons why the marriage didn't last. Terry wasn't comfortable with people who were sure of themselves.

Anyway, Terry's home was near our apartment, and a group of us would gather there to study. Terry was, almost always, inattentive. He needed the sessions more than anyone, but it was impossible to get him to concentrate. Again, I don't believe it was mental laziness, but a fear that if he did study *he still might not learn.*

Linda and I also attended parties at the Bradshaw house. Terry loved animals, big ones, and he always seemed to have a large dog or horse around. His laugh was unnaturally loud, another sign I interpreted as reflecting insecurity and immaturity. At one point he kept a bunch of pigeons around the house; he was trying to train them to be homing pigeons. The parties were of the southern variety—old-fashioned hoedowns where you could almost smell the hay. Terry was going out of his way to say, "Look, I'm country, nothing sleek or city about me."

Few people—Frenchy Fuqua was one— enjoyed partying more than Terry Bradshaw. He later made loud protestations about how important being a Christian is to him; he even berated reporters before a Super Bowl for wanting to talk about the upcoming game rather than Jesus Christ, but I have to wonder about this. During fourteen years in the NFL, I was always amazed by the guys who showed up most regularly at pregame chapel. The coaches were always there, but also in the pews, saying "Lord this" and "Lord that," were some of the wildest hell-raisers in the league. I wondered if they were trying to impress someone, or maybe themselves. For myself, I didn't find it necessary to advertise my belief in God.

Getting moved to Pittsburgh was a nightmare. I stayed with John Williams and his wife, Colleen, in Baltimore for a few days, and then Linda and a friend named Delores flew to Pittsburgh to look for housing while I stayed behind to look after Greg, with help from Colleen, John's wife. Linda, ever resourceful, got off the plane and asked a policeman where a good place to live would be. He told her, she went there, and she leased it (No point wasting time, I guess).

The problem was getting our furniture to Pittsburgh. Movers all over Pennsylvania were on strike, and strikebreakers trying to move furniture into the state were being shot at. The three of us stayed four or five days in that apartment—only Greg in the bassinet had a place to sleep—until I realized something had to be done. The strike might never end. Certainly tempers weren't cooling off: There were daily reports of windows being broken, trucks being overturned and torched. You could take furniture *out* of Pennsylvania, you just couldn't bring it in. I decided I wouldn't fit the definition of *scab* if I moved myself, so it was back to Baltimore for the rental of a big truck. I just hoped the strikers would realize that mine was a do-it-yourself operation. I drove the truck back to Coraopolis (in Moon Township— the community we moved to outside of Pittsburgh) pulling one of our cars, and Linda and Greg followed behind in the second car. Sometimes we switched assignments. Fortunately, the trip was accomplished without incident.

Remarkably, for a team coming off a miserable 1–13 season, a good deal was expected of the Pittsburgh Steelers in 1970. And the players had high expectations also. The Steelers were one of the three NFL clubs (along with Baltimore and Cleveland) to move to the American Football Conference following the merger. I thought, especially after we went 5–1 in preseason, with Bradshaw always very good and often spectacular, that with a break here and there we could reach the playoffs. I knew personally that I was ready to go. I was scheduled to alternate at running back with Dick Hoak, the club's leading rusher the year before.

Thus, the 5–9 record we actually posted was somewhat of a disappointment. But only somewhat. There wasn't a knowledgeable football fan anywhere who didn't predict that the Steelers were about to arrive with a bang. That it might be the biggest bang in the game's history no one could have foretold.

In any case, here is the game-by-game rundown of our 1970 season:

Pittsburgh	7	Houston	19
Pittsburgh	13	Denver	16
Pittsburgh	7	Cleveland	15
Pittsburgh	23	Buffalo	10
Pittsburgh	7	Houston	3
Pittsburgh	14	Oakland	31
Pittsburgh	21	Cincinnati	10
Pittsburgh	21	N.Y. Jets	17
Pittsburgh	14	Kansas City	31
Pittsburgh	7	Cincinnati	34
Pittsburgh	28	Cleveland	9
Pittsburgh	12	Green Bay	20
Pittsburgh	16	Atlanta	27
Pittsburgh	20	Philadelphia	30

Against the Colts, of all people, during the preseason, I'd rushed for 150 yards in just three quarters, which I thought was a "Take that!" performance against the team that had traded me, but in our regular season opener I gained only 33 (the team high) against Houston.

Terry Bradshaw started and had all kinds of trouble, misfiring on nine consecutive passes, and completing only four of sixteen before being benched in favor of Terry Hanratty. "I wasn't moving the football team," Bradshaw said afterward, identifying at least part of the problem. "The guys were open, but I wasn't hitting them. I was hesitating on passes, and I was calling bad plays."

True enough. But the real reason, which went unmentioned, was that he didn't sufficiently understand the Steeler system. He also made a silly error that cost us a safety, when he dropped back to pass and simply stepped over the end line.

In games two and three, losses to Denver and Cleveland, Bradshaw also gave up safeties, though these times he was tackled in the end zone. Terry had a much better day against Cleveland than he had had against Houston, which I think buttresses my argument that he hadn't worked hard enough mentally. The Browns played a much more basic defense than the Oilers, who at the time were mixing in plenty of tricks, and Terry could be excellent against teams that weren't sophisticated.

We won our fourth game of the season, 23–10, against Buffalo, ending a losing streak that had extended to sixteen games over two years. Terry Hanratty started instead of Bradshaw, didn't throw a single interception, and I had the pleasure of running the clinching fourth-quarter touchdown. The Buffalo game was my first look at O. J. Simpson as a pro, and you could tell how good he was even though we stopped him, holding the entire *team* to less than 100 yards rushing. O. J., of course, would later go on to establish the all-time one-season rushing record of 2,003 yards.

Even starting the season at 1–3, it was clear we had a strong defense, and could be overpowering if Joe Greene, L. C. Greenwood, Andy Russell, and Mel Blount received a little help. Joe Greene was just fearsome, with a reputation—and this was only his second year—as a hothead and a destroyer. The hothead part wasn't deserved. I think he got angry over losing so much, coming as he did from a winning program at North Texas State, but this was the sign of a competitor. That he was a destroyer cannot be questioned.

I remember a scrimmage we were having, offense against defense, everybody going about three-quarters speed. The coaches kept praising one of the offensive linemen—Bruce Van

Dyke, I believe—and Joe kept getting madder by the moment. You could just see him thinking, *They know this is just practice, don't they? That we're going three-quarters speed, aren't we?* But the coaches insisted on praising the offensive line, and Mean Joe finally announced, "I'm coming this time. Look out!"

He ran *over* the offensive guard when the ball was snapped, right *through* the quarterback, and *over* the two offensive backs. Then he turned around and smiled, at peace with himself. He was *the* man. It was important to Joe that everyone knew that.

The "Mean" part of his name didn't come from a nasty disposition, but from the nickname of his alma mater, the North Texas State Mean Green. Actually, Joe was a good guy off the field. People who remember the award-winning Coca-Cola commercial he did, where he handed a young boy his jersey, got a better look at the real man than did offensive linemen, whom he terrorized.

Joe had a winning personality. He was straight-arrow in his approach with people. "I'm not going to say much," he would begin, and then he would honestly set forth what he thought.

Mean Joe was a giant. He was six feet four, but in width and from back to front, he was as big as any man who played the game. Soon teams started putting two blockers on him, and still he was effective. More important, with two blockers on Mean Joe, the job of the linebackers was much easier.

L. C. Greenwood, defensive end, was tall and rangy, and had, in my opinion, one great quality as a football player: He could keep his hands and feet moving as he advanced like a missile toward his target. At first L. C. tried to be another Frenchy Fuqua, once wearing blue panty hose (I am not making this up!) in the locker room, but he eventually straightened out his act. We called him "Hollywood Bags" because he wanted an acting career (he has been seen doing a Miller Lite commercial with Bert Jones), and the gold shoes he wore on the football field were his trademark. A lot of athletes try to wear something distinctive. With eight-hundred-meter runner Dave Wottle it was a baseball cap, with Billy Johnson, his famous white shoes, for Joe Namath it was lowtops.

I don't think L. C. Greenwood was a good athlete. He was a

My mother, Mrs. Catherine
Pearson, at age sixty-two
(PRESTON PEARSON)

The Pearson home when I
was born (PRESTON PEAR-
SON)

The grocery store I passed each day on the way to school (PRESTON PEARSON)

Freeport Senior High

The 1972 Steelers training camp. In the foreground is Coach George Perles. In the background is Coach Chuck Noll. (*The Pittsburgh Press*)

One of Gerela's Gorillas in
football-crazed Pittsburgh
(*The Pittsburgh Press*)

Going over Oakland's Phil
Villapiano for a touchdown
(*The Pittsburgh Press*)

Stopping a car at the Steelers training camp during a strike. From left to right are Frenchy Fuqua, Roy Gerela, Moon Mullen, and Jack Ham. (AL HERRMANN, JR., 1974)

Hanratty handles the ball while Bradshaw (left) and Coach Chuck Noll look on. (AL HERRMANN, JR.)

On a Topps chewing gum card when I was with the Steelers (TOPPS)

On a Topps chewing gum card when I was with the Cowboys (TOPPS)

This was the first picture taken of me as a Dallas Cowboy. (*Dallas Cowboys Weekly*)

This was my first carry with the Cowboys. I'm following Burton Lawless. (*Dallas Cowboys Weekly*)

A touchdown catch in the 1975 playoffs against the Rams. The defender is Ken Geddes. Notice his right arm. It's dressed up perfectly to deliver "the bone," a shattering forearm shot to the head. (*Dallas Cowboys Weekly*)

I'm showing good concentration on the football in a playoff game against the Rams, despite being killed by Nolan Cromwell. (*Dallas Cowboys Weekly*)

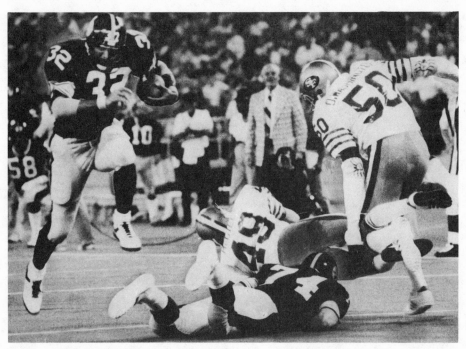

Franco on his way to a touchdown (AL HERRMANN, JR.)

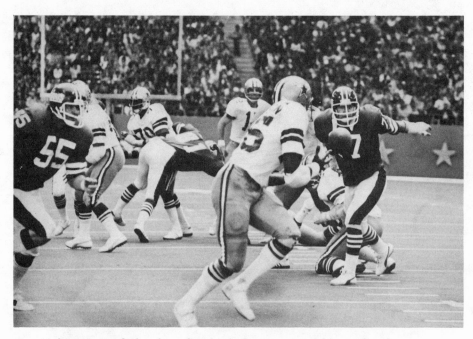

A pass completion from Staubach. It was easy pickings when isolated on a linebacker. Number 70 in the picture is Rayfield Wright, one of the linemen who helped make Roger what he is. (*Dallas Cowboys Weekly*)

Carrying the ball against Atlanta in the playoffs (*Dallas Cowboys Weekly*)

Looking for a place to run against Atlanta (*Dallas Cowboys Weekly*)

I designed this caricature. It alludes to the fact that most passes I caught were for first downs (or touchdowns).

Scoring a touchdown against the 49ers; one of two I had in the game. (*Dallas Cowboys Weekly*)

The Vikings' Paul Krause, all-time pass-intercepting safety, is about to miss me. (*Dallas Cowboys Weekly*)

My hands were banged up in this game against Oakland. Incidentally, there's nothing wrong with carrying the ball this way in certain situations, despite what many TV announcers say. Notice the way the ball is held firmly in the fingers. (*Dallas Cowboys Weekly*)

This was my last touchdown, December 21, 1980, against Brenard Wilson and the Eagles. The form here is good. I'm catching the point of the ball, not the fat, and staring it right into my hands. (UPI)

very effective *football* player, but I don't think he could have excelled in anything else, even basketball, where his six-feet-seven height would have to be an advantage. At tennis or golf he would be ludicrous.

On the other hand, wide receiver Frank Lewis, who would soon join the team, was one the best athletes you'll ever see. This graduate of Grambling was good at everything, and I think he would have made a remarkable decathlete. Frank Lewis was a whiz at basketball, at almost any sport you could name, and if he'd never played the game, he could pick it up in minutes.

Lewis was more Chuck Noll's type of athlete than L. C. Greenwood was, I think. Noll, and Shula and Landry also, looked for athletic skills more than specialized ability on the football field. All three can look at a good athlete and project into the future, imagine almost exactly how much he will grow, and how a few years down the road he might be much more valuable than the individual who has had no other experience but in football.

Oddly enough, neither Joe Greene nor L. C. Greenwood really caught my attention when I first reported to Pittsburgh's training camp. There were a lot of big men on hand, and although maybe I just wasn't looking, physically they didn't stand out. I remember one big guy, 285 pounds and almost as fast as a halfback, who missed curfew one night and the next day was on the waiver list. This was more effective than a dozen screaming sessions, as far as getting players to know what was expected of them. Word of why the big man was waived spread like wildfire through the camp, and the wise took heed. In such a manner, without trumpeting fanfare, Noll started to shape up the Steelers.

My roommate that first season in Pittsburgh was Dave Smith, a multitalented wide receiver who also had been a college basketball player. Smith and I were good friends. He was very cocky—I could have used a *little* of this—and it led to his getting in trouble. At a Dapper Dan banquet in Pittsburgh, sporting a lustrous Afro, he embarrassed Dan Rooney by announcing that he wanted to be traded, and Chuck Noll by intimating that the coach didn't know what he was doing.

Dave Smith, of course, got his wish. He was waived to

Houston. He told me the first thing he was told when he arrived in that Texas city: "*We,* not you, run this show."

Smith was waived again and then was out of the league. I can't prove it, but I, along with many other players, suspect there is a blacklist that operates in the NFL. I think Dave Smith got himself on it. I don't think the blacklist is so crude as to consist of a sheet of paper with names written on it, but it's real nonetheless. Word is passed that "so-and-so is a trouble-maker, stay away from him," and usually teams do. It is possible that even if a blacklist doesn't exist, management would like the players to think it does. Just the thought keeps athletes in line.

When I came to the Cowboys in 1975, I was asked, by Dr. Pat Evans of the Cowboys, "How's the knee?"

I gave him a blank stare. Nothing had ever been wrong with either of my knees. "It's fine," I said.

"You're sure it's okay?" he asked.

"It's fine."

Now where did Dr. Evans get the idea my knee was bad? All I could think was that somehow I'd gotten myself on a list. I'd been union-player representative for the Steelers in 1974 during the bitter strike action, a position guaranteed not to endear myself to the hearts of management. The job of player rep is hard and largely thankless. I figured there was a very good chance the rumor going around about my knee had something to do with union activities.

Our fifth game of the season, a 7–3 win over the Oilers in Houston, demonstrated the kind of defense we could play. Our only touchdown was a Bradshaw-to-Ron Shanklin thirty-three-yard aerial on which the Oiler cornerback, Leroy Mitchell, fell down. Terry Bradshaw just wasn't moving the team. He started only about half the games, mostly because Chuck Noll couldn't make up his mind. The team seemed to function better with Hanratty, but then Noll would look at all of Bradshaw's raw talent and get him back in there.

It was just a terrible year for Bradshaw, as bad as the following statistic would indicate: He threw six touchdown passes and was intercepted *twenty-four* times.

I scored another touchdown the following week against Oakland, but Bradshaw threw four interceptions and we were thumped 31–14. What a contrast this game provided: perhaps the most mature, experienced quarterback the game had ever known, the ageless George Blanda, against one of the least knowledgeable to start an NFL contest, Terry Bradshaw. This is not meant to be hard on Terry. His four Super Bowl rings speak for themselves. What I'm saying is merely the unvarnished truth: He was not prepared mentally to play in the league.

The next week against the Bengals underscored Chuck Noll's dilemma: He wanted to build a championship team, but it was important to win also. Often the two are mutually exclusive. To build a winner, Bradshaw needed to be given experience; to win a few games immediately, we were better off with Hanratty. In any case, against the Bengals, Bradshaw, four for twelve passing, was relieved in the third quarter by Hanratty, who went seven for eleven and led us to two final-period touchdowns. We were in second place in our division, at 3–4 only a game behind Cleveland.

Terry Hanratty started the big game the following week against the Jets, and hit the winning touchdown pass to Frenchy Fuqua. Joe Namath was injured and not in action that week, but there was still something special for me in beating the Jets. I knew the Super Bowl loss would forever retain its sour taste.

Against the Super Bowl champion Chiefs (the biggest team I've ever seen), it was Bradshaw who replaced Hanratty in the third quarter in what turned out to be a 31–14 loss. Terry did throw two touchdown passes, but was intercepted three times. This game, perhaps more than any other, highlighted the growing pains the Steelers were experiencing. We didn't know whom to use at quarterback, yet we were knocking at the door of the playoffs. Two weeks later, when we crushed the Browns 28–9, holding the great Leroy Kelly to *zero* yards rushing on ten carries, we were tied with Cleveland and Cincinnati with 5–6 records and only three games remaining. It was, in retrospect, a remarkable achievement, a 1–13 team the previous year still in the running for the Super Bowl.

The pivotal game was against Green Bay in Three Rivers Stadium. The big park was packed with howling fans who had *never* known a championship team. We stormed down the field on the opening kickoff, determined to take charge right from the start, and Larry Krause ran right by us, one hundred yards for a touchdown. But the game wasn't over yet, nor were our dreams of a first-ever Steeler championship. Running effectively, slowed up only by Terry Bradshaw's worst day, we got into position for four Allen Watson field goals and were down only 13–12 heading into the final quarter.

But Bart Starr—what a contrast he was to Terry Bradshaw this day!—hit John Hilton with a sixty-five-yard scoring strike that made the final tally 20–12. I don't think I've ever even *heard* of a worse game than the troubled Bradshaw had. He completed *three out of twenty* passes. He had more interceptions, four, than he had completions.

It wasn't a good game for me either. Throughout the contest veteran linebacker Ray Nitschke had been shouting to his teammates what our next play would be, and he was invariably correct. We were such a young, immature team that somehow we were giving away what play was coming next, and we weren't able to figure out where the leak was coming from. But if Nitschke said Frenchy Fuqua was going to run an end sweep, you could bet that's what Bradshaw had called, or if he yelled to look out for a post pattern, you could make book that a post pattern was coming. It made us sick, Nitschke standing back there, not bothering to conceal his contempt.

In any case, Bradshaw called a draw play with me carrying the ball, and I heard Nitschke call out where we were going to run; I even saw him point to the spot. As the saying goes, my mother didn't raise a fool for a son, and I made up my mind right then and there that after I took the hand-off I'd head for another spot. Nitschke could guard the spot where the play was supposed to be coming for as long as he wanted. I was going to head in another direction. I had visions of breaking one all the way.

There was one fatal flaw. The lineman—I won't name him—who was assigned to block Nitschke, keep him away from the hole, did exactly as he was supposed to, forcing the fearsome linebacker to change direction. I had thought the lineman had seen Nitschke point, heard him yell out where the play was coming, and would think along with me and let Nitschke get to that point. I surely wasn't going to be there. But Nitschke, forced to change direction by the proper (improper, I say) block, ended up on a collision course with me and my newly designed route.

I saw this monster only a moment before he hit. Just an instant before, not enough time to prepare myself, and it felt like he was tearing my head off. He hit me on the right side of my face and flattened me. It was the kind of hit that can break a man's back. I saw Nitschke as I was going down, and he had a wild look in his eyes. His mouth, incredibly, seemed to be foaming.

I wasn't knocked out, but it was the closest I've come. I was stretched flat on my back on the Three Rivers turf, snow falling in my face, my head feeling as if a bomb had exploded in it, and the trainer, smelling salts to my nose, was saying, "You okay?"

Of course I wasn't okay. I'd just been hit by a train. But every ballplayer answers "huh?" when asked that ridiculous question, and until he can say "yes," he is not considered fit to play.

"I've never been hit that hard," I told my friend Tom O'Malley after the game. O'Malley was an advertising man who lived close to our apartment. "It was scary. I doubt if it's possible to ever be hit that hard again."

"You should be happy, then," he said. "The worst is in the past."

And it was. Of all the hits I took in fourteen years, the one from Ray Nitschke stands as the hardest.

Although we mathematically still stood a chance at the playoffs, the defeat by Green Bay really spelled the end for us. It was surprising that we had come as far as we had, with the turmoil at quarterback and so many inexperienced players. We lost our next-to-last game against Atlanta and our finale, 30–20, to the Eagles.

Frenchy Fuqua (finally in shape?) gained 218 yards in 20 carries against Philadelphia, breaking the all-time Steelers one-game rushing record. He scored on runs of 85 and 72 yards, and I thought the triumph at least partially belonged to me. Many of his gains came on a play called "counter-15," with my block on the defensive end being the key. In this game I was usually paired against Mel Tom, a 255-pound defensive end, and the result established me as a superior NFL blocker. Time after time we trapped Tom, and then I would bang him with all I had, opening huge holes for Frenchy.

Bill Nunn, a Pittsburgh scout, paid me a high compliment. "Forget Frenchy Fuqua," he told a reporter. "Preston Pearson was responsible for those runs."

The counterplay with the trap block would become Pittsburgh's bread-and-butter play, just as the sweep was for the Packers. Sports fans can close their eyes and still picture Franco Harris cutting behind a halfback block and heading upfield. It was my honor to be Franco's partner in the backfield when he broke in with the Steelers.

Right near the end of the final game of the 1970 season, against Philadelphia, Joe Greene, never having accustomed himself to defeat, took off his helmet and tossed it high into the air. It seemed to soar to the top of the stands at Franklin Field (this was one of the last games played there) and above, somehow a fitting signal, as it fell to earth, of our disappointed hopes. But maybe, as it soared upward, it symbolized also the direction we were headed.

Joe wasn't fined for throwing his helmet, though usually such a practice is automatic. Perhaps it was viewed as a step toward maturity for the great tackle. Throwing a helmet wasn't as serious as the numerous fights he'd gotten into in the past, fights that stemmed solely, I think, from his utter abhorrence of losing.

Joe was growing up. So were the Steelers.

8

Joe Greene, Ernie Holmes, and Other Friendly Folk

My good friend Jon Kolb, Steeler offensive lineman and perhaps the strongest man in pro football, was largely responsible for getting me interested in weight lifting. It was just what I needed to build up my strength, and it came at a good time, during my fourth and fifth years in pro football. If I'd taken it up seriously earlier, I think I might not have developed other important athletic attributes—speed, grace, fluidity—as well as I did. But now what was needed was the muscular structure to withstand the terrific pounding that was a weekly occurrence in the NFL. Jon Kolb, who was punished on every play by defensive behemoths, had built for himself the sort of body that could take it, and at the same time he had acquired awesome strength. I saw him bench press 555 pounds.

Working with weights quickly shot my own weight up to 218 pounds, from a norm of 196. There were people who only half-jokingly said I could be a contestant in the Mr. Universe contest. Indeed, when I wanted to show my muscles it was almost as if I didn't have skin, so clearly could each muscle be outlined.

Later, with the Cowboys, I was given a variety of tests aimed at determining the amount of my body fat. One of these, being dunked in a pool of water, was administered at the famed Aerobics Center in North Dallas. It turned out I had less than 3 percent body fat, lowest of any of the Cowboys (and if you know Tom Landry, you understand that there is no such creature as a fat Dallas Cowboy). The truth is that I really might have been undernourished, but I suspect such an extreme example of conditioning is not good in pro football. *Some* body fat is needed to cushion the hard blows.

The year 1971, through the draft, brought more of the players who soon would form the championship teams. One of the most important was Jack Ham from Penn State—Linebacker U.—known for producing players for that position, just as USC is famous for running backs, and BYU, now, for quarterbacks.

It was clear from the beginning that Ham had been well versed in the fundamentals by someone, probably Joe Paterno. He was small for a linebacker, and was another example of Chuck Noll's ability to see more in an individual than raw statistics. During his rookie season Ham replaced injured corner linebacker Henry Davis, promptly intercepted two or three passes, and was a starter for the rest of his career.

I liked Jack Ham. He was a guy who didn't feel he had to tear your head off on every down. If he could avoid a block and make a tackle, he would. He didn't need to go out of his way, like other Steelers, to pop somebody. He took the game seriously, but not *too* seriously, and he knew how to have fun. I guess you'd call him the strong, silent type, and he was looked to as a leader, not because of his mouth but his actions.

Ham was shy, but very popular with women. Some of them weren't hesitant to come right up to him, after a game when we'd met in some restaurant for a drink, and make it clear they *wanted* Jack Ham. It was enjoyable to watch him. He would wriggle and squirm, finally escaping by taking down their names and phone numbers and saying he would call. We always asked him if he followed through, but he wouldn't say.

He was on one of the first *Superstars* competition, and, rare for him, kept bragging to me about how much money he was going to win. He came back almost empty-handed and I asked him what happened.

"Hey, man," he said, "those guys are superathletes. Wait till you get there, Pres. You'll see."

I did see. I also saw a lot of athletes, like Jack Ham, who thought they would enter the television competition and pick up a wad of easy money. It usually didn't happen. Even winning a single event was difficult, especially so for football players. The competition took place right after our season ended, and there really wasn't time to get ready for it. Baseball players might have been practicing for the events for months.

Jack Ham was as good an outside linebacker as I've seen. He was excellent at dropping back into pass coverage, and good also at coming across the line of scrimmage. Just as I got my game baptism of fire from Herb Adderly, Ham got his from St. Louis Cardinals running back MacArthur Lane. Lane was a tough guy. Ham came after the quarterback on a blitz, and Lane, part of the pass protection, caught him with a terrific wallop right underneath the chin. It was a lesson he didn't forget: The big running backs can hurt you.

Jack Ham had a graceful way of running, a bounding gait, and he was a good overall athlete, not just at football. He and I were on the Steelers' basketball team, which was not an untalented congregation. He was enjoyable to be around. He had a good sense of humor, a quick wit; he knew what he was about. I even liked Jack's lisp.

Tight end Larry Brown also joined the Steelers in 1971. He was a nice guy, on a team not known for an oversupply of them. He was tall and thin, 225 pounds, had great hands, and didn't say much. He also was a basketball player, could dunk the ball with either hand, and was yet another example of Chuck Noll's being able to see what a player will become somewhere down the line. Larry took up weight lifting and went up to 260 pounds. And it was a powerful 260. He is a *specimen*. He is now offensive tackle Larry Brown, and, according to my pal Too Tall Jones, who ought to know, one of the very best.

Then there was Dwight White. "Mad Dog" we called him.

Dwight was undersized for his position, and *mean*. He would grab face masks, hit an opponent, spit in his face. Dwight was always ready for a fight.

Dwight White was from Dallas and he hated the city for racial reasons. He hadn't been treated well, I gathered, and he had a special dislike for the police, whom he gave the following imitation of: "Boy, don't y'all realize this here ain't no highway. Y'all in a residential area."

Dwight always seemed to get into fights with Doug Dieken, an offensive tackle with Cleveland. Again, with Too Tall Jones as my source, I've heard that Dieken is a quiet guy who doesn't look for trouble on the field. I would guess the cause of the difficulty was Dwight White. Anyway, White loved to play the Cowboys, and nothing gave him greater pleasure than beating them.

I considered Dwight White a dirty player. He didn't just respond to violence, he initiated it. But he was also a good player. He could read keys, avoid traps—important skills which were taught to him by defensive-line coach George Perles. Today, Dwight is with a brokerage firm. I admire him for knowing how to approach the business world. If you met him you wouldn't think he had been that good, judging from his physical characteristics, but he was. He doesn't look like the popular conception of the behemoth lineman.

We called Ernie Holmes "Fats," though he wasn't, certainly not when he joined us in 1971. He was just *huge*. Squat. He weighed 285 pounds and was by far the strongest player on the defensive team. He shaved his head so that the only hair remaining was in the shape of an arrow. Everybody wanted a trademark, and understandably so. It gave them distinction, an image, something people could identify with. It served not only as ego gratification, but could pay off in commercial endorsements. Joe Greene was "Mean," Dwight White was "Mad Dog," L. C. Greenwood had his gold shoes, and Ernie Holmes had his arrow haircut.

I once saw Ernie Holmes eat thirty boiled eggs for lunch. He wasn't showing off, or winning a bet either. It was just that he was dead tired from a training-camp practice, knew he had to get some food into himself even though he wasn't hungry, and eggs were what he could get down easiest.

You had to be in good shape, even during practices, or Ernie Holmes would hurt you. He always wanted to go all out, even when common sense said a drill at three-quarters speed was wiser. He'd deliver shots in practice that nearly knocked you out of your shoes, and he wasn't the type of person to whom you complained.

Holmes and Joe Greene were as effective a tandem of tackles as ever played the game. Holmes, with his tremendous strength, could wreak absolute havoc in the middle of the line, and Joe Greene would maneuver around and through it to make hits that made your ears hurt. Greene and Holmes designed their own special defense, only the one seemed to know what the other was doing, and with their size, strength, agility, and meanness, playing against them was brutal.

I was somewhat afraid of Ernie Holmes. He once had to be put away for a time. He'd come to Pittsburgh for some reason or other to borrow money from Art Rooney, who refused. Holmes went on a spree. Speeding down a highway, shooting guns out the window, he was eventually chased and trapped by police. A helicopter hovered overhead, and Holmes shot at it, wounding a policeman. Holmes was that way.

Ernie Holmes always looked like something was going to snap in his head. He had a blazing look of anger in his eyes, and seemed often to be on the verge of losing control. I've seen the look in the eyes of other men, but not as frequently as with Holmes. You just know that pain or civilized behavior doesn't matter to them, that they are capable of almost anything. It is frightening, that ferocious, hateful, on-the-brink-of-going-over-the-edge stare, even in a very small man, but it was terrifying coming from the 285-pound Holmes.

Holmes liked to drink cognac in bars, always facing the door so he could see who was coming in. He would drink a fifth or two of the booze, and the only way you could tell if he was inebriated was when he got nastier. He would say something hateful, and you felt he would kill you if you answered back. Especially when he was drinking, Steeler players tried to stay away from Ernie Holmes.

Yet Holmes was very good with children. He genuinely liked them, and they loved to be around him. He could be the most charming individual with young people, then he would start to talk with adults and that wild stare would be in his eyes.

I think Ernie was jealous of Joe Greene. He didn't have Joe's charisma, and I believe that bothered him. He thought, correctly, that much of Joe's success was due to him. He could just rip open the middle of a line, a giant casting people aside, until only Joe Greene or a linebacker was in the path of the frightened ball carrier. I could understand Ernie's feelings about not getting proper recognition. With Frenchy Fuqua, and later with Franco Harris, it was rare indeed to see anything mentioned about the blocks being thrown that sprung them loose.

Pittsburgh in 1971 was a team right at the threshold of being a champion. A few of the key members of the future dynasty were not yet on hand, but most were. That we didn't blossom into one of the league's powerhouses until the next season was a result of not yet being precisely fine-tuned. We were close, but a player or two and a year or two away. Anyway, this is how our season log was in 1971, a 6–8 year:

Pittsburgh	15	Chicago	17
Pittsburgh	21	Cincinnati	10
Pittsburgh	21	San Diego	17
Pittsburgh	17	Cleveland	27
Pittsburgh	16	Kansas City	38
Pittsburgh	23	Houston	16
Pittsburgh	21	Baltimore	34
Pittsburgh	26	Cleveland	9
Pittsburgh	21	Miami	24
Pittsburgh	17	N.Y. Giants	13
Pittsburgh	10	Denver	22
Pittsburgh	3	Houston	29
Pittsburgh	21	Cincinnati	13
Pittsburgh	14	Los Angeles	23

The opening game in Chicago was important for two reasons. We were a young team on the way up, and we wanted to find out just how far we had come. Both the Steelers and the Bears had reputations, richly deserved, for being very physical, and the Bears were a good team against which to measure our progress. On a personal level, it was the first time my father had ever seen me play—anything!

I guess curiosity simply got the best of him. Also, the game was in Chicago, so he didn't have to travel far. He, my brother Ed, my brother-in-law Bill, and I got together the night before the game for dinner. Dad, never demonstrative, actually had an involuntary twinkle in his eye at the prospect of seeing me play. That meant he was *very* interested. Mom wouldn't come. It was a Sunday, and she didn't think a football game should be played on Sunday.

I wanted to play the best game of my life. I couldn't have been more excited if it had been the Super Bowl. And I scored the first touchdown of the game on a pass Ron Shanklin caught and fumbled into the end zone, which I was able to recover. It was a case of good hand/eye coordination, and somehow being calm enough inside to wait for the ball to bounce *up.* A football can take strange bounces, and many players in their overeagerness go after it when it's just hitting the ground. After I scored and accepted the obligatory congratulations from my teammates, I scanned the stands with my eyes, trying to see Daddy, but it was just as hopeless as when I'd tried to find Linda during Super Bowl III. But I knew how he looked. His facial expression never changed. A stranger wouldn't have been able to detect even a trace of pride. And Daddy wouldn't have wanted me to know he was proud. But I know *him,* despite his disclaimers, and how happy he was.

Most of the game was spent blocking Dick Butkus on trap plays. I hit him at least two solid shots, and a third time, when he was ready for me, I hit low down around the ankles and took him down. I learned my lesson on "hitting 'em in the numbers" from Bubba Smith. Butkus was steaming mad. "I'm gonna get you, Pearson," he screamed. "You S.O.B., I can't wait until you come back here again!"

Butkus meant it. He is what is called an intimidator—many of the Steelers were this way—and he could back up what he said. I smiled at him, but quickly experienced fear when in the very next huddle Bradshaw called a play that required me to go back after Butkus. Somehow I survived all of it. I thought once during the game how unusual my life had been. I'd been at Illinois when Butkus had been there, a great football player, just as he was now. I never imagined I'd be playing against him in Soldier Field, with my father watching.

Bradshaw still wasn't completely familiar with our offensive system, and this led to some trouble for me. It was the old story. We were on a drive and he asked his famous question, "What do we have here?" (Meaning what plays were in the game plan for the given situation?) I didn't think it was wise to say, "You're the quarterback, aren't you?" This would just have led to a time-out that we might have needed later. So I mentioned the plays.

The following Tuesday Chuck Noll called me into his office.

"I hear you're talking in the huddle," he said. "We don't want that sort of thing."

"I was just responding to the quarterback's question."

"Well, we'll have no more of that."

I don't know who told him I'd been talking in the huddle. But he was clearly upset with me. It didn't matter that I thought I'd done the right thing. Next time, though, I'd let Bradshaw use a time-out. That would really make Noll mad.

The fourth game of the season was a good one for me, gaining seventy-three yards on just seven carries in a 27–17 loss to Cleveland, but the game two weeks later—against Houston—meant much more to me. My mom, deciding it wasn't right that Daddy had seen me play and she hadn't, flew to Pittsburgh for the game. It was a quick change of heart from refusing to watch a sport on Sunday. "God," she reasoned, "must think football is all right on the Lord's day. He wouldn't have made my son to play it if it wasn't."

Linda and I showed Mom around Pittsburgh. It was a bigger thrill for me than it was for Mom. We took her to dinner aboard a riverboat on the Allegheny, and I don't think she enjoyed it. She said she was afraid of the water. And I know she didn't enjoy all of her meal. We persuaded her to try escargots, and made the mistake of telling her what they were. The best we could do was get her to take a few nibbles.

It was great having her in Pittsburgh. I'd wanted Daddy to come, but *he* was afraid of flying. Both at Soldier Field for the Bears game and in Three Rivers against Houston I'd invited

Rufus, but his presence was out of the question. He wasn't interested, and my parents didn't want him to come either. His attention span was very short, and it really was impossible to tell how he would react. I was disappointed that he couldn't be there. Had he not fallen sick, he would have been a star in the NFL.

My mother saw us win, 23–16. Bradshaw had four interceptions, but our defense as usual was solid. I wanted Mom to stay longer, but I knew she would go home to my father. Anyway, the ice had been broken for both of them, and I knew I had two more solid fans.

The week we beat Houston we were shocked to learn that Chuck Hughes of the Detroit Lions had collapsed during a game with the Bears and died. We felt terrible for his family (he had a wife and a twenty-three-month-old son), but it also made us realize again how dangerous the sport is. You could get killed out on the football field. In fact, a number of players had: Stan Mauldin of the Chicago Cardinals in 1948, Howard Glenn of the New York Titans in 1960, Stone Johnson of the Kansas City Chiefs in 1963, and Dave Sparks of the Washington Redskins in 1964. The wonder was that with the brutal hitting, more players hadn't died. Stone Johnson, for instance, had his neck broken. Later, Darryl Stingley, who lived, was paralyzed for life, and this on a hit that hadn't even been necessary.

In our ninth game of the season we showed signs against Super Bowl-bound Miami that we weren't far away from becoming an elite team. The Dolphins and Don Shula, with Paul Warfield catching 12- 86- and 60-yard touchdown passes from Bob Griese, beat us 24–21, but they had to wait until the last quarter to do it (we built a 21–3 lead). The next week against the Giants, my 77-yard kickoff return set up the winning touchdown in a 17–13 victory, and I also gained 53 yards rushing. I scored the following week on a pass from Hanratty in the Denver game, which was tied until the final quarter. The season was almost over and still the Steelers couldn't decide on a regular quarterback. If we got that straightened out, and just a few more players, we didn't think there would be anything stopping us.

Bradshaw was *third string* in game thirteen against the

Bengals. Hanratty started, was injured and replaced by Bob
Leahy, who in turn was ineffective, and *then* the future hero of
four Super Bowls was brought in.

Our last game was a 23–14 loss to the Rams, but I thought
it was an encouraging sign that I rushed for eighty-six yards in
sixteen carries. Not only was I given the ball more than anyone
else, but if we did get that premier running back, I didn't see
how I could fail to be chosen to block for him. However it
turned out, whether my chief duties were blocking or running, I
felt I was a valuable member of the Steelers.

It was time. The 1971 season concluded my fifth year in the
NFL, which meant my career had already lasted longer than the
league average for a player. And I still didn't think I'd come
anywhere near reaching my peak. I'd been used at too many
positions to really be able to settle into one. Now, at least, for
better or for worse, I was a running back, and I doubted there
would be any more experimenting.

Linda and I liked Pittsburgh, and we had made it our
home. And we'd made friends outside of football. Dr. Vaughn
Nixon and his wife were two, but also were many members of
the Pittsburgh Pirates: Willie Stargell, Al Oliver, Rennie Sten-
nett, Doc Medich, Dock Ellis, Manny Sanguillen, John Canda-
leria, and Roberto Clemente.

Stargell was a member of the national Sickle Cell Foundation, a chapter of which I would become a member in Dallas (I
have sickle-cell trait). Dock Ellis had sickle-cell anemia.

During the off-season I thought a good deal about the
Steelers' chances for the upcoming year, and they seemed very
good to me. One sign which I think was overlooked was that
many of the newer players were making Pittsburgh their home.
The older guys mostly lived in other places. They would come
to Pittsburgh, play out the season, and go home. It was far better, I thought, to be part of the community, to be year-long
friends with your teammates. A bond develops off the field—
call it friendship if you want; I call it love—that becomes very
important during a game. You *care* what happens to your
friends. This is a harder feeling to acquire for people who are
away half the year.

The same was true later in Dallas. Perhaps forty out of
forty-five Cowboys made their homes in Dallas, and guys were

always getting together for outings, parties, just to talk. Togetherness was built, and so was *love*. I've heard generals say this is important in battle. I know it is in football. And that's what was happening in Pittsburgh. Newer guys were coming and *staying*.

I remember telling Pittsburgh defensive end Lloyd Voss that I was throwing a party and he was invited. He seemed almost too excited. "Great!" he proclaimed. He thought it over a moment, then asked: "How much is it going to cost?" I assured Voss it wouldn't cost anything, that it was chiefly an opportunity for all of us to get together off the field. Evidently, with the older players this wasn't an idea that had gotten much testing in the past.

During the off-season I was still working for the computer firm, and I also conducted seminars that brought people (not necessarily football players) and businesses together. There was a lot of talent, I was learning, that was not being fully utilized because it hadn't been matched with the proper job. I got quite expert at bringing the right individual together with the right company.

A lot of athletes took advantage of the seminars. Often, business executives didn't understand how really intelligent an athlete with, say, only a C+ average probably was. A C+ can be excellent for an athlete, especially a basketball player. He is away from school on road trips for long periods of time. Even when he is at school, as I'd learned, the training and practice sessions make it extraordinarily difficult to spend as much time as needed to study.

Again, I was looking for ways to spend my life *after* football. It was even better if it could be spent in ways that benefited someone, as well as keeping me solvent. But I also was looking forward to the 1972 season. I thought the Steelers were about to do big things.

9

Knocking at the Door: The First Two Playoff Years

In 1972 and 1973, years when the Steelers were an eyelash away from making the Super Bowl, they managed to put together all but the final pieces of what would become the team of the decade. Franco Harris was drafted number one in 1972. He slowed somewhat as he pursued Jim Brown's career-rushing record, but as old-timers say, you should have seen him when.

Many have forgotten that perhaps three quarters of the football world, myself included, thought the Steelers made a mistake choosing Harris in the draft over Lydell Mitchell. All of us who thought this were proved wrong. Franco became one of the great running backs in NFL history.

Both Franco and Lydell Mitchell played at Penn State, and Franco had disciplinary problems in his senior year. I don't know what was involved, but I suspect the difficulty was Franco's unwillingness to work hard in practice. He simply didn't look good on a football field, except during the actual game. Then he was everything a player, coach, or fan could want. But there was this bad rap out on Franco (surely Penn

State's Paterno wouldn't have had to discipline him without excellent cause).

Noll's choice of Franco over Lydell Mitchell (who also had an outstanding career) was still another example of Noll's being able to see how a potential problem could be manageable. Franco never did become a great practice player, but he was largely responsible for Pittsburgh's unprecedented four Super Bowl championships.

Franco weighed 230 pounds. This is a big running back, especially when you realize that his legs were rather small. Franco liked to run around people, rather than over them, a fact that later drew the ire of Jim Brown. I think there are two ways to look at this. Negatively, it was true that Franco wouldn't take guys on at the line of scrimmage, or burrow like a tank for that extra yard, the way Earl Campbell or Walter Payton will, and on some key third-down plays this hurt us. On the positive side, not becoming a human battering ram undoubtedly prolonged his career and increased his own happiness at playing the game. I tend to agree with Jim Brown. Franco was 230 pounds. You expect a guy who is that big to do some head-banging. But maybe I have a double standard. I thought it was okay for me or Frenchy Fuqua on occasion to head for the sidelines and avoid some lunatic who was pursuing, but I reasoned that this only made sense. We didn't have Franco's size.

The trivia question on a 1983 *ABC Monday Night Football* telecast was to name the other back who started with the rookie Franco Harris. The answer was Preston Pearson, which was tough to get because most people think of me as a Dallas Cowboy.

I was always telling Franco as we broke from a huddle, "Get going now!" or "Let's go!" because I felt he needed a fire lit under him. Franco could be lackadaisical. I was pleased when he later said to the press that my constant urgings helped him learn the value of greater intensity. I think what he mainly lacked was confidence. He knew he was good enough to play in the NFL; at first he just didn't realize how *great* he could be.

Franco was shy. He seldom drank, even socially. He was very handsome, with his beard, mustache, and dark good looks. His mother was an Italian, his dad a black, and it wasn't long before Franco's Army, a fan club, was formed. A Pittsburgh judge even had FRANCO'S ITALIAN ARMY T-shirts printed, and he gave one to every Steeler to wear. Some of the players did. I refused. Franco didn't wear a PRESTON PEARSON T-shirt, and I didn't see why I should become a walking advertisement for him.

But Franco was a good guy. He was sensible, though not bright in a business sense. Fortunately he hooked up with Lee Goldberg, who previously had represented me, and was introduced to a number of off-the-field opportunities. Franco was able to supplement his football earnings quite nicely.

Franco was a good runner and a skilled basketball player, but I wouldn't say he was a great athlete. I remember his competing in the *Superstars* competition and being surprised by how badly he was beaten in the sprints. What he did possess was great vision, a marvelous ability to cut back, and tremendous high-leg action. Players who did tangle with him head-on often would have been grateful if he had opted to run out of bounds.

The Steeler offense needed exactly what Franco provided: a one-thousand-yards-a-season running back. No defense could sit back, with Bradshaw and the receivers we had, and wait for the pass. If they did, the six-feet-four Franco would simply chew up the length of the football field on the ground.

Playing with Franco guaranteed that the other running back would have a good season. Defenses so keyed on him, with Bradshaw's passing also on their minds, that the other back usually had splendid opportunities to run. Unfortunately for me, Noll later decided that the other back who should do most of the running was Frenchy Fuqua. I think he looked back to what Frenchy had done in the past, not what we were capable of in the present, and decided to go with Fuqua. Later, Rocky Bleier would start with Franco instead of me. Neither Fuqua nor Bleier was nearly as good a receiver, and I didn't think they were better as runners, but they took over in the backfield with Franco. The example of Rocky Bleier proves my point. Even his most avid fan wouldn't consider him a one-thousand-yard rusher, yet he was. He accomplished the feat because he was in the same backfield with Franco, and defenses practically ignored him.

There were mixed feelings on the Steelers about Rocky. He had shrapnel in his foot from a Vietnam War wound and couldn't walk right, much less run. He would limp whenever he tried to turn a corner with the ball. Yet he wasn't cut from the team. Jimmy Brumfield, a black, was cut to make room for Bleier. Brumfield was shy, never tooting his own horn, and he made mistakes, but he could play. Bleier was kept on, I believe, because he was a Vietnam War hero, white, and had a Notre Dame background. There was even a slogan that went around, "Don't knock the Rock." I have nothing against Bleier. He proved to be a friend of mine during the players' strike. But none of the good things that happened to him (like a movie about his life) would have occurred had he been a black man.

Our offensive line had also been built up to the point where, collectively, it was the finest I had seen before or since. These linemen never seemed to get the credit that was their due, but they were rough, talented, and supremely effective. These included Jim Clack, Gerry Mullins, Sam Davis, Jon Kolb, and Gordon Gravelle.

Another interesting addition to the Steelers in 1972 was Joe Gilliam from Tennessee State, who figured to have no chance as a late-round draft pick against quarterbacks like Terry Bradshaw and Terry Hanratty. But when these two were hurt, Gilliam came in and performed well. Joe acted as if it were no surprise at all.

Joe Gilliam ran on toothpick legs and outwardly seemed to be the most confident young athlete you would ever meet. "I can get 'em," he said to me, "anywhere, anytime. I'm bad." We called him "Jefferson Street Joe," and he was full of himself, effervescent, bubbling with cockiness and good cheer. He had a wonderful arm, a quick release, and was equally effective throwing both long and short. A lot of us thought he might provide more competition than Terry Bradshaw could handle. In 1973, in fact, it appeared that he might be *the* quarterback for the Steelers. He led us to a number of victories, but was replaced by Bradshaw after some mistakes (three interceptions against Miami) that might have been overlooked in a veteran.

Losing the starting job seemed to crush Joe Gilliam. He became very depressed, getting down on himself, taking to drugs, and taking himself, ultimately, right out of the NFL. It was a terrible shame because Gilliam was likable and talented. I also thought the Steelers did not give him an adequate chance

to prove what he could do, though of course that does not excuse Joe for losing control of everything. He later made a comeback in the 1980s in the USFL, but he was a shadow of his former self. What I like to remember was the cocky kid from Tennessee State saying, "I can do it all, man," and telling us about
his father (a coach at Tennessee State), and about this lineman
"you aren't going to believe." Gilliam was right. He could do it
all, and the lineman became known as Too Tall Jones.

In 1974, when the players' strike threatened to disrupt the
season, I was the Steeler union representative, and responsible
for making certain we presented a united front. A meeting was
called. Bradshaw had gone to camp, and we feared there would
be other defections.

"Are you with us, Joe?" I said to Gilliam.

"I'm here," he said. "I'm with you all the way."

"You sure?"

"All the way, man."

The next morning I heard on the radio that he'd reported
to camp. I felt sick.

"Why did you do it, Joe?" I asked him.

"I'm sorry, man."

"Just give me a reason."

"I called my father. He said I should go in."

"You're a man now, Joe. You don't have to check things
out with your father."

"He said Bradshaw had gone in. He said Bradshaw would
get way ahead of me. I couldn't let that happen."

"I understand," I said. And I did. Joe was convinced that
he'd never make up ground on Bradshaw if he were on strike
while Terry was practicing. And he thought he'd score points
with Coach Noll if he showed up, a proposition I find dubious,
though no head coach would discourage the idea. Yet I felt that
deep down a coach might wonder about a player's commitment
to his teammates if he broke ranks with them. How, then, would
he stand up with them when things got tough on the field?

In 1974, the Steelers were one of the teams most solid behind the strike, despite the action of Bradshaw and Gilliam.
The players really were with one another. They would stick together, for better or for worse. The same was later true with the
Cowboys. The Cowboys were very strong during the 1982 strike

action. I think it's not coincidental that both teams were of championship quality and valued the one-for-all concept.

People often ask me why it is that baseball players have a much stronger union than football players. I think a big part of the reason is that baseball players are not as spoiled. A football player often comes off a college campus where he already has been a hero, and thinks he can make it on his own, no help needed from anyone. Thus, he doesn't see the need of a union as clearly as a baseball player does. These athletes have often spent years in the minor leagues. They have not been treated as mini-gods. They see themselves as workers, which they are, despite the high pay, and thus are not too proud to be in a union. The "independence" some pro-football players think they get by opposing united action can be costly indeed.

The 1972 season, which saw us post a 12–4 record, served notice on the nation that the Steelers had arrived:

Pittsburgh	34	Oakland	28
Pittsburgh	10	Cincinnati	15
Pittsburgh	25	St. Louis	19
Pittsburgh	13	Dallas	17
Pittsburgh	24	Houston	7
Pittsburgh	33	New England	3
Pittsburgh	38	Buffalo	21
Pittsburgh	40	Cincinnati	17
Pittsburgh	16	Kansas City	7
Pittsburgh	24	Cleveland	26
Pittsburgh	23	Minnesota	10
Pittsburgh	30	Cleveland	0
Pittsburgh	9	Houston	3
Pittsburgh	24	San Diego	2
Pittsburgh	13	Oakland	7
Pittsburgh	17	Miami	21

The first game against Oakland was very important. They were a team that loved to intimidate. The Raiders were hard hitters, physical, a lot of opposition players would call them dirty. The Steelers, though not proven, were much the same type of team. We were the new kids on the block where intimidation was concerned, and we had the personnel to do it. Mean Joe Greene by himself could strike fear into an opponent, but a large number of the other Steelers were just plain tough guys. The Raiders didn't like it when we defeated them at what they thought was their game, plenty of rough stuff and threatening.

Previously our biggest rival had been Cleveland, but after the Raider game at the beginning of the 1972 season, it was Oakland. Incredibly, the fans in Oakland considered *us* a dirty team. The Raiders practically had a patent on the title.

Anyway, you could feel resentment building between the two cities and the two teams. The Raiders didn't like that we gave back as hard or harder than we received. They could see us getting stronger and stronger. They could tell we wouldn't be intimidated. Unpleasant as the reality may be, intimidation does play a big part in the NFL, and the team that does it best, the meanest and roughest, often walks away with the laurels. The Steelers in that first Raider game were indeed a rough bunch. I don't think we were dirty yet: That would come later.

This first game was marked by an oddity that should be mentioned. George Blanda, celebrating his forty-fifth birthday, threw a touchdown pass. I watched Blanda out on the field and the impression he gave was that he would just deteriorate in front of your eyes. He *looked* old. But Blanda was smart, and he had a great offensive line, led by Highway 66, Gene Upshaw, to protect him.

Joe Greene, in a newspaper interview, expressed what a lot of us thought during this triumphant season: "When the Steelers drafted me, it should have been the happiest day of my life, but I couldn't be happy about it. I couldn't find anything good about it. And in my rookie year, 1969, we were 1–13, and it was awful. But the next year I could see something happening. And now I wouldn't want to be on another team. This is history happening.

"You grow to love this team. Every year Mr. Rooney knows every rookie's name, and he's the owner. There's a lot of owners can't do that. That's why even if we get in the playoffs as the wild card team and win the Super Bowl, it won't be the same unless we win that first division championship."

We did clinch the division championship, the first time in forty years, the first ever for Pittsburgh. *The New York Times* called us "a vigorous young team full of speed, muscles, and enthusiasm." We were all of that. We were a tough, talented group of football players.

The city of Pittsburgh was delirious all week long before our first-ever playoff game, against, fittingly, the Oakland Raiders. For three straight nights Pittsburgh fans stood outside the Hilton Hotel where the Raiders were staying, and chanted, "Steelers! Steelers! Steelers!" An Oakland player trying to return to his room was clubbed by a policeman. Everything on radio, television, and in the newspapers was about *the* game. They can talk about the mania of the Mets fans when they pulled their 1969 miracle, but it couldn't have been anything like this.

When we took the field for the kickoff, the noise was so loud I couldn't make myself heard to a teammate standing next to me, though I was shouting at the top of my lungs. I believe it was the wildest, most enthusiastic crowd ever to watch a pro game. The noise was deafening, and it seemed never to stop. Such a crowd inevitably provides an advantage to the home team.

The game matched two utterly intimidating defenses. The only points in the first fifty-eight-plus minutes were field goals by Roy Gerela, which gave us a 6–0 lead. It seemed fitting. In seven of our fourteen regular season games, *no* touchdowns had been scored against us. Then, with one minute and sixteen seconds to go, Ken Stabler, who had relaced Daryle Lamonica, scrambled thirty yards for a touchdown, and ancient George Blanda added the extra point that made it 7–6.

We started on our own twenty. I was on the sideline, screaming words that were lost in the pandemonium. Bradshaw, who seemed finally to have straightened himself out (there would later be relapses), threw five passes. The fifth, from his own forty, was probably the most famous ever thrown. It's become known forever as the Immaculate Reception.

The ball was zipped down to the Raiders' thirty-five, whistling over Franco Harris's head as it went, to Frenchy Fuqua. But the ball struck Oakland safety Jack Tatum and was propelled in a high arc back seven yards to Franco, who was trailing the play. He caught the ball at his shoe tops in full stride and went the remaining forty-two yards for the touchdown, the most famous in Steeler history. There were five seconds left in the game.

When I saw Franco catch the ball I ran down the sideline, if not exactly with him in body, certainly in spirit.

It took a long time for the officials to confirm that it really was a touchdown, and NFL officials viewed a television replay before confirming it. The supervisor of officials, Art McNally, said the TV replay did not influence the decision, a questionable assertion, but in any case it showed that Tatum had hit the ball before it came catapulting back to Franco (had it hit Frenchy Fuqua, no touchdown would have been allowed). I know there was never any doubt on our sideline that the touchdown would stand, though maybe there should have been.

When Franco scored, hundreds of fans poured onto the field. I've wondered what would have happened if the touchdown had been disallowed. This was a blue collar, shot-and-a-beer crowd, and I believe, no, I *know* it would have been ugly. The game officials might have been killed, so rabid was the group that burst from the stands, and the Raiders might have been in danger also. It could very easily have developed that the Steelers would have had to come to the defense of the Raiders.

On numerous occasions I've seen fans pour onto the field. I've always wished they wouldn't. They invariably go for a souvenir, usually a chin strap or wristband, the latter being something that is *taped* to your hand. If you're at a visiting park, they spit at you or challenge you to fights. Washington is one of the worst places. I've seen Danny White have to fight his way off the field. The best thing to do is to get into the locker room as quickly as possible.

But this was a joyous crowd in Pittsburgh, since, luckily, the Immaculate Reception was allowed to stand. Interestingly, the game is remembered for that catch, not because it was our first appearance in any sort of postseason game. "I was damn lucky," Franco said about his miracle catch.

He was also good, gaining 1,055 yards in his rookie season, and he was outstanding also in the AFC championship the next week. Said linebacker Nick Buoniconti of the Dolphins, as if he were possessed of the gift of prophecy: "Franco Harris is going to set a lot of records."

Our opponents for the AFC championship were the Miami Dolphins, 15–0. Interestingly, I'd be going against two old friends, Earl Morrall, now the Dolphins' quarterback, and Don Shula, the man who drafted me for Baltimore. The Dolphins were shooting to become the first team ever to go undefeated for an entire NFL season, but such was the respect we'd earned that they were established as only three-point favorites.

They beat us by four. The biggest play was a fake fourth-down punt in which Larry Seiple, seeing our defense dropping back into blocking coverage, ran thirty-seven yards for a first down on our twelve.

The final was 21–17 (two weeks later the Dolphins won the Super Bowl, 14–7, against Washington, completing the undefeated season), but you could see they were relieved to get past us. This was the game they had feared. They knew how strong, talented, and bursting with life we were, how we were fast becoming masters of intimidation.

The word *intimidation* can't be used often enough in describing the Steelers. Seventy-five percent of Noll's pregame instruction centered on beating up on the player who was opposite you. Many teams talk about this, the importance of dozens of one-on-one confrontations, but none practiced it the way the Steelers did. In reality, one of the few teams that didn't constantly talk about the intimidation factor was the Cowboys. Landry was a "finesse" coach. But talking was one thing. Doing it, which the Steelers did, was what counted.

It seemed different on the field for the Miami game than it did against the Raiders. The fans were ultranoisy, as usual, but not maniacal as they had been for the Raiders, practically tumbling out of the stands, hanging from rafters. We weren't quite as high either. The Raiders had become a special enemy for us. No one had anything much against Miami.

I've never understood why the 1972 Dolphins aren't mentioned more often when the great teams are discussed. Perhaps no NFL squad will ever match that 17–0 record, and the teams they defeated, usually with ease (I believe we were their toughest game) were hardly pushovers. I think the strength of the

Dolphins was their offensive line, anchored by Larry Little and Bob Kuechenberg, but their No Name Defense, coached by Bill Arnsbarger, was smart, quick, and devastating. People don't think of the Dolphins as intimidators, but they were.

Of course, they had three outstanding running backs: powerful Larry Csonka, Mercury Morris, and Jim Kiick. Two good quarterbacks, Bob Griese and Earl Morrall. And the brilliant receivers, Marv Fleming and Paul Warfield.

For a while our defense was known as No Name II, but that couldn't last. Soon we would be dubbed the Steel Curtain. Maybe the reason the Dolphins aren't thought of so quickly when the subject of great teams is brought up is because their roster wasn't jammed with players bearing colorful nicknames: Mean Joe, Frenchy, the Italian Stallion, Mad Dog. I do think our 1975 Super Bowl champion team would have defeated the undefeated Dolphins.

The Miami game was played on New Year's Eve, and the next day I received some terrible news. The great Roberto Clemente, a Good Samaritan if ever there was one, was killed in an air crash on his way to Nicaragua to make sure that emergency supplies were being delivered to earthquake victims. I was chosen to represent the Steelers at the funeral. It was one of the most touching experiences of my life. Literally, all of Puerto Rico mourned his passing.

I'd gotten to know Roberto, since we both played in Pittsburgh, and knew he was much more than just a player who could do it all on the field. His four batting championships, three thousand base hits, thirteen years hitting over .300, and National League Most Valuable Player Award testified to that. His only living peers were Willie Mays and Henry Aaron. The great and the powerful attested to his worth.

"Words seem futile," said baseball commissioner Bowie Kuhn, "in the face of this tragedy, nor can they possibly do justice to this unique man. Somehow, Roberto transcended superstardom. His marvelous playing skills rank him among the truly elite. And what a wonderfully good man he was. Always concerned about others." "He was one of the greatest persons I knew," said John Galbreath, owner of the Pirates. "If you have to die, how better could your death be exemplified than by being on a mission of mercy? It was so typical of the man. Every time I was down there, someone was always saying how he contributed to the youth and needy of his island; how he was going to make that his life's work. He did these things without fanfare or anything—just what he thought was right to help somebody else." Governor Luis A. Ferre of Puerto Rico issued a proclamation ordering three days of mourning.

But I think what would have meant the most to Roberto was what I saw at his funeral. Ordinary Puerto Ricans, many with children scarcely old enough for school, tears tracking down their cheeks, standing in mute but eloquent testament outside the church. Roberto had been their champion, and they would never forget. For me, it was simply an honor to represent my teammates.

In the winter of 1973, the man for whom I worked at the computer company asked if I would visit a high school in Aliquippa, Pennsylvania. There was a top basketball player in Aliquippa, and it was just one of those things a pro athlete does. It means something for a pro to stop by. I know it would have for any of us in Freeport.

I met the basketball player, whose name I can't recall, and several others, and also a football player who was the star of the high-school team. "You look very small for football," I remember saying.

"You're too small to ever play pro football," the player recalls my saying. I don't believe I ever would have said that to anyone, though I might have thought it.

The young high-school star was Tony Dorsett, and when we became teammates with the Dallas Cowboys, he never tired of telling the story. I just know it never happened the way he says.

Linda and I visited Freeport in the winter of 1973. It was good to see that most of the people at home were treating Rufus very well. He'd had some problems, my brother Ed told me, but generally folks were compassionate and understanding. One time, however, while playing pool at a local hangout, a bully kept moving balls on the table. He thought he could cheat "dimwitted" Rufus. This bully had formerly idolized Rufus when my brother had been a star running back, but now he taunted him, called him cruel names. He kept it up. Finally, Rufus administered a well-deserved beating, and thought the matter was history. Soon, however, the same guy showed up at our house with two of his brothers. Ed figured there would be trouble, and so did Daddy, but before they could get to the door it was over. Rufus could be very enterprising when he had to. He had stuck his head out the door when they knocked, but did not allow them to see his hands. This frightened them and they took off.

Mom and Daddy were doing their best with Rufus. You couldn't tell anything was wrong with him unless you caught him at the wrong time. This unfortunately was a frequent occurrence. He would go into a sort of trance, just stand still and stare into space. Or he would start jumping up and down, drool coming from his mouth. But a lot of people in town protected Rufus. He hadn't been able to keep his job long, his attention span was simply too short. His mind couldn't stay focused more than a few minutes on any subject. But he was very good when playing with children, and youngsters loved being with him.

Rufus had always been my number one fan in the Pearson household. He and my brother Ed. Each Sunday during the season Rufus would ask Ed if a game I was in was being televised, and if it was, he would sit faithfully and watch. He never showed much emotion. But I wonder if a great deal wasn't present in his mind. Ed, Rufus, and I had often dreamed about playing in the same backfield together. I wonder if he remembered those times. Ed thought that because he never fulfilled his great potential, Rufus was a bit embarrassed. But he would sit there and watch, and seemed happy whenever my team won. Mom and Daddy, after they finally got their feet wet, became avid fans. Daddy got to know the rules better than most NFL officials.

I asked Ed if he'd seen the Immaculate Reception.

"Missed it," he said. "So did Rufus. But Mom saw it."

"What was the matter with you and Rufus?"

"I was disgusted with you guys. Thought you'd never score a touchdown. I walked out of the room that last minute. Mom kept saying, 'Come back, Preston's team is going to do something,' but I said, 'Why should they? They haven't done anything all day.' Then I heard a whoop of joy, and Mom yelling

Franco Harris's name, and then, 'I told you they'd do something! I told you!' "

"She was happy?"

"Like she'd gone to heaven."

"What about Rufus?"

"Someone had come to the door earlier. You know about that."

Yes, I did. If someone came to the door, Rufus would retreat to a back room. It was an improvement over earlier times, when he would pull his T-shirt over his head to hide, and let his fingernails grow grotesquely long, like miniature swords. Yet there were still many things about him we would never know.

I was treated like a celebrity in Freeport. I was the only athlete from the town ever to make it in the pros, and this was considered a big deal. Ed told me that whenever the Steeler games were on TV, Freeport was a ghost town. Everyone was home watching. The Bears were the big draw in Freeport, but not when the Steelers played.

I tried to get through to Rufus, but he just wasn't with me much of the time. He wasn't with anybody. He seemed to have hallucinations quite often. But I fantasized too. It would have been something, with Rufus as the star running back, Ed blocking for him, and me catching record numbers of passes. By this time in my career I figured the proper position for me was wide receiver, though I knew it was too late to convince my coach of that.

Ed played for a semipro team in Rockford. He told me about a conversation he had had with an opponent who had played against us in high school.

"How's your brother?" the opponent asked.

"Preston? Where have you been? Preston is big time. He's with the Pittsburgh Steelers."

"Not Preston. Who cares about Preston? I mean Rufus. Now there was a football player."

I wholeheartedly concur.

The 1973 season probably proved that we'd gone about as far the previous year as we deserved to, maybe a little farther. Our draft wasn't outstanding, and although we won a wild-card berth in the playoffs, it was evident we needed one or two more pieces before we put together the entire puzzle and climbed to the summit. Our 10–5 year looked like this:

Pittsburgh	24	Detroit	10
Pittsburgh	33	Cleveland	6
Pittsburgh	36	Houston	7
Pittsburgh	38	San Diego	21
Pittsburgh	7	Cincinnati	19
Pittsburgh	26	N.Y. Jets	14
Pittsburgh	20	Cincinnati	13
Pittsburgh	21	Washington	16
Pittsburgh	17	Oakland	9
Pittsburgh	13	Denver	23
Pittsburgh	16	Cleveland	21
Pittsburgh	26	Miami	30
Pittsburgh	33	Houston	7
Pittsburgh	37	San Francisco	14
Pittsburgh	14	Oakland	33

We had had too many injuries toward the end of the season to be a threat to make the Super Bowl. Terry Bradshaw suffered a shoulder separation, Franco had a bad knee, Hanratty, broken ribs, and Frenchy Fuqua, a broken collarbone. Joe Gilliam performed well at quarterback, but when he lost his job to the recovered Bradshaw, it sent him into a depression that would ruin his NFL career.

Before the 1974 season could begin, there was the players' strike. When it was called, Andy Russell, our union representative, even though he identified with and supported management, resigned his job. I was elected to take his place, a job that is often thankless and can actually be the kiss of death for a player's career. Most owners hate a union, but of course they can't fire every player who belongs to one. What they can do is let their enmity focus on an individual who seems to represent all they dislike, and that often is the athlete who represents other athletes. I knew this before I took the job, but I also felt very strongly that players needed an organization that could represent their interests. In a real sense the owners were united as a single group. Why not the players?

One problem that still exists is the draft, in which a player must play for the team that selects him. If you are, say, O. J. Simpson from USC, you still must play for the Buffalo Bills, if they happen to draft you. Now Simpson never received a nickel from Buffalo while he was developing his great skills, but he nonetheless was forced to play for them if he wished to pursue a pro career. And if he didn't like what the Bills offered, it was too bad for him. This situation would not be tolerated in other forms of business, where a college graduate is able to choose the company for which he will work. Lockheed and Boeing, for example, do not draft outstanding engineers.

Owners say the draft is necessary to maintain parity in the NFL, but actually it is a reward for incompetence. Few teams (the Steelers are an exception) of outstanding merit have relied chiefly on high draft choices. The Cowboys and Colts, long powers in the league, usually drafted late in the round, but maintained themselves as contenders year after year. They were intelligent and did their homework. It took the Steelers a long time to catch on. Before holding on to Terry Bradshaw, they let go such quarterbacks as Sid Luckman, John Unitas, Lenny Dawson, Jack Kemp, Bill Nelsen, and Earl Morrall. The draft doesn't so much maintain parity as it gives a team power in contract negotiations. One need only look at the great Dolphin teams built by Don Shula. Larry Little and Bob Kuechenberg were free agents, as were Jake Scott, Doug Swift, Manny Fernandez, and Garo Yepremian. Nick Buoniconti and Paul Warfield were acquired in shrewd trades.

But this was just one of a dozen or more issues, most of which we ended up losing. The owners proved they had more solidarity than the players, though I thought a great deal of courage was shown by the vast majority who stayed out. The owners were financially independent men who could survive for a long period without football. The players were not. And, oddly, sadly perhaps, those players with the highest salaries, who could have survived, were often the least strong during the strike. The highly paid Terry Bradshaw, for example, could far easier miss a paycheck or two than one of the men who blocked for him in the front lines.

Of course, at the bottom of the strike was economics, specifically the question of whether an individual could go to a team that needed him, wanted him, and was willing to pay him what he could get on the open market. The issue was one that was very near to me. I was in my eighth professional season and still not playing on a regular basis. There were plenty of teams, I thought, where I could have played, even starred, but I was not being given the opportunity I thought I deserved in Pittsburgh. I'd developed myself into a highly skilled pass receiver and blocker, but wasn't really being used. That was Chuck Noll's business. But it wasn't fair to me. That I wasn't simply dreaming, overestimating my own ability, would be proven later during the peak years of my career in Dallas.

I must say I was plenty steamed with Andy Russell for forsaking his duties when he heard there was going to be a strike. When there hadn't been any need for him he'd had the job, but when push came to shove he was gone. Anyway, the home Linda and I had bought in Mount Lebanon (some eight miles outside of Pittsburgh) became strike headquarters for the Steelers, and I set up a special room for an office. Linda was very supportive, and the kids weren't really in the way. My second son, Matthew Jay, had been born September 29, 1971, and thus was a "terrible two" at this time, but there really wasn't that much difficulty. This was good, because lately there had been strains in our marriage. A lot of them were caused, I think, by my own resentment. Linda, through necessity, had largely been responsible for most of the decisions in our family, many of them financial. It was partly because I hadn't known much about business, partly because I was lazy. But now, I felt, I was learning more, growing up, and felt I should have a bigger say in what was going on. Previously, even if a salesman came to the door, it was Linda he talked with; I guess he could just look at me and figure I wasn't the one to be consulted. Our system had worked well during the earlier years of our marriage, but now there was the beginning of friction, as I felt I had matured more than I thought Linda was willing to admit.

Much of my day during the strike was spent on the telephone, operating various business machines and keeping my teammates appraised of progress. There also had to be time set aside to walk the picket line.

Dan Rooney was probably the best possible owner I could have played for, as far as the strike was concerned. He knew I had to champion what the players wanted, that it was my job, and he didn't treat me as most owners would have—as an ungrateful traitor. Still, I was afraid my career was being put in jeopardy, and I had good reason to fear. There was a terrific vendetta against player representatives after the strike ended. Many were either cut by their teams, waived, or treated very poorly. Kenny Houston of the Oilers, for example, a good ballplayer, was simply released. Kermit Alexander, the talented safety of the Eagles, was let go. Tom Keating of the Raiders was traded to the Steelers and treated horribly. He never saw any action and was humiliated by Chuck Noll, who made him practice alone.

Kermit Alexander fought back courageously. He filed a class-action suit against the NFL and won. Every player who was in the NFL at that time still receives money from this suit. I get eight hundred dollars a year, ending in 1985.

We did win a few points, such as getting pay for rookies for preseason games (previously they got zero) and higher pay for veterans. We also won per diem allowances. Many players today don't understand why they have these benefits. It is because many of us put our careers on the line to win them. It makes me mad when the highly paid Dan Fouts refuses even to pay union dues, when it is that same union that won him so many of his benefits.

In any case, we lost more points than we won, which doesn't mean the battle shouldn't have been waged. We did win some. And in this instance the strike was over before the regular season began.

10
Super Bowl IX

In 1974 we intimidated our way to the AFC Central Division championship, the AFC championship, and a chance at Minnesota in Super Bowl IX in New Orleans. It was almost that simple. We were the roughest, meanest, most physical team in professional football, and these qualities are often what count the most. Forget about fancy moves or trick plays, trying to outsmart somebody. We beat up on the other guy. We were intimidators, a rugged, no-frills, blue-collar team from a blue-collar town that loved us.

The 1974 draft had filled in the final pieces. We acquired two great wide receivers, Lynn Swann from USC and John Stallworth from Alabama A & M, and linebacker Jack Lambert from Kent State. The most important of these three, I felt, was John Stallworth, who became one of the great receivers ever to play the game. He could do everything well. Lynn Swann was vastly talented also, and received the lion's share of the publicity, but I did not think he was Stallworth's equal. John was much more reliable and just as brilliant, though in a less flashy way. Swann received more attention, I believe, because he was considered handsome and had caught the fancy of Howard Cosell. Cosell constantly sang his praises, which helps an athlete, no matter what anyone may think. It may not have hurt that Swann was light-skinned (Stallworth was dark-skinned). Or that

Swann came from a glamour school, USC, while Stallworth played at unknown Alabama A & M. Of course, Swann did make catches that were utterly fantastic. And he did it with an easy grace and fluidity of motion that was beautiful to watch.

Lynn Swann could remind you of a little boy. He would catch the ball and you could almost hear him singing "nyah nyah nyah-nyah nyah" as he held it in the defender's face and taunted him. He was a great athlete, and he knew it. Butch Atkinson, the fierce defensive back of the Raiders, didn't like Swann, and told him to stay out of his territory. Atkinson meant it. He would try to hurt Swann when he ventured into Atkinson's part of the field. It was almost as if Butch were saying, "If you're such a hotshot, this hit shouldn't hurt at all."

Swann reminded me of Sugar Ray Leonard, in that he was an athlete who could speak for himself. He looked good in front of a camera, and sounded intelligent. Stallworth's voice was high-pitched, and he didn't seek publicity. He was rangy, wiry, with no unusual physical characteristics. His selection by Noll out of Alabama A & M was another example of this coach's ability to spot talent in unusual places. Stallworth's chief abilities as a football player were quickness, concentration, and consistency. But really there weren't a lot of differences in their abilities. Most coaches would give their eyeteeth for either Swann or Stallworth. I just want to record my feelings that Stallworth, who never received enough attention, was superior.

I was walking a picket line one steaming summer day in 1974. Truckers stopped, wished us well, and refused to cross a union line. Steelworkers walking by wished us well. It was a good day, hot and humid, and we would rather have been having a cold drink, or watching TV in an air-conditioned living room, or even on the field getting ready for the coming season. But this was important for us, and for players who would come after us, so we held our placards high and walked with pride. Suddenly I saw a car coming toward us. It kept coming and drove right on through. I noticed one face in particular. It belonged to a rookie. He just stared straight ahead as his car went by.

I'd just gotten my first look at Jack Lambert.

"Hey," I said to him when I got a chance. "We don't have

any problems with you going into camp. We'd just like you to hear us out. A lot of this is being done for rookies like you." Then I gave him as oblique a warning as I could. "You're going to be one of us someday, you know."

Lambert wasn't impressed. He let us walk the picket line while he went in and tried to get a head start on everybody else. I didn't hear, however, that he refused the benefits we won for him.

Sam Davis, Frenchy Fuqua, Rocky Bleier, and myself were among the firmest union members. We were allowed inside camp to talk to the rookies. It wasn't a pleasant task. Chuck Noll and the other coaches were there, and it didn't take special insight to know which side they were on. Lambert was still not impressed by our efforts and continued as a strikebreaker.

My first impression of Jack did not improve as time went by. He and Frenchy Fuqua became practical-joke-playing buddies; things like calling the other to a telephone for an "emergency" and having the telephone rigged so it would spray shaving cream in the ear. Once, Frenchy must have gotten the best of Lambert, because the linebacker came into our room (Frenchy and I were roommates) naked, and got "even" by spreading the cheeks of his naked rear on one of the pillows. I told Lambert I didn't like what he was doing, that it was crude and in bad taste, but this didn't phase him any more than my talk about the union.

Lambert wasn't crazy about me either. I believed he was a bully, but I would never back off from him. I knew for a fact that if Lambert and I went into a dark alley to fight, I'd be the one who came out. Lambert, I believed, wouldn't stick it out in an all-out fight. He didn't like people who weren't afraid of him.

I do not think Lambert was a great football player, regardless of the accolades TV announcers have bestowed on him, and I'm not alone among former teammates who feel that way. Certainly he can't be mentioned in the same breath with Dick Butkus, Ray Nitschke, or Willie Lanier. These were real hitters. They could knock down a wall of blockers and still break the bones of a running back. Lambert made a lot of tackles because they were *easy* tackles. Ernie Holmes and Joe Greene made Jack Lambert's reputation. They would demolish a runner's interference and leave him easy prey for Lambert. I don't believe a highlight film of great Jack Lambert tackles could be made. He often got to runners just as they were cutting, or when they were hopelessly hemmed in. There are plenty of films of Butkus hitting a runner head on, the man in full stride, and literally bowling him over.

In my opinion Jack Lambert was one of a number of Steeler players who could be classified as dirty. In a pileup he seemed not to mind aiming a knee at somebody's groin. He wanted people to be afraid of him. I wasn't—and that's one reason we didn't get along. Nor did Lambert waste any time trying to get a psychological hold on Ernie Holmes. A bully he might have been. But he wasn't crazy.

I don't know if Lambert really was tough, or if he just tried to convince himself of the fact. I know he went into a nightclub one night, got into a tussle with two guys who weren't impressed by his football reputation, and reports I received were that he came out second best.

This is not meant to imply that Lambert wasn't a good football player. He was. He just wasn't as good as many contemporary commentators would have you believe. *Any* pro linebacker playing behind Joe Greene and Ernie Holmes would have been in on a lot of tackles. In fact, it was the *Steeler plan* that Lambert make the tackles. The Steel Curtain Front Four demolished everything in his path, and Lambert was left with relative setups.

Anyway, the addition of Swann, Stallworth, and Lambert filled in the last pieces of what would become a Steeler dynasty. The two receivers, to go along with Ron Shanklin, Frank Lewis, and Larry Brown, gave us an awesome passing attack. But what cornerback could sit back and wait for the pass? We were a running team. We had a bone-crushing offensive line, and our entire attack started with Franco, who was just beginning his long march on Jim Brown's career-rushing record.

What needs to be said about our defense? Has there ever been a better one? The front four were Dwight White, L. C. Greenwood, Joe Greene, and Ernie Holmes. Ham, Lambert, and Russell were the linebackers. The defensive backs were Mel Blount, J. T. Thomas, Mike Wagner, and Glen Edwards.

The oddsmakers installed us as three-point favorites to defeat the Vikings in the January 12 Super Bowl, but a lot of so-

called smart money was bet on Minnesota. They had been to
two previous Super Bowls, losing each time, and it was thought
they would go to any lengths to avoid a humiliating third defeat.
Actually, the two teams matched up pretty well. We were
young, tough, and on the rise. They were older, tough, and at or
just past their prime.

The main man of the Vikings, Chuck Foreman, was to my
way of thinking just about the ultimate back. He was a threat as
both a runner and a pass receiver, and had great speed and size.
The only other running back I'd known with such versatility
was Lenny Moore, and he didn't have Foreman's size. Of course,
receivers didn't come any better than Ahmad Rashad, and the
Viking quarterback was the scrambling Fran Tarkenton. We
would have plenty to worry about.

The Viking defense was known as the Purple People
Eaters, and their reputation was well deserved. Alan Page was
the only NFL tackle ever to be voted the MVP. Not defensive
MVP. Just plain MVP. He was quick, strong, and smart. Defensive end Carl Eller was big and fast and another with a reputation for meanness. Middle linebacker Jeff Siemon was one of
the best.

We arrived more than a week early in New Orleans and
were put up in a hotel close to much of the city's nightlife. The
first few days would be for taking it easy, having some fun if we
wanted, getting acclimated to our new surroundings. Chuck
Noll was indeed a student of Don Shula, as he would prove
more than once during the Super Bowl week.

The Vikings were headquartered quite a distance from the
night life of New Orleans, far out by the airport. As history
would prove, the team that lives the most spartan life during
the week before the Super Bowl is not usually the one that wins.
One night Frenchy Fuqua, Terry Hanratty (my roommate in
New Orleans), and I went to a nightclub and ran into Fran Tarkenton and running back Ed Marinaro (now a star on *Hill
Street Blues*). We joked about how isolated they were way out
by the airport, with nothing to do but get mad at one another.
Tarkenton winced. I think we hit a nerve.

Our wives arrived the Wednesday before the Sunday game.
I'm sure Noll planned it this way. Let the players sow whatever
wild oats they had to, usually drinking and staying out late par-

tying, then put them in a more domestic atmosphere. We started to practice seriously that Wednesday, and each day we seemed to get higher and higher. It was like a gang building itself up for a street fight. The Vikings had the big reputations, but we felt we were tougher than they were. That was it as far as our attitude was concerned. We were tougher than anybody else, and toughness decides football games.

One thing against us, if history was to be a guide, was that a first-time Super Bowl team usually doesn't win. We really didn't think much about that. We were confident, but not the same way the Colts had been prior to the disaster against the Jets. We weren't *sure* we would win. We weren't even sure we were the better team. We just thought we were the toughest team, and no matter what the score read, the Vikings were going to take a physical beating.

We had no trick plays for the game, not one. Our game plan consisted basically of just two things: run to the right side, and pound on the guys we were paired against. On their right side were Jim Marshall, Alan Page, and Wally Hilgenberg, a linebacker. Marshall was listed at 240, but was closer to 215. Page was also a smallish type lineman, though very quick. Hilgenberg, we felt, was slow and perhaps past his prime.

Jim Marshall had trouble against big offensive linemen who came right at him. He relied on finesse, and it often didn't work if a big man just charged him. Jon Kolb, who was assigned to Marshall, was perhaps the strongest man in football.

There were great matchups in Super Bowl IX. The best might have been Mean Joe Greene against Ed White. White was the largest guard in the NFL, and a champion arm wrestler. His battle with Joe Greene would be one of titanic proportions. Then there was Ron Yary against the towering L. C. Greenwood, Ernie Holmes against Andy Maurer. We felt the terrifying Holmes had a big advantage here.

Defensively, we wanted to keep Fran Tarkenton from scrambling sideline to sideline. It wouldn't be possible to stop his scrambling altogether, but we wanted him going backward. We didn't want to be beaten on a broken play.

The weather had been good most of the week, but Super Bowl Sunday turned out to be miserable. It was cold, twenty-two degrees, and a vicious blustery wind blew. The artificial turf of Tulane Stadium, soon to be torn down, was wet and slippery. Equipment manager Tony Parisi had supplied us with nonskid, rubber-cleated shoes, and these would prove a major help on the slippery field. The Super Bowl, of course, was sold out, more than eighty thousand, but the weather was so miserable there were almost one thousand no-shows.

There were only fifteen thousand hotel rooms in New Orleans, yet more than fifty thousand came from out of town for the game. Unlike the first Super Bowl in which I participated, this event was now *the* most important on the American sports calendar. The New Orleans Chamber of Commerce described it as "the biggest weekend in New Orleans history."

The Vikings thought this miserable day was their type of weather. Many of their fans had come, dressed in purple Viking hats, and many had bet large sums of money on their favorites. The same was true of Pittsburgh. "The fans in Pittsburgh," Art Rooney said, "don't think it will be a contest." The fans from the Steel City were the most avid followers of any sport I have ever known.

I did not expect to see any more meaningful action than I had in my first Super Bowl appearance. I was an eight-year veteran, and once again relegated to special teams. Needless to say, I wondered what kind of career this was. I'd been kicked in the back of my right leg during an early-season game with Cincinnati, and though the pain was terrific then, it was nothing compared to what I experienced when I got home. I called Pittsburgh trainer Ralph Berlin at three-thirty A.M., and he knew I wasn't someone who exaggerated hurt. He told me to go straight to Presbyterian Hospital and check in. By this time it looked as if I had a bag hanging from the back of my leg.

It turned out to be a blood clot. The leg was opened up and coagulated blood was scraped out. Today the wound looks like I'd been shot by a large bullet. The pain was the type that made you want to scream.

Frenchy Fuqua was in the hospital at the same time. He had *two* broken wrists. I smile when I hear football players are overpaid. A few, like forty-million-dollar-rookie Steve Young, may be, but most earn little more than a competent executive. The executive isn't lying in a hospital with two broken wrists.

Nor can he be almost assured that his career will last fewer than five years.

I didn't get back into the starting backfield after the injury. Rocky Bleier had replaced me, and he got better and better with each game. He had his Notre Dame background going for him, and that wound from Vietnam, and, yes, the fact that he was white, and he became a fixture in the Steeler backfield. He even would post a one-thousand-yards-plus season. But he did this because defenses keyed on Franco, just as Holmes and Joe Greene made Jack Lambert's life easier. I liked Rocky. He had courage. He stood up for the union when it might have been easier to go the other way. But I felt I was a better player than he was. Certainly I was the superior blocker, and in catching passes there was no contest. Later, with the Cowboys, I think I proved these points.

But I tried to make the best of my special-teams assignments, and was considered a leader of these units on the field. It was personally embarrassing, though maybe it shouldn't have been, to have eight years in the league and still be having the least sought-after job, but I didn't let myself give up. In fact, the job seemed to me important. Special teams played about 25 percent of the time, and it was important to set an example, mostly for the younger players. The Steelers had other leaders. On offense, Terry Bradshaw had suddenly matured, and on defense, Joe Greene.

One thing motivating us was the chance to win for Art Rooney. It became almost a win-one-for-the-Gipper type of game. Everyone cared about Mr. Rooney, who had gone more than forty years without taking *the* championship. I know for a fact that no player would get excited winning one for Joe Robbie of the Dolphins, or Robert Irsay, who recently moved the Baltimore Colts to Indianapolis. Mr. Rooney is one of those rare people it is just a pleasure to know. If winning a game was important to him, and it was, we had an obligation to deliver. Joe Greene is hardly a sentimental man, yet he can't say enough good things about Art Rooney.

The weather didn't bother us during warm-ups. We loved it. We intended this to be an "ugly" game, and what could be better than a miserable day? A beautiful day would have taken something away from what basically was going to be a one-on-one administration of brutality.

Noll's pregame talk could have been delivered by his mentor, Don Shula. It occurred to me that I'd heard this speech before, and that it was a good one. "This is what you've been working for," Noll said in an emotional talk that didn't require any fireworks. "It's been a long time for the Steeler organization. It doesn't matter what they do, you're better than they are. Just go out there and hit them."

Only once—with Dallas in a Super Bowl—have I seen a team as up for a game as this one was. These were people who *enjoyed* violence. We came roaring through the tunnel; blood in the eye would be an apt description. It turned out we were lined up right next to the Vikings, who were coming out of a different tunnel. I knew we were going to win the game when Glen Edwards, a not-large defensive back, turned to a Viking defensive giant and said, "You better buckle up your chin strap, 'cause we're going to lay it on you." That big lineman could have played volleyball with Glen Edwards. What I saw in his eyes was fear.

The weather was just miserable. Many people will tell you it was the most boring of all Super Bowls ever played, but they just don't know what the game is really supposed to be. Football is a violent, elemental game, and in this respect Super Bowl IX may have been the best example the sport can provide.

On the opening kickoff I experienced the inevitable déjà vu. I'd been here before, six years ago, Baltimore versus the Jets. I'd had ups and downs, but I was still waiting for a kickoff. I had some money now, and eight years in the league, which could probably be traded for something, but I thought my life was in trouble. The Steelers really had no use for me. I was a veteran, but not part of their starting scheme. I'd been a union leader, and no matter how understanding the Rooneys were, their view was that *they* were fair, and I was a militant stirring up the waters of discontent. It occurred to me that this might be my last game. *Well, make it a good one then,* I thought, *and make a hard hit to start the proceedings.*

Super Bowl IX was a clinic in violence. I'm sure what happened to us has happened to most people. You make a monster, a fearsome foe, out of your opponent, and then the confrontation turns out not to be so tough. Going against a boss, for example, expecting him to be tough where a raise in pay is concerned, but he is perfectly willing to give it. The Vikings in person were not as tough as we thought they would be.

The Vikings put the ball in play six times in the first half: from their 33, 14, 21, 23, 6, and 20. Bad field position. Terrible field position against a team of maniacs, which we were, headed by awesome Joe Greene and the crazed-eyes Ernie Holmes. This game was a slaughter. Forget 38–9 with the Raiders defeating the Redskins in 1984. What we did to the Vikings was more lopsided, regardless of the final score. Imagine Ernie Holmes and Joe Greene *simultaneously* attacking 230-pound Viking center, Mick Tingelhoff.

And consider these statistics: The Vikings gained 17 yards on the ground the *entire game;* Chuck Foreman had 18 yards in 12 carries, a 1.5 average; Dave Osborn carried 8 times for −1 yards. I believe football has never seen a more impressive defensive effort than the Steelers put on in Super Bowl IX.

How to describe Mean Joe Greene? Or Ernie Holmes, fearsome even in the best of times? L. C. Greenwood, a man gone wild? Tarkenton ran, literally, for his life, the guttural roars of Greene, Holmes, and Greenwood in his ears. Dwight White was effective also. He had come off a sick bed—"This is the Super Bowl," he said—to replace Steve Furness, and was an inspirational force. But the biggest mismatch was Ernie Holmes versus Andy Maurer. Holmes reminded me of a wrecking ball. He couldn't be handled. And this freed L. C. Greenwood, who spent the entire day chasing an increasingly terrified Tarkenton.

You have to hear the language in the war that goes on in the line to believe it. No adult, much less a starry-eyed youngster, needs to listen to this. But imagine Ernie Holmes making threats. The thing is, he means them. You believe he is capable of carrying them out.

We roared encouragement to the defense from the sidelines, but after a while we stopped. We just watched, like the people in the stands. How do you keep roaring at a team that has no problems? The Vikings were going nowhere. The Purple People Eaters were being eaten alive.

The wonder is that the score wasn't 100–0 at half time. In

actuality, it was 2–0, the result of the first safety in Super Bowl history. Tarkenton pitched out to Dave Osborn on the Viking six, Osborn fumbled, and all Tarkenton could do was save a touchdown by dropping on the ball in the end zone. The 2–0 half-time score was completely misleading. Bradshaw had hardly passed at all. We ran Franco at the outmanned Marshall, the neutralized Page, and the aging Hilgenberg (also, Jeff Wright, right cornerback, who we thought might be vulnerable), and punted the ball in good Woody Hayes fashion. There was no need to gamble. We had come into the game to beat up the Vikings, and this was being accomplished in a way that hurt the eyes.

I came to abhor the way the Steelers played. These were hurtful hits to the head. Big, strong men beating up on weaker men. Violence carried much further than the founders of the game intended.

The Vikings did nothing. How could they? It was Minnesota Iron versus Pittsburgh Steel, and the Steel prevailed. Joe Greene and Ernie Holmes—in short, devastating bursts of violence—destroyed the pocket in which Fran Tarkenton hoped to sit, and the screaming L. C. Greenwood, appearing to be ten feet tall, batted down four passes.

We just didn't know how good we were. We read the Minnesota press clippings, and figured we had better be careful of these killers. Their reputations kept them from getting a worse beating than they did.

Franco off our left side, their right: That was the story of this game. Just as the 3-4 of the Jets doomed us in Super Bowl III, such simplicity can explain Super Bowl IX. I consider myself an expert on Super Bowls. Fans can rehash them forever, but a few simple factors separate the winners from the losers. In Super Bowl IX, it was simply that we were tougher. Better. Our wanting to win one for Art Rooney was equaled by the desire of the Vikings to avoid a third straight Super Bowl defeat. The result, with the psychological factor evened out, hinged on which team was stronger.

The Vikings should have sat in on us during half time. It consisted mostly of moaning and groaning. The Vikings would have considered they had the upper hand if they could have heard us. Everyone was complaining about injuries, including me. My hands were scraped raw from the artificial turf, and my elbow felt twisted into a painful corkscrew. A visitor to our locker room might have thought he'd happened onto a band of whining, oversized adolescents.

Big men crying. That's what we were. Ahead 2–0 and it hurt this much? I could see Chuck Noll perfecting a half-time speech. But it wasn't needed. Someone, probably Joe Greene, pointed out how much more the Vikings must be hurting. He was right. The Vikings had to be fearing a second half of Mean Joe Greene hits to the head and Ernie Holmes on the rampage.

It didn't take long in the second half to establish who continued to be boss. Viking Bill Brown fumbled the opening kickoff, and reserve Steeler linebacker Marv Kellum recovered at the Minnesota thirty. Now Bradshaw used his head. He was calling his own plays, and he did not go for the quick bomb. The Packers of old liked to pass for a touchdown after a quick turnover, but Terry felt we could just run over the Vikings. He handed the ball to Franco against Jim Marshall, Alan Page, and Wally Hilgenberg, and Franco roared to the six. After a three-yard loss, when most quarterbacks would have passed, Terry handed the ball again to Franco, who scored.

We led 9–0 after the Gerela extra point. The frantic atmosphere I'd witnessed during the "kill, Bubba, kill" 1969 Super Bowl, was missing from our sideline. No matter that fans or bettors thought a contest was still going on. This game was over. I could see it in the eyes of the Vikes as we lined up for the kickoff.

Andy Russell and Jack Lambert were both injured in Super Bowl IX, and backups Loren Toews and Ed Bradley played most of the second half. It didn't make any difference. Our front four was more devastating than any defensive group I've ever seen, before or since. The Vikings scored the only way they could, on a blocked punt in the fourth quarter, but the extra point was missed and we still led, 9–6.

It occurred to me that I might be reliving that nightmare against the Jets, where everything seemed to go wrong, but I put the idea out of my head. You could see the Vikings disintegrating. They reminded me of fighters who had taken too much pounding. No, this wouldn't be a rerun of the game with the Jets.

We locked up the contest on our next possession, driving 66 yards in 11 plays, 6 of them runs by Franco. The touchdown came on a 4-yard pass from Bradshaw to Larry Brown. I think this drive, engineered by Bradshaw, finally established him in the top rank of quarterbacks.

The Vikings ran only three plays after this. The lead in a *New York Times* story summed it up: "On the scoreboard the Pittsburgh Steelers won the Super Bowl today, 16–6, but in reality the score was 249–17. That reveals the domination of Pittsburgh's offensive and defensive lines as the Steelers rushed for 249 yards, including a record 158 by Franco Harris, and limited the Minnesota Vikings to 17 yards rushing."

Franco broke Larry Csonka's Super Bowl rushing record with 158 yards on 34 carries, and was voted the game's MVP. Once again I disagreed with the selection, though certainly Franco had an outstanding game. But the real MVPs were Joe Greene (he even intercepted a pass), Ernie Holmes, and L. C. Greenwood. If I had to name *one* of these three, I'd say Ernie Holmes.

We ran 73 plays to Minnesota's 47. Early in the second half the Vikings were already out of their game plan, with Tarkenton scrambling, mostly backward, in a desperate attempt to make something happen. Franco, of course, ran the ball only 13 fewer times than the Vikings had total plays. Terry Bradshaw played a conservative game, completing 9 of 14 passes for 96 yards. We probably would have won by much more if we'd used a more spectacular offense, but what we did was precisely what we should have done. The important thing was to win the game, and the surest way to accomplish that goal was to go nose-to-nose with the Vikings.

It was a happy locker room afterward. Everyone was just delighted for Art Rooney, who had waited nearly half a century for this. The only negative statistic, which may not be negative if you think about it, was that we were penalized 107 yards to only 18 for Minnesota.

One of the most touching moments was when we presented the game ball to Art Rooney. I looked at him and he somehow reminded me of my own father. Mr. Rooney had snow-white hair and was trying to hide his emotions, but it was clear he was deeply moved.

Winning the Super Bowl was an important, exciting event in my life, and the fifteen-thousand-dollar winner's share could certainly be put to good use. I intended to buy a car for Linda, remodel our basement, and get some things for the kids. I tried to blot out the fears I had, but was only partially successful. I had genuine cause for worry.

I didn't know if the Steelers would want me back. I would be thirty years old in just five days, and didn't know what lay ahead for me. Rocky Bleier obviously was the back Chuck Noll was counting on to team with Franco. Also, my being the union representative had not endeared me to the coach. It was a not-unwarranted fear that I had. I was afraid that after eight years it might be over for me.

Linda and I attended the Steeler victory party at the hotel, a fifty-thousand-dollar bash paid for by Mr. Rooney. Very few of the ballplayers stayed long. After a big game there is a long way to come down, and it hits you quickly. Linda and I stayed just a short time and then went to our room to sleep. As usual, she was more exhausted than I was.

The team received a gigantic reception when we returned to Pittsburgh. I carried with me my jersey, which I'd hidden in a suitcase (the Steelers wouldn't let you keep them). I still have it. Regardless, it's difficult to imagine more fervent fans than these were. They were the opposite of Dallas rooters, who perhaps have been spoiled by year after year of success. Cowboy fans are among the most staid in the NFL.

I tried not to think about what awaited me. And for a time it seemed I might be all right. Then, *just a week before the start of the 1975 regular season,* I was put on nonrecallable waivers. I had a wife and two kids and no job. It was probably too late, I thought, to catch on with another team. Who wanted someone thirty years old who was still on special teams? Everything I could imagine pointed to the fact that my pro-football career was over.

11

Tom Landry, and the First Year with the Cowboys

I was one day older than thirty-one on January 18, 1976, and the time was a year and six days since the Pittsburgh-Minnesota Super Bowl game, a contest I had thought might be my last. But here I was again, waiting for the referee to blow his whistle, waiting to catch the opening kickoff in a new Super Bowl.

The Steelers were back in the Super Bowl, ready to defend their championship, and I was back too. But I was playing for the Dallas Cowboys. I wanted to win this game more than any I'd ever been in, almost more than I wanted to take my next breath. As I looked up the field, I knew it wouldn't be easy. I knew how tough, brutal, and determined my former teammates were. *This* was going to be a football game no one would call dull.

It had been quite a journey from the waiver list to Super Bowl X. The 1975 regular season was less than a week from beginning when Timmy Rooney phoned me at my home. "We've decided to make some moves," he said. "We're keeping Mike

Collier." He was a rookie out of Morgan State. "We're putting you on nonrecallable waivers. That means even if we wanted you back, we couldn't have you."

I didn't say anything. What could I say? I just wondered what I would do with my life.

"We've tried to deal you," Timmy Rooney said. "San Francisco, Green Bay, San Diego, and Minnesota showed some interest. But we couldn't swing anything definite."

I still didn't say a word.

"Good luck," Timmy Rooney said.

No matter that the Steelers would deny it, I still believe I was dropped because of my union activities. Joe Greene would later try to persuade me I was wrong. "You just got caught in the numbers game," he said, meaning the Steelers had more good players than they could use. But I didn't accept that. Before the strike it had been my duty to tell Chuck Noll we were going out. I asked for an appointment (this was the wonderful job Andy Russell left me), and when I went into his office I could tell he was already mad. He knew something was up. He talked very loud, and my knees were shaking. I looked him right in the eye and made sure I never lost this contact, because I knew my voice was wavering and didn't want to appear even less strong by not eyeing him man-to-man.

"We're going to strike," I told Noll, who had by now seated himself behind his desk. "We'll be picketing the practice field."

Imagine Noll's reaction to this! Picketing *his* practices!

Noll leaned back in his chair. He put his hands behind his head. His eyes were ice cold. It seemed that he hated me. "What do you think we ought to do about that?" he asked, his voice a barely controlled hiss.

"We're doing this as a team," I said. I thought this might calm him. That maybe he'd see all the players were together on this. But I could see he was taking it personally. That this was an insult to *him*.

Our eyes remained locked. I didn't want to break eye contact because I thought it would be a sign of weakness, and he glared, his anger red hot. "I'm just telling you," I said. "It's my job."

"You've done it," he said. He didn't say any more. I'd have

been dead if looks could kill. No, I don't believe Joe Greene's talk about "a numbers game." Chuck Noll didn't want me on his team anymore. I was the messenger bringing him bad news. The worst part was that he waited until the following season was less than a week from beginning before he told me.

I sat at the dining-room table and talked with Linda. We might have been attending a wake. Greg, six years old now, came in and noticed how glum we were. "What's the matter?" he asked.

"Daddy isn't with the Steelers anymore," I said.

This didn't mean anything to him. "What are you gonna do?" he asked. He was cheerful and smiling. I wanted to cry.

"I guess I'll have to become a businessman," I said.

"Okay," he said, and ran outside shouting happily, "Daddy's gonna be a businessman! Daddy's gonna be a businessman!"

I smiled at Linda. It was good Greg didn't know what had happened. The two of us had enough unhappiness between us for the entire family. I just tried to get my thoughts together. It was hard to believe the Steelers could not find a single team willing to deal for me. Timmy Rooney had said there was interest, however. What teams had he mentioned?

The phone rang. Linda answered. "It's Gil Brandt," she said excitedly, returning to the dining room. "Gil Brandt of the Dallas Cowboys!"

Incredible, I thought. *Maybe my last game hadn't been played.* I'd just been waived and already a team was calling. Life on a roller coaster.

"Mr. Brandt? Preston Pearson."

"We want you to come down here," said Gil Brandt, director of personnel for the Cowboys. "We'd like to take a look at you."

"I can't come right away," I said. I don't know why I said it. What else did I have to do?

"We already have your plane reservations waiting for you."

I don't know why I said what I said next either, but I'm glad I did. "Things are moving too fast," I said. "Before I come to Dallas, I want to check with San Diego and Green Bay. I hear they're interested."

A good way to get management's attention is to say other teams are interested. This was just the truth, but I wasn't saying it as part of a clever bargaining position. I just wanted time to think.

Gil Brandt could make a player feel good. He started to talk about my *father*. How did he know about my father? He even mentioned Rufus (called him a "former great athlete") and two of my uncles. He knew my high-school team had been nicknamed "the Pretzels." All of this was very flattering, made me feel someone cared enough to learn about me, but I nonetheless told Brandt I needed at least a little time to think. Linda was right up to the receiver throughout the talk.

"We'd really like to have you," Brandt said in closing. "It will be best for both of us."

Where had I heard that before? And he'd only been interested in taking a "look" at me before I mentioned San Diego and Green Bay.

I sat at the table again. I went over in my mind what players these other teams had. Green Bay, I thought, needed a running back. Minnesota had Osborn and Foreman and were strong in my position. Also, each time I thought of Minnesota, I thought of snow, ice, and a hard, frozen field. I didn't know about San Diego or San Francisco. Dallas, I thought, needed help. I could think of only Doug Dennison and Robert Newhouse, and I believed I could beat out Dennison.

I called Tank Younger of the Chargers and he said I should fly to the West Coast; they'd like to look at me. Bart Starr said about the same thing in urging me to visit Green Bay. I thought about that cold weather in Green Bay, not a lot different from Minnesota, and believed if everything else were equal, Dallas might be the place. A decision had to be made quickly. The season was about to start.

Brandt called again the next day. He seemed familiar with every friend and relative I've ever had. Then he told me he'd had that reservation changed. Why didn't I come to Dallas? Right away.

I did. Cornell Green, a defensive back, met me at the airport and drove me straight to the office of Dr. Pat Evans. Dr. Evans kept asking about my knee, and poking all around it, but he finally decided, "You're in pretty damn good health."

I wondered if Chuck Noll had said something about a knee. Probably not, I decided. But I was willing to think bad things of him. I thought he had come close to ruining my career. In fact, at that moment I still didn't have a career. There was no contract yet, and I imagined the Cowboys were going to put me through a workout before offering one.

Dan Reeves, offensive-backfield coach, was the first person I met after Cornell Green dropped me off at the Cowboy practice field in North Dallas. Reeves, now coach of the Broncos, was younger than me, and we talked about my old teammate Bubba Smith. Reeves joked about the time Ralph Neely, Cowboy offensive guard, had said, "Bubba who?" in response to a question about Smith, and how Bubba had later given him a terrific whipping on the field. I met Tom Landry, briefly, and was all eyes, watching his every movement. I wondered if he was really the stoneface everyone said he was.

I was put up in the Twin Sixties Inn on Central Expressway that night. What little I'd seen of Dallas, I liked. Deep-blue skies. A new, bustling appearance. Roads that seemed much wider than those in Pittsburgh. *A nice place,* I thought.

Gil Brandt called that evening and asked how much I wanted if I were to sign. I said I'd take what Pittsburgh had been willing to pay before they released me, plus five thousand dollars to move my family to Dallas. He wouldn't commit on anything. He said they wanted to look me over the next day at practice.

At this practice, I could see a lot of the Cowboys wondering who I was. Especially the linebackers and running backs. I seemed about their size, and my presence made them feel one of *them* might be gone. At a team meeting, Coach Landry introduced me as "Preston Pearson, from the Pittsburgh Steelers." There were a lot of "ooohs," people feigning fright, because a Steeler had to be tough, but actually there were players who were worried. A few of the veterans didn't "oooh." They booed. I didn't take it personally—they just didn't like Pittsburgh.

On the field when practice was over, Landry had Roger Staubach toss passes to me. My patterns were crisp, and I think Landry was impressed that I caught the ball *in my hands,* then always headed straight upfield. I knew any career I expected to have with Dallas would depend on how I impressed the coach right now. But it was impossible to tell what Landry was thinking. He had an unreadable mask over his emotions.

Landry wanted me to run forty yards against rookie linebacker Thomas "Hollywood" Henderson, the fastest Cowboy. We were going to start on the snap of a football. I shook hands with Henderson, who had a gold filling in his mouth in the shape of a Dallas Cowboy star. I knew he planned to run me into the ground.

This is it, I thought. *You're running for your career.* I tried to get closer to the ball that would be snapped, figuring I might see it sooner. I was prepared for the test of my life.

I beat Henderson at the start by half a step and at the finish by two steps! That day I felt I could have beaten Bob Hayes. Just as I finished the forty yards I felt a sharp pain in my thigh, and before I could think not to grab for it, not to indicate I was hurt, I reached down and held my leg. Landry, of course, saw this. He saw everything. Hollywood Henderson was already lobbying for a rematch, and the coaches had said we would do it twice, "as a truer test," but Landry said that was enough. Henderson still wanted me to run again.

But I was okay. I noticed Jethro Pugh and Rayfield Wright had been watching the race, and they both seemed very tall. Many of the Cowboys were tall and lean; like Cowboys, I guess. Anyway, Jethro Pugh was smiling broadly. He'd wanted me to beat Henderson.

I stayed a little longer, catching some more passes from Roger, and then Brandt came over and said I could have that contract.

"What about the five thousand dollars?" I said.

"I can't make a commitment on that."

"Well, it will cost that much to move my family here. I need a commitment, or I can't sign."

"That will have to be Coach Landry's decision."

"Ask him." I was feeling pretty good. If you could believe what the Cowboys said about Henderson, I would be the fastest player they had.

Brandt did ask Landry. Landry said to pay me the five thousand dollars. Later I learned that's the way things worked with the Cowboys. If Landry wanted someone paid, he was paid. I don't think Chuck Noll had that sort of authority with Pittsburgh.

Right away I sensed there would be a change for the better in Dallas, at least where my career was concerned. It was clear that as soon as I became familiar with Coach Landry's system, not an easy task, I'd be alternating with Doug Dennison at halfback. We'd carry in plays from Landry to Staubach, and for the first time I thought my skills would really be used extensively. I was slated to do a lot of ballcarrying, but there were also numerous pass plays where I'd be in the pattern.

Personally, I wasn't sure what to expect. Linda paid a visit to Dallas and pronounced that she wouldn't be happy here. I think she partially feared a less-progressive racial atmosphere, but also she'd grown to like Pittsburgh and our home there. She was attending classes that ultimately would lead to her becoming a CPA. Since Greg was already registered in school in Pennsylvania, we decided Linda and the kids would remain there. I took a North Dallas apartment, and wasn't sure what the future held for our marriage. As I've mentioned, I felt I was maturing a good deal, and was interested in taking chances in the business world. Linda was more conservative.

The answer to another trivia question: The player who was released when Preston Pearson joined the Dallas Cowboys was Jim Zorn, later a quarterback of some note with the Seattle Seahawks.

I saw spot action in our first four games—all victories—and became a regular for the Green Bay contest. This was another bit of déjà vu. My first game as a professional, when I was activated from the taxi squad, was against the Packers.

The Cowboys had missed the playoffs the previous year for the first time in years. Now we were without Duane Thomas, the troubled but gifted running back; Calvin Hill and Walt Garrison were both no longer with the team; and the great Tony Dorsett was still in college. Landry had to accomplish a *great* coaching job, and this season was perhaps his personal best. We had twelve rookies and no big name at running back; Landry compensated by turning our offense into one of the most creative in pro football. Often we ran from a spread (or shotgun) formation, with Staubach equally dangerous as either a passer or a runner.

We lost the Green Bay game, but ended at 10–4 and the wild-card berth in the NFC playoffs. We'd been picked by a Dallas newspaper to finish third in our division, and by a nationwide poll to finish last. We were eight-point underdogs against Minnesota in the opening playoff round, but a last-second pass, perhaps the most famous (except for Franco's Immaculate Reception) ever thrown, from Staubach to Drew Pearson, pulled the game out for us. Drew's catch was truly remarkable, caught virtually with one hand down around his hip, and the Minnesota crowd was wild with anger. A bottle came out of the stands and hit a game official on the head. Other bottles and debris poured onto the playing surface. Once again I thought someone might be killed by fans, but somehow we got out of Minnesota. I rushed for thirty-four yards against the Vikings, only two fewer than team leader Doug Dennison, and led the Cowboys in receptions with five. I was a major part of the team, and it felt great.

In the NFC Championship in Los Angeles, as 9-point underdogs, I caught 7 passes, 3 for touchdowns (18, 15, and 19 yards), and we crushed the Rams to reach the Super Bowl—and the matchup with the mighty Steelers. My 3 touchdown catches still is an NFL playoff record. The most sensational of these was one Roger told me he was trying to throw away to keep it from being intercepted. For me, the throw was like magic. I saw the ball all the way. I dove for it, and I swear that just before it hit my hands I could read the print on it. The most important thing was it made us the first wild-card team ever to reach the Super Bowl.

"Preston has to be one of the keys to our season," said Roger Staubach. "I don't know anybody who runs the screen better. He's also helped our younger backs, bringing a lot of experience to this team."

"The guy's super," said Lee Roy Jordan. "He's a big key. Preston and Roger made some big plays."

I knew this Super Bowl game was going to be different for me. In the previous Super Bowls I'd been almost strictly a special-teams player. I'd be a starter against the Steelers, a major part of the Dallas offense.

I'd really enjoyed my first year in Dallas. This year was the closest football ever came to being fun for me. There were WEL-COME PRESTON PEARSON signs in Texas Stadium, though I had no idea who brought them. I played the "inside back" on the spread formation, lined up right behind the tackle, and it didn't take long to see on the films that I was often open for passes. Increasingly, the Cowboys began throwing to me. It took pressure off Drew Pearson, Golden Richards, and our other receivers, and gave a large added dimension to our attack. For the regular season I rushed 133 times for 509 yards, and caught 27 passes for 351 yards.

The Cowboys' system was more sophisticated than any I'd had to learn before. Minor differences complicated matters further—for example, even-numbered plays at Pittsburgh had gone to the right; in Dallas they went left. I was glad I didn't have to learn Dallas's famous flex defense. It was Bob Lilly, the great tackle, who said, "By the time you've mastered the flex, you're too old to play it."

Super Bowl X was scheduled for the Orange Bowl, and Linda came from Pittsburgh for the game. She was still adamant about not moving to Dallas. I certainly didn't want to quit football to live in Pittsburgh, now that my career had turned so dramatically brighter. We were at an impasse. Still, it was good to have her with me in Miami for the big game.

Fran Tarkenton, among many others (Pittsburgh was a seven-point favorite), didn't give us much of a chance against the Steelers. He said we couldn't score more than seven points against the Steel Curtain, and that wouldn't be enough. Tarkenton, I thought, still had fresh memories from the beating his Vikings had taken the year before. I had no illusions about the Steelers being easy to score on. But I thought we'd do a lot better than Minnesota had.

I went to the Steeler locker room a few hours before kick-off. I just wanted to let my old teammates know I was still around. They were very aware, of course. I didn't want to run into Chuck Noll, however. I still had trouble even thinking about him without getting angry. That he'd done me an unintentional favor did not alleviate my resentment toward him.

But it was good to see my old teammates. Ernie Holmes was particularly friendly, as was Joe Greene. Ernie had been quoted in newspapers as saying I was his "friend." I'd tried to be. It's just that I thought he had problems, and it was hard to be close to him. But I'd appreciated what he said.

Dwight White was the only Steeler who felt he had to play tough guy before the game. "Tell Staubach," he said, "not to jump up and get mad in front of everybody. I'm gonna hit him."

"Work that out with Pat Donovan," I said to White, referring to the Cowboy offensive lineman he would have to get past before he even thought of maiming Roger.

I made a point of seeing Mike Wagner and Jack Ham. Joe Greene also had good words to say to me, and I shook his hand. Mel Blount came up to me. "I've been following you guys," he said. "I want you to know I think you should be the Cowboy MVP." That was nice, though not true.

Coach Landry had been pounding into our heads all week that the Steelers would try to intimidate us. He said we shouldn't fight back. Let them take penalties, he said. Landry said the Steelers wanted us to retaliate. It would get us out of our game plan, away from thinking about football, and into a sort of street fight at which they excelled. I thought Landry's advice was a prescription for disaster. I knew the Steelers. They weren't the kind of people who would stop if you turned the other cheek. If they slugged you and you didn't slug back, they would do it again and again. If they spit, cursed, punched, and kneed, and you gave tit for tat, they would back off (not down).

"Our game plan," Roger Staubach described accurately, "was to shoot the works. At the time Super Bowl games had a reputation of being conservative and boring. Since we were heavy underdogs we accepted the challenge of taking chances to make things happen."

I mentioned in some of the team meetings that I did not think Landry's advice was correct. But I didn't make a big thing of it. And what I said didn't have any effect. Most players thought Landry was a genius, and he probably is. Why should they listen to me?

Landry was certainly right when he said the Steelers intended to beat us up. But they were going to have more trouble than against the Vikings, mainly because we were so tricky. If they merely came charging in, intent on playing gutter ball, they would find we had finessed the ball right past them into the

end zone. The Steelers were going to have to be more sophisticated than they had been with Minnesota.

There was a period of relaxation before beginning serious
preparations for Super Bowl X. In this regimen, Landry was the
same as Shula and Noll. But his system was much more complicated. He used a computer to show the "tendencies" of the
other team, that is, what they were likely to do in a given situation. And this, we felt, would be especially helpful against the
Steelers, hardly a team that relied on surprises to win.

The longer I knew Coach Landry, the more he impressed
me. He always had great assistant coaches—a sign, I thought,
that he was sure of himself, not afraid someone else might steal
his thunder. And he spent a lot of time with the defense, developing his beloved flex. His game plan always showed that a
great deal of thought had been put into it. No one ever doubted
that he'd done his homework. I doubt if anyone has watched
more film than Landry.

Landry worked harder than any player. And, amazingly,
more than 75 percent of the time he would be right if he said a
player or team was going to do a certain thing. Also, like Noll
and Shula, he had the ability to see what an athlete would be
able to do in the future. Wouldn't this be something if we could
do it with people in everyday life—spot a great actor, for example, or a scientist, when they are just kids?

Coach Landry was a cold man. I think he had to be. He had
to deal with perhaps fifty players, and there would have been
trouble if he'd gotten chummy and let his emotions rule. But
Landry hadn't always been this way. From old-timers I heard
that more than once he'd broken down in front of the team and
cried when he'd had to let a player go. This, he learned, didn't
help any, and it could hurt.

We were supposed to be men, it was made clear from the
first. No fiery speeches from Landry. He would tell someone, or
the entire team, what was needed, and conclude his talk with
"Okay." Just, "Okay." Then we were expected to do it. No one
should doubt that in the Cowboys' scheme of things, where the
team was concerned, Landry was in charge. General Manager
Tex Schramm had some authority, a lot of it, but Landry made
the final decisions about the team—who was kept and who was
not, what plays were used, and so on.

Both Chuck Noll and Tom Landry were quiet men. Each could delegate authority. Each recognized talent. Noll had to get his word in more than Landry, however, and he occasionally made it seem he knew everything about everything. He fancied himself an expert on food, wine, politics. Both were religious, though Landry wore his belief in God on his sleeve. Both could be cold. With Don Shula, you always knew where you stood. Not necessarily with Noll or Landry. Noll played favorites, which may not have been bad in his case. He got close to Joe Greene, for example, and persuaded him he could be a leader. Mean Joe is still an "honorary coach" of the Steelers. It is a position without authority, but conveys the esteem in which Joe is held.

Noll also played favorites with Terry Bradshaw. Joe Gilliam would have been just as good as Terry, I think, had he gotten an equal opportunity. I believe Landry understood football better than Chuck Noll. I think that's why Noll so frequently went for physical players. They took the pressure off him. A big brute may not be as effective as a player with finesse, but the man with finesse needs more coaching.

I wonder what kind of player Terry Bradshaw would have been had he played for the Cowboys. A better one, surely, at least early in his career. Landry called all offensive plays from the sidelines. Noll let Bradshaw call his own plays. With the pressure taken off Bradshaw, I believe he would have become a star earlier than he did. With a quarterback like Bradshaw, the coach *should* call the plays. Perhaps Noll didn't think he had the expertise. On the other hand, I wish Landry had let Staubach make his own decisions on the field. An intelligent player in the middle of the action has a better idea than the coach of what is going on, no matter how brilliant the coach may be. I wonder if both Bradshaw and Staubach might have been superior quarterbacks had they been able to switch coaches. Perhaps not. I'm not sure how the straight-arrow Staubach would have related to the assassin-type football played by the Steelers.

We had our "Dirty Dozen" rookies, but we also had a sprinkling of top-notch veterans, and I thought the oddsmakers who were writing the wild-card Cowboys off might be making a mistake. One of these was Jethro Pugh, six feet seven, and 260, one of the nicest people I've ever known. Jethro rarely said anything on the field. It's interesting: You could meet Jethro's kids, and if you knew Jethro, you could guess to whom they belonged. They had absolutely perfect manners, without ever giving the impression they were anything other than regular kids.

Ed Jones told me about being in a defensive huddle with Jethro Pugh. The Cowboys were losing; worse, they were not playing well. In a quiet voice, Pugh said, "Let's go." Anyone else, Jones said, would have had to deliver a ten-page tear-the-walls-down oration for the Cowboy defenders to react as they did. They knew they had better straighten out if Jethro Pugh said, "Let's go."

Jethro's situation was similar to what Ernie Holmes experienced, living as he did in the shadow of Joe Greene. For years the Dallas press praised the brilliant Bob Lilly, but in the process forgot about Jethro. Lilly never did. He'll tell you Jethro was one of the best the game has ever known. Holmes tried to do something to get into the limelight, but Jethro was just constitutionally incapable of beating his own drum.

I became close to Roger Staubach this first year. He knew I was living alone and often invited me to his home. At first I didn't think Staubach was one of the greats, but he proved me wrong. What helped was that he was a very hard worker. He would always stay late after practice, working on my pass-catching routes. He was perhaps the highest paid Cowboy, but he'd be out there long after everyone else had gone, throwing the ball to me. You can count on one hand the quarterbacks today who will do this.

Roger Staubach was very religious, but he didn't beat you over the head with it, as Terry Bradshaw did. Roger just tried to live the way a good person should. He didn't run the streets. I think I saw him drink maybe one beer in six years. He cared a great deal about his family. But he wasn't perfect. I remember his getting hit late once by Washington defensive back Pat Fischer, and Roger got up and gave him a terrific cursing out. Pro football could turn a near-saint into an animal, at least for a moment. He usually said *fudge* instead of *fuck*, but you knew the latter was in his mind.

He and Landry were good for each other. Both were tremendously competitive. Both studied hard. Stauback knew the assignment of *every* offensive player. Most of us had trouble learning our own, especially in a system as intricate as Landry's. Roger had a great arm, especially for long passes, and he was a good runner. Both he and Johnny Unitas brought their teams from behind so often that it defied belief. I think this is because they were so competitive. Roger never thought a game was over until the players were in the locker room and the crowd had gone home.

A player just as competitive as Roger was Lee Roy Jordan. He was from Alabama, bona fide all-pro. I felt he gave us a big advantage over Jack Lambert at the middle linebacker position. Lee Roy was as intense as a player can be. He was fiercely competitive even in practice, and had no use for anyone who didn't go all out. This meant he wasn't fond of Thomas Henderson.

Lee Roy Jordan was always yelling, trying to fire up his teammates, but his yells were genuine. He'd scream at you to congratulate, or to say you were messing up. It is possible to be too "cool" on the field, a problem no one could accuse Lee Roy of having. And Lee Roy was a fearsome hitter. He could knock a runner out from under his helmet. Lee Roy Jordan was a leader, someone who would get down in the dirt and fight with you, and he'd keep on going no matter how badly he was hurt. If I was faced with a life-threatening situation, I'd want Lee Roy Jordan at my side.

Then there was Ed "Too Tall" Jones and Harvey "Too Mean" Martin, two future greats at the start of their brilliant careers. You could observe these two and know that not anyone, not even the fearsome Steelers, was going to intimidate them.

That's why I hated to hear Coach Landry's message delivered over and over again. "Pittsburgh is a basic team. They will continue to do the same thing. Keep this in mind. Do not fight with them. If you fight with them you'll lose your poise and concentration."

But if we didn't fight with them, I thought, *they would keep beating on us,* and it is not good for the spirit to be a punching bag. A Steeler would knock you flat. If you got up and slugged him, he'd back off. If you did nothing, he'd knock you down again.

Nor were the Steelers going to intimidate Thomas Henderson, our rookie linebacker sensation. Henderson *could have been* the best ever to play his position. He enjoyed hitting, and if he didn't like a guy, he would go after him. I saw him go one-on-one with New England tight end Russ Francis, dubbed "All-World" by Howard Cosell, and dish out terrific punishment. Henderson was fast, and smart. He was a gambler, who often upset Landry by ad-libbing on an assigned defense. But often it worked out for the best. Hollywood, as he came to be known, was six feet three and 215, but he had extraordinarily long arms, which allowed him to play as if he were a seven-footer. Henderson was not just a great football player. He was a great athlete.

The superficial cause of Thomas Henderson's problems was that he got a big head. He got to think he was more important than the team. He thought he could come to practices whenever he wanted to, sleep during team meetings, and leave when he felt the urge. Today I don't think he has a friend left from the Cowboys. Ed Jones lasted the longest, but Thomas turned on him also.

Thomas Henderson became heavily involved in the drug scene. Over a period of time I began to suspect something of the sort. He would show up late for a practice, either bubbling over with enthusiasm or dead to the world, unable even to keep his eyes open. No one was unhappy when he was let go, except a few members of the press who thought racism might be involved. It wasn't. Thomas got *more* chances, because he was so good, than almost any player would have. The reporters looking for a story could have come to any of the Cowboys and been told the truth.

Fame just came too quickly and easily for Henderson. He was from a small town in Oklahoma and just wasn't ready for everyone to tell him how great he was. He'd come from a broken family, and this had its effect. He called Tom Landry "Plastic Man," copying a description first used by Duane Thomas, but he did this only when he didn't get his own way. If he wanted to be late for a practice, and almost always was, Landry would be Plastic Man if he refused him. Hollywood would get players to confide in him, then go behind their backs and tell others what he'd learned. All that was necessary to get on his bad side was to refuse to cover up for him.

Thomas was very extravagant in the clothes he wore, though I never thought he showed particularly good taste. He was like a spoiled child. He'd sulk if he didn't get his way. Landry put up with a tremendous amount from Henderson, hoping, I guess, that the great talent would come to the fore, submerging the other part.

But it happened the other way. Later, when it was all over, both our careers ended, I had Thomas Henderson on my Dallas television talk show. He told me he loved the Cowboys, that all he ever wanted was to be a member of the team, and I believed him. Being a Cowboy had been important to Thomas, so much that he wore that gold-star tooth filling. He also said he would "do things differently" if he could live his life over. I wonder. Just recently he was in trouble again with some young girls in California. Watching Thomas early in his career, I'd predicted he would soon be dead or in jail. Something went wrong for Thomas. It is a shame when it happens to anyone, but worse because it was him: *He had so much talent.*

Don Shula gave Thomas a chance after he left the Cowboys. It didn't work out. Thomas suffered a broken neck. I wondered what he was thinking about when after breaking his neck he talked about catching on with another pro team.

But all this was in Henderson's future. Now he was simply a wunderkind linebacker, and not in the least in awe of the Steelers.

Another teammate I'd gotten to know very well was Mel Renfro, one of the only five players to be honored in the Cowboys Circle of Fame. Renfro was one of the best ever to play cornerback. I hung around him, in an all-black area of the locker room called Ghetto Alley, mainly to listen to him talk. He was rightly considered a sage, an old head, and a group of us, including Benny Barnes and Drew Pearson, tried to pick up whatever wisdom Renfro was handing out that particular day. "You don't get to be a fourteen-year veteran," I remember him saying, "by being a fool." He advised veterans against practicing when they were hurt, and against drugs, alcohol, and running around. It was old-fashioned common sense that came from Mel Renfro, but because it was *him,* we listened.

Mel Renfro could have been a great coach, or at the least a brilliant defensive coordinator. But he never got the chance because of prejudice against blacks holding these positions. He retired with a bitter taste in his mouth, and he had every justification. Take the case of Charlie Waters, another Cowboy defensive back, but not nearly as gifted as Renfro: All kinds of opportunities were waiting for Waters when he left football. Not so for Mel. The reason, I think, is that white people generally control the money in our society, and they would much rather deal with a white than a black. They can identify with the growing-up experiences of a white. What do they know about a black?

Renfro was the best one-on-one defender I've ever seen. He had both speed and quickness, and was a sure tackler. This made him doubly valuable in the Cowboy scheme of things, where the defensive back was expected to make a lot of tackles because of the flex. Mel Renfro came up as a wide receiver, could have excelled at that position, but was switched to the corner. I believe he also would have been a first-rate running back.

Then there was Robert Newhouse, five feet ten and 220, a running back. Everyone thought Newhouse had gigantic thighs, and though they were a good size, they appeared bigger because he was short for a pro player. Newhouse was another who helped me in my first weeks with the Cowboys. If I didn't know what to do on a certain play I'd ask him, and he always had the right answer.

Newhouse was just tough. He wasn't fast, and he wasn't big, even though 220 pounds makes him seem so. He and I became good friends. He was a player who always gave it all he had, and that's something. I'll never forget the numerous times he literally would crawl for an extra yard, risking life and limb because the *team* needed it.

No, I didn't think the Steelers would bully us the way they had the Vikings. We had too many good players: Randy White, Drew Pearson, Larry Cole, Blaine Nye, Billy Joe DuPree, Jean Fuggett, Bob Breunig, and Herbert Scott. Before we took the field for Super Bowl X (where I had the unforgettable joy of being introduced to the crowd and the vast TV audience as a starter), we listened to the final words of Tom Landry. We had heard them before.

"Don't descend to their level. We know what to expect from them. We know how to counter that. Okay."

Maybe it would be okay. Because we did feel we knew the rather basic material Pittsburgh would throw at us (they were predictable), and because we did have a brilliant general in Landry, we thought we had surprises for them they wouldn't be able to handle. I knew Coach Landry was figuring this way. I just wish he had let us off our leashes.

12
Super Bowl X

So I waited for the ball to come down. I wasn't nervous, not this time. I merely wanted to win this game. It had occurred to me that it would be a great joy to return to my Pittsburgh home and wear a Cowboy hat the entire off-season. It might be fun for my son Greg too. In football-crazed Pittsburgh, he'd been told numerous times how the Steelers were going to "pound his father." Even walking down a street with his mother, people would yell at them from cars about the beating I was going to take. Greg himself was a little confused. I have a picture of him in a Steeler jacket and a Cowboy hat. But I knew he wanted his daddy to win. I wanted to go to Pittsburgh and make myself visible, show the Steelers what a terrible mistake they'd made.

I was starting at running back, but it didn't occur to the Steelers that it was unusual that I was standing under a kickoff. They remembered me chiefly from special teams. They figured it was good I'd be running the kickoff back. Gave them a little extra inspiration, not that they needed any to get worked up about decapitating me. They wanted to show me a few things too. They'd race down the field like maniacs to get at me.

Coach Landry had probably figured all this out. The Steelers would be eager to get their hands on a former teammate, a "traitor." Of course he'd figured it out. He thought of everything. And there wasn't a chance in the world the big, bad Steelers would kick away from me, as the Jets had. They wanted to come down the field and tear me apart.

I caught the ball and headed smoothly up the field. The Steelers came screaming and cursing, as we'd figured they would. They'd try to show us who was boss from the start. What they didn't notice was Thomas Henderson, coming from my right. I slipped the ball to the rookie sensation and he went sailing up the sideline. Score one for brains, for planning.

Henderson went fifty-three yards before the last player with a chance, kicker Roy Gerela, was able to knock him out of bounds. Gerela suffered a cracked rib on the play. The first injury was to a Steeler!

Out came the Steel Curtain onto the Orange Bowl turf, and I knew exactly what to expect from this bunch. My teammates would learn soon enough. They had been worried because the Steelers were more experienced. I didn't think this should be a major concern. What we needed to become accustomed to were dirty tactics, which have no place in what, no matter how important, is still a game. The Steelers were very tough, we knew that, but we weren't afraid, and actually we were more relaxed than they were. They had the pressure of having to defend a title. We hadn't expected even to make the game.

Jack Lambert was screaming from the beginning—he didn't need a warm-up to get his lungs working—and the Steeler Front Four charged like bulls going at a red cape. Immediately the Steelers started to pick on Golden Richards, our wide receiver with the long blond hair. He was one of the smallest players on the field, which made him a perfect target for Pittsburgh. Even when he wasn't involved in a play he could expect to take an unnecessary hit. Once he was kneed in the groin right in front of an official, who told the offending Steeler, "Don't do that again."

Don't do that again! What kind of talk is this? It was a flagrant foul, and there should have been a fifteen-yard penalty, plus, I think, a game disqualification for the Steeler involved. But Golden had courage. He kept soaking up punishment the entire game. They finally broke his ribs.

We didn't move on our first possession after the Henderson

kickoff return, but neither did the Steelers. Bobby Walden dropped back to punt for them, dropped the snap, and we recovered at the Pittsburgh twenty-nine.

Back came the Steel Curtain, using language you wouldn't hear in an X-rated movie, issuing threats that anywhere else would make them indictable. Perhaps the Steelers were too busy threatening to notice. We swung Drew Pearson over the middle on first down, and he was all alone in the end zone for Roger's gentle pass. Toni Fritsch made the extra point. Cowboys 7, Steelers 0. The crowd in the Orange Bowl was delirious.

Nothing of this sort had been expected. Pro-football fans had expected, if anything, a wearying trench war that the Steelers eventually would have to win. They just didn't know Tom Landry, and the bag of tricks he'd prepared. Drew Pearson's touchdown was the first the Steelers had allowed *all season* in the first period. Sixteen games! And no one had crossed their goal line in the first quarter until now.

The Steelers took the opening kickoff and marched straight back down the field, tying the game at 7–7. Both drives were typical of the two teams. We had struck dramatically, one play after a turnover, and Pittsburgh had used a crunching drive to manufacture points.

Blackie Sherrod of the *Dallas Times Herald* gave a good analysis of how we played the first half:

> Tom Landry contributed generously to the suspenseful plot. Usually when coaches bring their teams as far as the Super Bowl, their collars get tight as Jackie Gleason in a telephone booth. They steer with the timidity of a driver just given a traffic ticket. They fear their own mistakes. Who wants to be remembered as the Roy Riegels or Fred Merkels of the Super Bowl? Regardless of the daring that fetched them to the Super Bowl, coaches become Goldwaters. It's okay if you beat me, they say, but danged iffen I'm gonna beat myself.
>
> But Landry danced with the gal what brung him. His Cowboys had made it to the final day on flamboyant offense—trick plays, weird formations. Staid old football men rattle their wattles in disapproval, but

Landry deemed legerdemain necessary for survival.
And when he reached this rarefied air, he didn't leave
his game plan in his work pants.

Anyone who before the game did not have a team to root
for, I believe, started to cheer for us. We played wide-open,
imaginative, daring offense. If you liked rough stuff—dirtiness is
a better word—then you were for the Steelers. But I don't think
this type of football appeals to many fans.

"We just don't think you can beat people by fooling people," Dwight White said, but his eyes might have been opened
by half time. We had a 10–7 lead. The Steeler defense would
have been tough without all the questionable tactics—late hits,
kneeing, gouging, piling on—and we weren't exactly lighting up
the scoreboard (though we'd already scored more than Fran
Tarkenton thought we would), but Landry had been right. The
Steelers were a basic team. Our defense was stopping them.

It was clear that the Steelers were not physically superior
to us. We were just as big and tough. But they were dirtier.
That's the only word that can be used. More than half the players in our locker room had some complaint about a hurt inflicted by some illegal hit. "I think we have to stand up for one
another," I said at half time. I meant that we couldn't let guys
like Golden Richards be brutalized without one of our big guys
stepping in and putting a halt to the punishment. But no one
was listening. We had the lead, and Coach Landry wanted us to
play a clean game.

The Steelers had not a single yard in penalties in the first
half. Could anyone believe this? Fouls occurred right in front of
officials, and their responses were timid suggestions that Pittsburgh should please cut it out. I was convinced, as were my
teammates, that the Steelers had *intimidated the officials*. No
other answer sufficed. The officials were right down on the field
with us, they knew what was going on, and they did nothing
that would have been effective. *We* were not intimidated, but
the officials were. I did feel we would be beaten down, however,
in the second half, just as the Vikings had been, if we kept soaking up punishment without retaliating.

But it got even more unbelievable. Listen to Roger Staubach, whose truthfulness cannot be questioned: "I wasn't aware

until later that the Steelers hadn't drawn a penalty throughout the game. I remembered Lambert kneed Preston Pearson flagrantly and the referee only warned him, which was a joke. They should have called a foul right away."

I still have trouble believing it. The Steelers didn't get *a single penalty all day*. Here were players who boasted about their bad-boy images, who openly admitted it *helped* them to get more penalties than the opposition, and they were not so much as called for an offside. It can't be true, I tell myself, especially since I lived through the entire game (one of the dirtiest ever played), but it is. The most avid Steeler fan will admit that zero penalty yardage was impossible for a team such as this.

Football players do not like to sound like complainers. Especially where dirty play is concerned. The public has a macho image of them, and they often believe the he-man stuff themselves. If you complain about a dirty play, you open yourself up to the cry-baby label. "You're a big, strong man, aren't you?" a fan may justifiably ask. "Can't you take care of yourself?"

Yes, we could. But I know why we didn't. We had too much respect for what Coach Landry told us. It's why he is such a great coach—his players will accept what he tells them. The point is, the dirty stuff really has to be far out of line for any football player to complain. On the other hand, rules should be enforced. Officials should call flagrant fouls. Otherwise, let's not call the game football, but something else: war, perhaps?

We were still leading 10–7 early in the fourth quarter. But I was beginning to feel apprehensive, regardless of what the scoreboard read. Momentum, pushed along mainly by Pittsburgh's rough tactics, seemed to be going in the direction of the Steelers. The Steelers were not indiscriminately rough. They did not try to intimidate us as a *team*. That wouldn't have worked. Jethro Pugh or Too Tall Jones, for example, could not be intimidated, and the result might have been the opposite of what was intended. The Steelers intimidated *individuals*.

I cannot believe a baseball manager would continually let Dave Winfield be thrown at and not order retaliation. Nor would a basketball team stand idly by while Isaiah Thomas was brutalized. But in this game, we raised not a finger to the Steelers.

Early in the fourth quarter Reggie Harrison blocked one of our punts out of the end zone, and the score was 10–9. But this meant we had to kick from our own twenty, and Pittsburgh drove into position to kick a field goal for a 12–10 lead. Gerela should be given credit. He booted the goal despite the cracked rib he suffered when he drove Hollywood Henderson out of bounds. Many fans were surprised Noll went for this field goal. It was on a fourth down and a half-yard to go from our twenty. It was thought he might try sending Franco for the eighteen inches.

I wasn't surprised. The Steelers, I knew, were a conservative team.

The intensity of the game was scintillating. I'm still happy I was part of it. It gave me pleasure, even though we trailed, to notice the difference in the Steelers from the year before against Minnesota. The Pittsburgh players were just as ferocious, but they weren't beating on corpses this time. There was worry in their eyes.

With six minutes, thirty-seven seconds left in the game, the Steelers made it 15–10 with another Gerela field goal, set up by Mike Wagner's interception of a Staubach pass intended for Drew Pearson. Wagner returned the ball to our 7, but still the Steelers and Franco couldn't get the touchdown. This was a different Super Bowl for Franco. He gained 83 yards, but had to carry 27 times to get them; it was hardly the cakewalk he'd enjoyed against Minnesota.

Lynn Swann was the hero this day. He caught 4 passes for more than 160 yards, including the game-winner with three minutes to go. We blitzed Bradshaw, getting to him just an instant late (he was knocked out of the game by a Cliff Harris hit), leaving Swann with one-on-one coverage, and the result was a 64-yard touchdown catch. Gerela missed the extra point, but it was 21–10 and very little time was left.

Swann was brilliant this day, but he had to, as always, ice the cake a bit. One catch he made, against Mark Washington, he said could be credited to his training as a dancer. This was ridiculous. I've watched the catch dozens of times, and dancing had nothing to do with it. He caught the ball because, luckily, he didn't get tangled up and fall until an instant before Washington did. Had the positions of their legs been reversed, Swann would have gone down. It's a matter of physical laws.

We really didn't think we were beaten. Certainly Roger didn't. He marched us right down the field, hitting Percy Howard, a former basketball player for Austin Peay, with a thirty-eight-yard touchdown pass with just one minute, forty-eight seconds to play. It was 21–17 when we lined up for the onside kick. The Steelers had even stopped trying to intimidate us. It was life or death for them now.

Our onside kick was recovered by Pittsburgh on our forty-two. But still we thought we were alive. The Steelers ran three straight times, gaining only one yard, and we used up our three time-outs by stopping the clock after each play. Then Chuck Noll made a mistake that almost cost his team the game, an error I don't think Tom Landry ever would have committed. Instead of punting on fourth and nine, he ran Rocky Bleier up the middle, and our defense held.

"We felt," said Noll, immediately after the game, talking about the decision not to punt, "we could hold them at that point of the field. Besides, we almost had two earlier punts blocked. They needed a touchdown to beat us and we felt the defense would not allow it. If they could have won with a field goal, we would have punted."

I know very few players who believe this explanation. I think Coach Noll knows it isn't true. Reports out of the Pittsburgh locker room were that Noll thought the clock would keep running after the fourth-down play, when in reality it was stopped by the change of possession. It was a terrific mistake for a coach to make. We were set up with reasonable field position on our thirty-nine, and one minute, twenty-two seconds still to go.

We were just a small miracle away from beating the Steelers, and they knew it. They were as tired as we were when we lined up for the crucial last series. The only difficulty was that we were out of time outs. Still, it was not even a big miracle we needed. Just a small one. The big one we'd used on Drew Pearson's Hail Mary catch against the Vikings.

It had to be the most exciting finish in Super Bowl history.

Actually, the outcome was in doubt until the last three seconds.

Operating from the spread, Roger scrambled for 11 yards to midfield. The clock kept moving. We hurried for the next play. Roger threw it to me over the middle for another 12 yards and we were at the Steeler 38. Just one more, into the end zone, and we'd be champions of the world. I'd wear that Cowboy hat in Pittsburgh every day of the off-season. I would have said a prayer, but I was too busy concentrating. Come on, Roger!

Twenty-two seconds remained. We had three more plays. On the first, Roger had to retrieve a low snap from center and throw a hurried incompletion over Drew Pearson's head. Our second-to-last play was a pass batted down in the end zone. On the very last play of the game, Roger was back, throwing it into the end zone, victory one catch away. But Glen Edwards caught this ball, and the Steelers, by the skin of their teeth, were champions once again.

I've never been more crushed after a game. We were *so close*. It had been a good season, we'd come much further than anyone had expected, but I was just inconsolable. Someone once said *losing* a Super Bowl produces more pain than winning one produces pleasure, and I agree.

The game was relatively even statistically. Bradshaw was 9 of 19 for 209 yards; Roger was 15 of 24 for 204. We'd held Franco to just 3 yards a carry, and virtually shut out the Steeler receivers, except Lynn Swann. So why did we come up short?

I think Pittsburgh was a better team at this time. Their personnel was slightly superior, reflected perfectly by the narrow margin of victory. That was the reason we lost. But we could have won. The Steelers were not *much* better than we were, and our coaching and imaginative style of play could have overcome the slight talent differential. These could have been the winning ingredients if the officials hadn't called a disgraceful game.

One example out of many sticks in my mind. Roy Gerela missed a field goal, and Cliff Harris did a little finger-tap on Gerela's helmet, sort of a congratulations-in-reverse. Lambert slugged Harris hard, right in front of God and everybody, and then hurled him to the ground. The referee asked him sweetly not to do that in the future.

I won't say the referees cost us the game. Only that their

officiating was terrible. We lost because we weren't as good as the Steelers.

But I tell you, that last drive, with Roger throwing one after another into the end zone, being out there, hearing the noise, seeing the fear in the eyes of the Steelers, it was something to remember on long, hot summer nights.

13
Too Tall Jones, Roger Staubach, and Others

Playing in Dallas was not for the slow of mind, not with the complicated system Tom Landry had perfected, and expected us to know backward and forward. We probably had more plays than any other team in the NFL, and this was just on offense. A very bright person could learn the offense. On defense, perhaps only one person—Tom Landry—entirely understood our flex.

I'm sure we also had the most elaborate "fine schedule." I reproduce it here, word for word, exactly as it was given to the players:

1. Failure to report to training
   camp on date specified (per day) $500

2. Late for meetings (MEETING
   CALLED TO ORDER) $ 50
   Late for practice (complete
   warmup routine—WHISTLE
   BLOWS) $ 50

Late for trainers' and doctors' appointments $ 50

3. Late for any scheduled transportation $100
    (Miss plane: Pay own ticket, fine discretion of head coach)

4. Missing meeting—missing practice, may be reduced at discretion of head coach in extenuating circumstances $500
    Missing trainers' and doctors' appointments $100

5. Curfew violations: (In dorm by 11 PM, in room by 11:30 PM)
    Disturbance after 11 PM $ 75
    Late for bed check:
        First 15 minutes $100
        Next 45 minutes $ 50
        Each additional hour $100
    (Report to Coach Landry on arrival, otherwise fine runs until next scheduled meeting) (maximum fine $500)
    OUT AFTER BED-CHECK
    NIGHT BEFORE GAME   GAME
                                                                        CHECK

6. Sprained ankle without protective wraps $250

7. Weight control: All players subject to fine per lb. $ 25
    (No allowance except for tape)
    Overweight repeated $ 50

8. Loss of notebook $500

9. Headgear touching ground or helmets off in drill, or chinstrap unfastened in drill $ 25

10.	Improper dress while traveling as a member of the team	$200
11.	Penalty: Will not receive final check until playbook turned in	
* 12.	Throwing ball into stands	$100
* 13.	Players leaving bench area during fight	*
* 14.	Players thrown out of game	*
15.	Conduct detrimental to club	GAME CHECK SUSPEN- SION

In addition, the Commissioner may impose fines (and other appropriate discipline, up to and including suspension from the League) for conduct detrimental to the NFL or professional football. Among the types of offenses for which such disciplinary action may be imposed are: betting on NFL games; associating with gamblers or engaging in gambling activities; accepting a bribe or failing to report a bribe offer; improper use or circulation of drugs; fighting, commission of flagrant fouls, leaving the bench area while a fight is in progress and other game-related misconduct.

* LEAGUE FINES—NO SET AMOUNT—DEPENDS ON FLAGRANCY OF VIOLATION. ALL FINES DOUBLE PREVIOUS OFFENSE, CONTINUED FINES DISCRETION OF HEAD COACH.

NOTE: Fines will be withheld each payday, including training camp. Other fines may be levied at the discretion of the head coach and will not accumulate in the special fund unless so stated.

Some of these fines were pretty stiff. Twenty-five dollars for each overweight pound (escalating to $50 at a second weigh-in) could curb the heartiest appetite. Missing a bed check the night before a game cost you the pay for that game: a $10,000 fine if your salary is $160,000—expensive for a party. And how about $25 for taking your helmet off and letting it touch the ground?

Being late for a normal bed check meant you had to report to Coach Landry when you got in, or the fine kept going up until the next scheduled meeting. But who wanted to face Landry? Does he look like a person who would be understanding with an athlete, breath smelling like a brewery, who wakes him at four-thirty A.M. to "report"?

The schedule of fines was more intricate than those which other clubs imposed, but then everything about the Cowboys was different. The mood was set by Landry, and it wasn't a bad one. We were professionals, and he expected us to act that way. One rule the Cowboys make public—that a ballplayer is not allowed to date a Dallas Cowboy Cheerleader—I know has been broken. Not surprisingly, two of the players who went out with cheerleaders were Ed Jones and Thomas Henderson.

I must have broken a bunch of rules myself when after about my first two weeks with the team, figuring I knew my offensive assignments, I allowed Ed Too Tall Jones and Harvey Martin to take me out on the town to "see Dallas." An individual needs only to look at this pair to imagine the attention we got upon entering each new night spot. Jones is six feet nine and 270 pounds; Harvey is six feet six and 265.

We went barhopping. Too Tall, whom I now consider to be perhaps my best friend, drinks *only* beer. But when he's in the mood, he can drink a lot of it, and perhaps faster than any man alive. He was in the mood this night. And people's eyes just bulged when they saw this behemoth coming. This first night wasn't any different from many others I've spent with Too Tall, at least in one respect. Inevitably, he attracts numerous gorgeous women. I've known guys to hang around him just to meet the ones he's not interested in.

Ed Jones seems to be as unpopular with men as he is popular with women. It drives some of them crazy, the appeal he has, and I remember at least one instance where the resentment led to bad judgment. A short guy with a weight lifter's build came up to our table, put his head right next to one of Too Tall's gigantic arms, and insisted that he wanted to fight. He had a big mouth, and a dirty one too, and he kept after Ed. Ed could have swung that big arm and taken the guy's head off. But he tried to ignore the taunts. The insane person (what else could he be?) left to get a drink, and Ed, who hadn't said a word, looked at me.

"Hear what he said?" he asked.

"I heard."

"I don't want to hurt him."

"Don't."

For one year during the peak of his football career, Ed left the Cowboys to become a professional boxer. His first two or three fights were on national television, something I don't believe occurred even when Muhammad Ali turned pro. Ed went undefeated. He fought maybe twenty times. I don't think he could have defeated Larry Holmes or Ernie Shavers, but if he'd devoted perhaps three years to the sport he might have. He was graceful and enormously strong. And what could anybody do against someone his height? His arms are much longer than the average man's.

I admired Ed for taking a chance. He'd always wanted to try to become a fighter, so he did. It didn't matter that he was walking away from an All-Pro football career. I saw Ed when he was in his peak shape for boxing. He'd dropped from 270 pounds to 242, and looked just great. When he did decide to come back to the Cowboys, he didn't lose his penchant for risk-taking, for trying to broaden himself. He immediately cut a record album. A black Elvis Presley?

Too Tall, on the football field, was one of the game's most feared players. He was good against both the run and the pass, and his great height made him almost impossible to throw over. And his strength! I've seen him take a ballcarrier down with *one finger*.

Harvey Martin, my other companion that memorable night, was no fighter. He was too gentle. Harvey didn't want to hurt anybody. It was always interesting to watch him before a game. He had to psyche himself up to be tough. You could see him working on his own mind, transforming himself so that he could perform the rugged work he had ahead of him.

Harvey had perhaps the greatest outside pass rush the game has ever seen. He was just too quick for the offensive tackles who tried to stop him. And Harvey was likable off the field.

He was another one with charisma. A big ear-to-ear smile. I think, despite difficulties this likable man has had, he possesses the qualities needed to be a good businessman.

Talk about two bodyguards. I didn't have any fears that night we spent on the town. I walked between these two bookends, and probably no one knew I was there. It was a good night with two good people.

I became friends with a lot of the Cowboys. It's one of the main reasons my career in Dallas was so pleasant. One of these was Randy White, the great defensive tackle, nicknamed "Manster" (half man, half monster). It was not a fair name. Randy wasn't a monster. He wasn't brutish or destructive, like others I've known. He liked nature and being left alone. He was a good ol' boy, an all-American guy. He would fish *all* summer.

Randy gave 100 percent 100 percent of the time. He thought nothing of playing hurt, and never complained when he did have an injury. He was strong, like Jon Kolb (which meant Randy was one of the strongest men in the world). He was a power-lifter, something the Cowboys encouraged, which requires fast movement along with strength. Have you ever wondered why two football players can hit each other, and the larger one is knocked to the ground while the smaller one continues forward? It's because the impact will be heaviest from the guy who is moving the fastest with the greatest strength. Randy could just explode when he hit an opponent.

At first Randy liked his nightlife, but he soon settled down. He was always helpful with rookies. He was never too busy to take time to help the lowest person on the roster. And you always felt good with Randy White on your team. Like Lee Roy Jordan he'd just get tougher and tougher, as the situation required. No one on his side had to worry about a dangerous situation arising and finding Randy White had deserted his teammates.

I really liked Dallas. I can't imagine a city where there are more business opportunities. And especially for a football player, even if he is black. The people in Dallas love football, especially the brand the Cowboys play. The image of Dallas as a bastion of reaction, largely caused by the assassination of John Kennedy, has gradually changed, and the modern, supersophisticated, state-of-the-art Cowboys played a role in that transformation.

What was best was being an important part of one of the class teams in the NFL. In 1976 I was a starter, along with Robert Newhouse, but unfortunately both of us missed a good portion of the season with injuries. The team finished 11–4, after a heartbreaking 14–12 loss to Los Angeles in the playoffs. Nevertheless, I caught 23 passes for 316 yards (13.7 average). "He had more moves," said Washington safety Mark Murphy, asked to describe my pass catching, "than a wide receiver."

The next year, 1977, my eleventh in the NFL, was perhaps the Cowboys' greatest season. Everything came together for us. Here is our 15–2 record:

Dallas	16	Minnesota	10
Dallas	41	N.Y. Giants	21
Dallas	23	Tampa Bay	7
Dallas	30	St. Louis	24
Dallas	34	Washington	16
Dallas	16	Philadelphia	10
Dallas	37	Detroit	0
Dallas	24	N.Y. Giants	10
Dallas	17	St. Louis	24
Dallas	13	Pittsburgh	28
Dallas	14	Washington	7
Dallas	24	Philadelphia	14
Dallas	42	San Francisco	35
Dallas	14	Denver	6
Dallas	37	Chicago	7
Dallas	23	Minnesota	6
Dallas	27	Denver	10

Tony Dorsett, by way of Aliquippa and the University of Pittsburgh, joined our team in 1977, and it was clear from the beginning that he was the franchise running back the team had been looking for. But I kept him on the bench for the first nine

games, the first eight of which were victories. Then we lost to
St. Louis, 24–17, in a game in which I played well but the team
performed poorly. Coach Landry told me that from now on
Tony Dorsett would be starting. I appreciated that he had come
to me, not let me find out in the press, but I was disappointed
and bitter. The timing made it seem as if I'd had a bad game
against St. Louis. It bothered me also that the job hadn't been
taken away from me in any competition with Dorsett; it had
just been given to him.

But what could I do? I'd always considered myself a team
player, and raising a big fuss wasn't going to help. But it hurt
very deeply. I'd finally become a major part of a team that
started 8–0, and now I wasn't a regular. In this regard, Landry
tried to help. For the rest of my career he always referred to me
as "a starter," and it was true I was always inserted in key passing situations, but it didn't seem to me to ring true.

Landry explained his move of replacing me with Dorsett to
columnist Sam Blair of *The Dallas Morning News*: "Naturally
we had to have some special plans for Dorsett after giving up so
much to get him in the draft. I anticipated he would be starting
about mid-season but I didn't know he would be hurt in training
camp. So we had a delay and then we found ourselves in a difficult time of the season, trying to settle down for the stretch run.
When we made the change after the ninth game my timing
wasn't the best because we were going to Pittsburgh. That's
Preston Pearson's home too, and it hurt him. It took him a
game or two to get over it. But I had to do it to get Dorsett
ready for the playoffs."

Said Tony Dorsett: "Preston was playing excellent football. I knew I had the talent but I didn't know if I'd get off the
bench. I didn't want to complain but naturally I wanted to be in
the lineup."

"I hold no animosity toward Tony Dorsett," I was quoted
as saying. "We're friends and teammates. He's still a rookie and
I help him any way I can. There are so many things a running
back gains through experience, little things that can be the difference between making six yards and six points. I want to help
him and I want to help this team."

Sam Blair ended his column with a nice remark about me:
"The man has class, all right."

But it was painful. I really wonder if, as Landry said, he had intended to insert Dorsett earlier but was deterred by an injury. Or was it that I *couldn't* be replaced as long as I was a major part of an undefeated team? We lost one game, and I was out.

Even Tex Schramm tried to soothe feelings: "It's very unusual for a back to be so productive at his age. With the notable exception of Jim Brown, most running backs have short careers and a lot of injuries. Preston has a great knack of getting open, even when other teams are expecting us to throw to him. Physically, he's a unique individual to have lasted so long."

Some people thought I lasted so long because I didn't have to take a pounding for long periods of time, carrying the ball about twenty times a game. I'm not sure I agree with this. When I wasn't starting, I was playing special teams, and how about the pounding you get there?

It didn't take long for me to think that Tony Dorsett might become the greatest running back of all time. I've never seen anyone quicker. He was fast, also, but plenty of backs have speed. Tony could literally turn on a dime. He was so good, in fact, that I don't think the Dallas fans gave him enough credit. He made things look *too* easy.

Over the years, I don't think Tony worked as hard as he should have during the off-season. And I thought he could have spent more time studying defenses than he did. This would have made him a better pass receiver. Old-time baseball players Jackie Robinson, Ty Cobb, and Ted Williams come to mind when I think of players with great ability who also pushed themselves to the limit. Tony didn't do that. But he still was among the very best ever to play the game.

Dorsett is a lot stronger than people think. He has power when he runs. And he's beautiful to watch. I wish people would try to make the moves Tony does. Maybe then they would know how hard it is, how rare is his talent. But I don't think Tony is a leader, though he could be. Staubach, Pugh, and Lee Roy Jordan were leaders. I don't think Tony wants to be.

I like Tony. It would be silly to hold resentment that he replaced me. He didn't make the decision, any more than I decided to leave the Steelers. Tony's son is a good friend of my youngest, Matthew.

I think Tony has suffered unjustly from innuendos. He was going to marry a beautiful black woman who died suddenly of an unusual illness. Somehow this was thought to be partially his fault, though the idea is patently absurd. Another woman who was referred to as Tony's girlfriend died from an overdose. In reality he'd dated her maybe three times, and hadn't seen her for a long time before she died. She wasn't his "girlfriend" at all.

Tony Dorsett is an example of the black athlete who gets shortchanged on off-the-field opportunities. He's good looking and has an attractive manner. Yet you seldom see him doing commercials. Danny White, on the other hand, sometimes seems to dominate the Dallas airwaves. Imagine what opportunities would await a *white* running back with Dorsett's ability and accomplishments.

My role in 1977, after being replaced by Tony, was to come in on obvious passing downs. Defenses started to look for me. But they couldn't stop me. I wonder if anyone has had a better year coming off the bench: I was a running back who caught 46 passes for 535 yards (11.6 average) during the regular season.

I don't think there should be any mystery about why I succeeded. I would catch 25 to 50 passes every day *before* practice began. I would try to catch them in every possible position. I would kneel down, lie down, fall down. I'd dive for balls. I even would close my eyes and try to catch them without seeing. Often you have to turn suddenly and the ball is right on you. If I could catch a ball with my eyes shut, I could catch it with just a moment to get a look at it.

It was also important to know the game. This came from hour after hour of study. I'd study a defense so long I figured I knew exactly what it would do. I knew where the defenders would be. I anticipated any adjustments or changes the defense might make, and then decided what I would do to compensate. I tried to figure what the right move was against every conceivable defense. It seemed not unlike chess. You can't be certain what the opponent will do, but you can prepare a counter to whatever it is.

Drew Pearson was another of the great Cowboys. People constantly asked if we were related. We each said no, relying on what our parents told us. But I wonder. I've met Drew's parents, his brothers and sisters, and of course know Drew very well. His family has many of the mannerisms of mine. It's almost startling. And Drew reminds me a lot of myself. He can fly off the handle, just as I can, and since our lockers were right next to each other's, we had our share of disagreements. I remember one in particular.

He brought me a football to autograph. The team autographs a lot of footballs, sometimes it seems almost a full-time job, but it's always been a task I welcome. Still, there had been a lot of them this day, and I said, jokingly, "How many are there?" my voice feigning weariness.

Drew leaped all over me. "If it was for a white boy, you'd do it right away," he snapped.

The football was for a man who couldn't have been more deserving. A black man who worked around the practice field, always helping out the players. He'd wash their cars, take care of any detail he could. He was just a nice man. When I'd made my remark I wasn't even thinking about who the football was for, and Drew completely misunderstood what I meant. Anyway, I resented what he said, and felt I could match any devotion he had to the rights and dignity of black people. But the argument was far from the only one we ever had. I guess we liked to fight with each other.

Drew was not fast, but he worked terrifically hard. He would stay after practice to perfect his skills, and he was generous in community work, just as I was. Drew would share his considerable knowledge with young players. He could run the most beautiful pass patterns you'll ever see (except for Ray Berry's), and he could catch the ball over the middle. The reason, I think, why he and I could catch the ball in a crowd, when others would drop it, was because we knew defenses. It wasn't that we had more courage. But *knowing* where a defender is going to be gives you confidence. The real fear is of being hit by someone you don't even know is around.

Drew Pearson was a free agent, along with such players as Benny Barnes, Dextor Clinkscale, Everson Walls, Cliff Harris, and Raphael Septien. The Cowboys were adept at tapping the free-agent market. I think being a free agent motivated Drew to work so hard. He is, of course, now the all-time Cowboy leader in pass receptions. He was not big, but he taught himself concentration, and he was a great clutch performer. His Hail Mary grab against Minnesota will never be forgotten by any who saw it.

Another colorful Cowboy was backup quarterback Clint Longley. He got into a couple of well-publicized fights with Roger Staubach and was sent to another team. What finally shoved Longley over the edge was the arrival of Danny White as backup quarterback. Staubach was always saying good things about White, which had to rankle Clint.

Longley had a couple of outstanding games for Dallas. In one of these he threw a fifty-yard touchdown pass to Drew Pearson in the last seconds for the winning touchdown in a 24–23 game against arch-rival Washington. Personally, I liked Longley. I think he just let things get to him. I wonder if Roger knows that after one of their fights Longley went to get a rifle he owned. The fracas could have ended up tragically if Longley hadn't had a change of heart.

I wasn't always crazy about Clint Longley's sense of humor. He once brought three rattlesnakes into the dressing room and turned them loose. I've never moved so quickly in my life. So did everyone else. After he'd had his fun, Longley calmly picked up his snakes and put them back in the bag.

The 1977 season was the third I was spending in Dallas alone. Linda refused to move, and I felt I just couldn't leave a career that grew better with age. Also, numerous opportunities were opening up for me in Dallas, and I was active in a variety of community affairs. So actually I had two homes. During the season I lived in Dallas. During the off-season I lived in Pittsburgh. It wasn't a healthy arrangement.

It surprised me how fans boo a player when he is sent to another city. But it happens all the time. I was unpopular with Steeler fans even though I'd had nothing to do with leaving the team. That was another reason why it hurt so much when Dorsett replaced me for the Pittsburgh game. I'd been eager to play in Three Rivers and have a big day. One teenager—eighteen, I believe—told Greg, "Your father is a bum. He's through as a football player."

Actually, the best was to come, but I didn't know that, and certainly Greg was too young to understand.

We took the Bears apart in our first 1977 playoff game, 37–7. *The Dallas Morning News* described what happened:

"Dallas totally, thoroughly destroyed the Bears in what was one of the most lopsided NFL playoff victories in memory. The Cowboys moved so well offensively that they were able to lose fumbles on their first two possessions and still steamroll over the Bears. They played so well defensively that Payton had just 31 yards on twelve carries (a 2.6 average) through three periods when the score had mounted to 34–0."

Charlie Waters intercepted three passes, and Too Tall and Harvey never gave the Bears a chance even to hope. D. D. Lewis was also outstanding, intercepting a pass and recovering a fumble. Both Robert Newhouse and Tony Dorsett outgained Payton (Newhouse had eighty yards, Dorsett had eighty-five, and Roger had to pass only thirteen times, completing eight).

I was injured and didn't play against the Bears, but was ready for the NFC championship against the Vikings. It was a good game for me, and the Cowboys. I made the key block on Carl Eller that let Tony Dorsett loose for an eleven-yard touchdown gallop, and caught a screen pass from Staubach for a thirty-two-yard gain, setting up a field goal by Efren Herrera. The final was 23–6, and I think the game marked the beginning of Ed Jones being recognized as a superstar. He was awesome. One of the most memorable hits was put on Viking punt returner Manfred Moore. Mark Washington grabbed him, and as he was trying to step away, Thomas Henderson blasted Moore head on. It was a sickening sight. Reporter Bob St. John wrote, "Moore appeared to be dead as the ball flew loose and Jay Saldi got it and went nine more yards to the Viking 35."

Robert Newhouse led all rushers with eighty-one, an effort you couldn't help but admire. Newhouse always played hard. I was filled with admiration for how he squeezed every ounce of performance out of talents that were not spectacular.

Harvey Martin recovered two fumbles in the Minnesota game, and Too Tall Jones had twelve tackles. One of these was a tremendous hit on Chuck Foreman, stopping him dead in his tracks and forcing him to fumble. Forcing is the right word. A runner hit this hard has no control over whether he holds onto the ball.

So it was on to my fourth Super Bowl. I knew many players never made a single one. I was getting a lot of recognition now, as the player Dallas called off the bench when we *had* to have yards, and also because I had set a Dallas record for those forty-six receptions by a running back. I intended this to be my best Super Bowl, though it clearly would be tough: We were going against Denver and their much-feared Orange Crush defense.

14
Super Bowl XII

Both teams entered Super Bowl XII with 14-2 records, but one of Denver's losses was to us. We had defeated the Broncos, 14-6, in the last game of the regular season, but their starting quarterback, Craig Morton, had played only a few downs. We knew we hadn't seen the real Denver team that day. The Broncos were thinking ahead to the playoffs, and were mainly concerned with not suffering any injuries.

I think the Broncos probably defeated slightly tougher teams than we did in the playoffs. They had knocked off mighty Pittsburgh and then a strong Oakland Raider team. It had been good to hear the Steelers moan. They contended they were a superior team to Denver. When we had complained about their dirty tactics in the Super Bowl, they replied with, "Who won the game?" That was my reply to them when they fell to the Broncos.

Coach Landry, in preparing us for the game, talked not only about the enthusiasm the Denver players would have, but about how fired up their fans would be. Landry thought of things like that. The Denver fans that year, in my opinion, second only to the Steeler fans in enthusiasm, really could be a factor. They were Denver's "twelfth man."

It didn't take a football wizard, however, to know what Denver's strength was. It was that magnificent 3-4 defense, the

Orange Crush, especially Denver's four linebackers. We particularly feared Randy Gradishar, Tom Jackson, and Bob Swenson, who were always aggressive. The Broncos also had former New York City street fighter Lyle Alzado at one defensive end, and Rubin Carter at nose guard. Jackson, Gradishar, and Alzado were all-pro.

The game was a big challenge for Roger Staubach. He and Craig Morton had vied for the starting role in Dallas, and although Roger ultimately won, many Dallas fans thought Morton should have come out on top. Craig had many boosters in Dallas. For Staubach to obtain the unanimous acclaim he deserved, he would have to do well against his friend. Our challenge was to match Denver in enthusiasm, while not getting so fired up that we would make stupid mistakes.

That was what we aimed for in our preparations: to get as high as we knew Denver would be, Rocky Mountain high. I wondered if it could be done—if a team could pump itself up artificially. It didn't require any effort to get enthusiastic for a Super Bowl. But what would it be like when one of your major goals was to get enthusiastic? It was important that this occur. Denver was riding a season-long adrenaline high, and they'd be on top of Pike's Peak by the time the whistle blew. We couldn't let the Broncos steamroll us off the field.

The Super Bowl was once again in New Orleans, but this time at the Louisiana Superdome. A ticket cost thirty dollars, but it was no problem getting three hundred dollars for one. People from Colorado flocked to the game. Of course, football-crazy, free-spending Texans weren't going to be discouraged by a high price either. There was a reason why the game, an economic bonanza for New Orleans, was scheduled for a five P.M. start, and it wasn't just because of television. "It goes without saying," said Super Bowl PR man Bill Curl, "that the merchants in this city are extremely happy with the five P.M. starting time. That late start means another night in the hotels, an extra night out on the town. And since most fans can't leave until Monday anyway, they just might stay over an extra day or two. Also, from the city's point of view, two better teams couldn't be playing here. I know that we've had a lot of Dallas Cowboy fans in New Orleans the past two weeks. Dallas people are spenders. They bring money and they spread it around. The merchants wanted them here. Denver will be the same way, I'm sure. This is a first-time team in the Super Bowl. Their fans have gone crazy. They'll be down here spending it up."

Because Denver was new to the Super Bowl, they were considered a "mystery" team. They weren't a mystery to us, of course. We knew all about them and how tough they were. But many fans didn't know about them. They weren't on national TV as often as the Cowboys, by now called America's Team. That nickname, by the way, was certainly a promotional stroke of genius, but some of us liked to think we had something to do with it also. We were a wide-open, exciting team. We never quit, as dramatically illustrated time and again by seemingly impossible come-from-behind wins. Many people told me they did indeed identify with us. We were known as a team with brains —this was to Landry's credit—not just a bunch of grunting muscle men. But the Cowboys were a team that didn't quit.

We had bigger "name" players than Denver. Staubach was the NFC's leading passer this year. Harvey Martin was voted MVP in the NFL on defense. Tony Dorsett had been offensive rookie of the year.

Our statistics were more impressive than Denver's. Staubach has passed for 2,620 yards to Morton's 1,929. Forgotten here, however, was that Morton suffered a conference-low eight interceptions. The Broncos rarely turned the ball over. It was said, not altogether in jest, that the job of the Bronco offense was merely to hold the ball, then punt the opponent back into its own territory. Scoring opportunities would be set up by the special teams and defense.

Denver's leading rusher was Otis Armstrong, with just 489 yards. The *leading* receiver was Riley Odoms, with 37 receptions. As a player used mainly in critical situations, I had 46! But we knew statistics weren't the measuring stick for this game. The Broncos had one of the great game-breakers of all time in Rick Upchurch. A major part of our preparations was aimed at Upchurch. We didn't want him beating us on a sensational run or catch.

Players experience a great deal of apprehension before a Super Bowl. I think this is why so many of the games have been conservatively played. Who wants to make a mistake in this biggest of games? You might be remembered forever for the wrong reason. I always felt comfortable in a Super Bowl, even in that first one with Baltimore. Because I'd studied so hard, prepared myself, I felt it was impossible I would forget what I had to do.

Super Bowls should feature the very best in execution. The teams competing are the cream. The stakes are the highest. It is inexcusable for a player to miss an assignment.

We knew Denver's chief aim would be to stop Tony Dorsett. If a team can advance the ball on the ground against you, you're in trouble. We wanted to use the aggressiveness of the Denver linebackers to our advantage. We intended to do a lot of trapping on Randy Gradishar. We thought he would take fakes. Against Tom Jackson, who liked to drop deep on pass coverage, we intended to pass underneath.

In the locker room just before heading out for the kickoff, I knew we had succeeded in getting ourselves up. Yes, it can be done. A team can manufacture a high by telling itself to. This game would be known for ferocious but clean hitting, and I could tell, just by looking at my teammates, seeing how pumped up they were, that they were ready. Denver was a three-point underdog; the wise money was with the Cowboys.

Coach Landry talked to us before we went out. He is a bigger man than many people believe, having seen him only on television. He is six feet one and a solid two hundred pounds, and you might guess he'd been a former defensive back in the NFL. He said, "Denver is going to be very high. We have to match this. But at the same time we must maintain our poise. It will be very noisy out there. Okay."

Maybe I'd seen what he hadn't, though I doubt it. Landry knows what is going on. But we already were high. What was good about his always-short talk was the reference to noise. It was terrific when we emerged onto the floor of the Superdome. I'd expected not to be able to hear. What I wasn't ready for was the blinding flash of color. Everything was a bright splash of Denver orange. The colors seemed bright as sunlight. I looked around, a bit surprised, and then I saw it: A lot of silver and blue was in the stands too. It just didn't register as quickly as the orange. Never let a player or fan tell you that a crowd isn't important. I think a crowd can often be the difference in a game. I knew we didn't want to play in front of a wholly Denver audience.

A contest went on in the stands, as surely as one took place on the field. The Orange versus the Silver and Blue. I thought the Bronco fans were louder, though not by much. It was bedlam, yet the crowd did not seem about to lose control of itself in a violent manner. I've seen this happen, and it can worry you. This crowd almost lifted the roof off the Superdome, but it was good, healthy, hearty cheering, from the first row to those who sat twenty stories high.

"The only thing flat in this game," wrote Sam Blair of *The Dallas Morning News,* "was the artificial turf." It was true. Both teams were sky-high, and so were the fans. Perhaps the only time things looked dark for us was on our first, failed offensive play, a double reverse, typical of Landry's daring style of play.

There were more than forty players on each team, but the outcome was determined by nine of them. Denver's five offensive linemen, and our four defensive linemen. It was a mismatch.

Statistically, Craig Morton had a terrible day, but it wasn't his fault. No man alive could have thrown the ball accurately under the pressure we put on. Morton just didn't have a chance. Harvey Martin, Randy White, Jethro Pugh, and Ed Jones were in his face from the beginning. At the start of the season, Denver had feared mainly that its offensive line wasn't strong enough, but this had been forgotten in the glow of a 14–2 season. Yet the worriers had been right all along.

Morton threw *four* interceptions in the first half. At this rate, he would have as many interceptions in *one game* as he'd had all year. Let Craig Morton himself explain: "We did the very thing today that we hadn't done all year and that's turn over the ball. Dallas is everything everyone says it is, but I knew that all along. They really put it to us today. There's no excuse. My hip felt fine. It had nothing to do with the way I played. Their line covered me up, and everything I tried to do against them, they had the right defense for it.

"As usual, Dallas was very well prepared. I tried to audible on them several times, but they'd slide over into the right defense. However, the interceptions had more to do with the pass rush they put on. On two of those my arm was hit when I was throwing. Another time I underthrew Moses when I was hurried, and the last time I just put a bomb up there trying to get us something in a hurry."

Randy Hughes intercepted two passes, setting up ten points, and also recovered two fumbles. We forced *eight* turnovers (four fumbles to go with the interceptions) in the game. The hitting on the field was as hard as I've ever seen.

It was hard on both sides. I have the utmost respect for the Orange Crush defense. Denver would have suffered an even greater defeat if the defense had not played such an outstanding game. I doubt if we would even have won had we also turned the ball over eight times.

The two interceptions by Randy Hughes were the key to our 13–0 lead at half time. Tony Dorsett made it 7–0 in the first quarter with a one-yard run, and Efren Herrera added thirty-five- and forty-one-yard field goals. He also missed three field goals, and our offense was sputtering at best. We just couldn't take advantage of the many opportunities the Broncos presented us. This was because the Denver defense was as good as advertised.

Tony Dorsett was injured, and he describes it with typically good humor: "They kept saying they were going to get me, and I told them the only way they could get me out of the game was to hurt me. And they did."

But this wasn't a dirty game. Twenty penalties were called, but they didn't have anything to do with the high road both teams followed. I can get steamed up contrasting the twenty penalties in this game with the *zero* infractions levied against the Steelers two years before.

The game was no nail-biter. Denver couldn't get past our big, talented front four. And Benny Barnes and Mark Washington also had interceptions, while sacks were recorded by D. D. Lewis, Randy White, and Harvey Martin (two). The crowd noise remained a deafening constant throughout—nothing could dampen the enthusiasm of those orange-clad Denver rooters—but the Broncos were being thoroughly beaten at the line of scrimmage. Ed Jones was a towering force. It was almost as if he should have been in another league. Aaron Kyle recovered a fumble when Jones and White simultaneously hit Craig Morton. Sights like these were guaranteed not to allow me to go overboard about the "fun" aspects of life in the NFL.

Coach Landry could have gotten on the offense at half time, but he didn't. He warned us that Denver had a deserved reputation as a "fourth quarter team," and that we should have a big incentive in taking that away from them. He also warned of Rick Upchurch, the game-breaker, who could set his teammates afire if we let him get loose for one of his spectacular runs.

Denver cut the lead to 13–3 in the third quarter on a forty-seven-yard field goal by Jim Turner, just a yard short of the Super Bowl record, but we didn't feel the Broncos would get any closer. It was clear who was dominating the game. Our front four was too big, tough, and talented. Most of the concern on the bench was with our performance on offense—we had lots of trouble with this tough bunch of Broncos—and with our special teams, who were playing poorly. But lose the game? That wasn't a big concern, at least to me. I knew the Broncos would be strong in the fourth quarter, but so would we.

We went up 20–3 on a Butch Johnson forty-five-yard touchdown catch from Roger. Butch described the play: "As I started to leave the huddle, Staubach told me to change my route and run a strong, deep post. Drew Pearson and Billy Joe DuPree had both cut across the middle, and I had a lot of open space out there." What Butch didn't mention was that his catch was spectacular, and it was made despite a finger that had been broken earlier in the game.

The Broncos had one last gasp. Rich Upchurch took the ensuing kickoff and roared back upfield sixty-seven yards, a Super Bowl record. This had to gall Landry. It was just what he'd warned against. The special teams just had an off day. But I could almost feel Landry thinking, *If I could just make these guys play as well as I coach*. Teams didn't surprise us very often, nor were we ever in my six years with the Cowboys beaten because Landry hadn't properly prepared us.

The Broncos started on our twenty-nine after the Upchurch return. On first down Morton threw a pass right into the hands of a surprised Too Tall Jones. Ed, with seventy yards of open field in front of him, dropped the ball, and a chance at everlasting fame. When I'm in the position where I know I can get away from him, I like to tell him about his poor hands. His missed chance at a record that would probably stand forever: longest pass interception in Super Bowl by a six-feet-nine lineman.

Coach Red Miller of the Broncos pulled Morton from the game after this throw. Morton was hurting, and there wasn't any chance in his psychological state that he would rally the desperate Broncos. Craig was a talented, heady quarterback. This day he just never had a chance.

Norris Weese relieved Morton, and the Broncos crossed our goal line for the only time shortly afterward. The big run was seventeen yards by ex-Cowboy Jim Jensen. Rob Lytle carried it in from a yard away. The third quarter ended with the Cowboys leading, 20–10, and that ocean of orange going crazy in the stands.

During the break before the fourth quarter, Denver Coach Red Miller held up four fingers, indicating "fourth quarter, Bronco time," and the impossible happened: The good people from Denver raised the volume! I didn't think it could get any louder. I'm sure the noise was magnified over other Super Bowls I'd been in because this was the first ever played indoors, but it would have been awesome anywhere.

The noise, I could see, made the Broncos stronger. It invigorated them. They had indeed been a fourth-quarter team, especially in Mile High Stadium, and they might have thought they were there now. That they'd gotten a lift from the crowd I didn't doubt. But we were professionals, and winning championships isn't easy.

Cliff Harris put it well: "They talk about emotion. Well, we have emotion. But it's an iceberg. You only see the tip. But it's there and it runs deep. We were ready. Just because we weren't jumping up and down doesn't mean we weren't emotional. We had been building to this for days, while everyone kept talking about Broncomania and all that stuff. No way we were going to get caught short for this game."

The Broncos never could get going, despite the increasingly frantic pleas from their fans. They gained a *total* of 156 yards the entire game! Their final hope disappeared when Harvey Martin crushed Norris Weese and Aaron Kyle recovered on the Bronco twenty-nine.

Landry sent in the next play: "Brown right, X-opposite shift, toss thirty-eight, halfback lead fullback pass to Y."

I love Robert Newhouse's description of what happened: "In the first place, I had just put a big glob of stickum on my hands before the play came in from the bench. Roger called it, and I said, 'Oh no, the ball will never get out of my hands.' Preston Pearson handed me a rag just before we broke the huddle and I did my best to wipe off as much of the stuff as I could. Then, after I got the ball and got to the outside, I looked down-field and saw so much open field that I thought seriously about running with it. But I knew it was one of Coach Landry's all-or-nothing plays, so I threw."

The result was a touchdown pass to the wide-open Golden Richards and a 27–10 lead. When Richards heard what New-house said about how he almost ran, he quipped: "Don't even tell me about it. It worked too beautifully to think that it might never have happened."

As for my own modest role: What good is a veteran if he doesn't have a rag handy when it's needed?

The countdown to the final gun was thrilling. At last the good Bronco fans were quieted, and now we could hear the din from the Cowboy rooters growing louder and louder, almost to a crescendo. It is greatly rewarding to work an entire season at the highest physical and mental levels and to know that you've accomplished all there is, that there isn't any more. You can't do better than to be a world champion.

Just before the final gun, Thomas Henderson, in a no-class display, lifted an Orange Crush cup above his head and crushed it in his fist. He shouted something about this being what we had done to Denver.

But I wasn't going to worry about Henderson. I prefer to remember what Sam Blair wrote in *The Dallas Morning News*: "Then it was over, Center John Fitzgerald reached down and picked up the game ball and the Cowboys started galloping to-ward the ramp to the locker room as the cheers thundered down through the massive stadium. And with that top on the Super-dome, they really do thunder!"

Harvey Martin and Randy White were voted co-MVPs of

the Super Bowl and were awarded new automobiles. "Why stop there?" said Bronco guard Tom Glassic. "Give everybody on defense a car. They damn sure deserve it."

The Broncos were a different act from the Steelers, who continued to complain that "the best team wasn't in New Orleans." Said Bronco center Mike Montler: "I think it's very fair to say that they whipped the hell out of us. There's just no nice way to explain it. Maybe a lot of things could have changed that, a lot of things being all those turnovers. But it is too late to do anything about that now."

Once again, the perceptive Tom Glassic: "As a unit, it's the best front four we've seen this year, and with our schedule we've seen some good ones. But the Dallas people complement each other so well, especially Martin and White on that one side. One guy will always give himself up to get another guy free. It's the total team concept with the Cowboys, and they have the talent and the coaching to go along with it."

The Cowboys dominated the game statistically, as well as on the field. We outgained the Broncos 325 to 156, an edge of more than 2 to 1, and Roger hit on 19 of 28 with no interceptions. We ran 71 plays to their 58, and held the ball for 38½ of the 60 minutes. It was a good game for me also. I was the game's leading pass receiver with 5, as our plan to go underneath Tom Jackson's deep pass drops presented us several excellent opportunities. With Tony Dorsett out, I was once again in my regular position, helping to make the fourth quarter ours, not Denver's.

The Cowboys' owner, Clint Murchison, accepted the Vince Lombardi trophy, given to the Super Bowl champion each year, from Commissioner Pete Rozelle, and Murchison had generous words for his coach: "I'm going to give this to Tom Landry, who is not only coach of the year, but coach of the century."

This was high praise. But was it just given in the joy of the moment? I thought about coaches, the few I'd known, and the many I'd read and heard about. Surely there were those who were Landry's superior in one area or another of the game, and all the other aspects that comprise the sport (motivating, scouting, judging talent, and so on), but I wonder if any of them really understood the overall tactics of the sport better than our coach.

Everything considered, however, the difference in this

game was our defensive line. They won it for us. I find it interesting that most Super Bowls have been won by the defense, and this was one of the clearest examples of why. Even though our imaginative and potent offense had an off-day, Denver wasn't going anywhere against us, and all we needed was a few big plays: those touchdown passes to Butch Johnson and Golden Richards. Again, all the analysis in the world can be thrown out and this substituted: Our defensive front four outplayed Denver's offensive front five.

The Super Bowl win over Denver was the last game for fourteen-year-veteran offensive guard Ralph Neely. "I'm going in for my fourth knee operation when I come back from Hawaii next month," he said, "and four is a good number to quit on." What he said next, about his teammates, would be exactly what I would later feel: "I'll miss them, but I won't miss the physical part of playing football."

Clint Murchison footed the tab for a big victory party, which began the next day at one A.M. Players who wanted to get a short rest before partying could do so. Entertainment included Waylon Jennings, Charley Pride, and Willie Nelson.

John Denver, another singer, was seen hugging a little girl in an Orange Crush T-shirt after the game. "Hey, John," a Dallas fan called to him. "If you had changed your name to John Dallas, you'd have a party to go to tonight."

"I'm loyal to the Broncos," Denver replied.

Once again I spent the off-season in Pittsburgh. It was clear the marriage wasn't what it once had been. Linda and I were apart too much, and going in different directions even when we were together. I think we both knew the handwriting was on the wall, but we didn't talk much about it. Of course, we tried not to let Greg or Matthew know anything was wrong. When I had to head back to Dallas for my twelfth season, I kissed them good-bye, as I'd done before, but I was worried about what the future held for all of us.

15
Super Bowl XIII

I would never grow tired of it, no matter how often it happened. Here it was, January 21, 1979, just a little more than a year since we had demolished Denver, and we were back again for Super Bowl XIII, my fifth. I wonder what life would be like if it were all a Super Bowl. I keep thinking I'd love it.

We were playing none other than our old friends, the Pittsburgh Steelers. The memory of the fiasco of Super Bowl X, with the Steelers getting away with aggravated assault and battery on down after down, was still fresh in our minds. For newcomers and rookies, we painted a vivid picture. We wanted them to know what to expect.

Pittsburgh hadn't changed much. Maybe a little, I guess: for the worse. The Steelers had added a cornerback, Ron Johnson, a player I consider overaggressive and dirty. I thought he should fit right in with the Steelers. Also, Donnie Shell, a rough player, a terrific hitter, but not dirty. And linebacker Dennis Winston, who in my opinion was and still is one of the dirtiest players the game has ever known. Winston seems to enjoy hitting people on the head with his forearms and fists. None of this is necessary. It just causes injuries. I think the philosophy of the Steelers encouraged dirty play. In other words, the fish stinks from the head. Coach Noll wanted the Steelers to intimidate, and it was just a small step from there to a "dirty" brand of ball. Dennis Winston, incidentally, was nicknamed "Dirt."

So the Steelers hadn't changed. I hoped we had. I knew we were older and wiser. We hadn't had Tony Dorsett in Super Bowl X. Harvey Martin, Randy White, and Ed Jones were much improved. They were genuine all-pros. And this time *we* were the defending champions. The Steelers would have to take the title away from us. I knew this was a game *players* would pay to see. It was going to be something.

I'd had my greatest season, breaking my own Cowboy record (it still stands) for receptions by a running back, 47, good for 526 yards. I did this despite the fact that defenses *knew* Roger would be throwing to me. I was successful because I knew what they were going to do to try to stop me. I was now the dean of all NFL running backs, the running back with the most years of service. Newspapers sought me out for interviews. *Pro Football* magazine did a nice article on me, titled PRESTON PEARSON—KING OF THE SUPER BOWL. But I knew I would trade every moment I'd ever had on the football field for a win over the Steelers in Super Bowl XIII.

Each team came into the game on a roll. We had crushed Los Angeles, 28–0, for the NFC championship, and the Steelers brutalized Houston and Earl Campbell, 34–5. Against the Rams I caught several balls, including an important eighteen-yard pass from Roger on third and ten that took us to the Los Angeles three. The oddsmakers thought the Steelers were four points better than us. Each team was trying to become the first ever to win three Super Bowls, a considerable incentive. The Steelers were coming into the game 16–2. We were 14–4. There was no doubt whatever that we were the best of each conference.

At tight end the Steelers had 250-pound Benny Cunningham, a tank, backed up by Randy Grossman. We started Billy Joe DuPree, with fifteen-year veteran Jackie Smith replacing injured Jay Saldi as backup. The Steeler wide receivers were Lynn Swann and John Stallworth. We countered with Drew Pearson, Tony "Thrill" Hill, and Butch Johnson. Primary running backs would be two of the best the game has seen:

Tony Dorsett and Franco Harris. The opposing quarterbacks were Roger Staubach and Terry Bradshaw.

Jon Kolb would go against Harvey Martin when the Steelers were on offense. Perhaps the strongest lineman in the league against perhaps the quickest. Ray Pinney, just 240 pounds, against Too Tall Jones, was a mismatch, we felt. I expected to see Larry Brown replacing Pinney. Sam Davis and Mike Webster were expected to double-team Randy White, with Gerry Mullins against Larry Cole. I hoped Ed Jones would do the sort of job Ernie Holmes had done with Andy Maurer in Super Bowl IX.

On defense for the Steelers, Holmes had been replaced by Steve Furness, a solid player. Joe Greene, Dwight White, and L. C. Greenwood were back. The starting linebackers were Ham, Lambert, and Robin Cole.

I hoped Tom Landry would change just one aspect of his preparations for the Steelers from what we'd employed in Super Bowl X, but it was not to be. He saw as clearly as anyone the type of tactics they would use, but he continued to champion the turn-the-other-cheek philosophy. Perhaps he just couldn't believe the jobbing we'd gotten from the officials the first time around. But that's not what he said, and he's a man who can let you know his feelings. He continued to say we would lose our poise and concentration if we retaliated. Maybe he was such a purist about football that he hated to see the symphony he conducted on the field, right down to calling every offensive play, disrupted by activity that had no place in the game. Perhaps he felt that *his* team would play as it should. I don't know what he felt, only what he said: "Don't fight back."

Dallas columnist Skip Bayless described what he thought the game would be like: "It's macho vs. chivalry. Blood and guts vs. head and heart. Ugly vs. pretty. Snarls vs. smiles."

We were hardly as nice as Bayless described. Many Cowboys might take offense at being called "pretty." But Bayless wasn't far off the mark. I didn't think many fans, unless they were from Pittsburgh or related to one of the Steelers, would be cheering against us.

There were some anonymous death threats made against players before the game. This shook everyone up a bit, I think, and certainly added to the tension. Incredibly, CBS had scheduled the movie *Black Sunday* to air shortly after Super Bowl XIII concluded. In *Black Sunday,* a group of terrorists hijack the Miami-based Goodyear blimp for an attack on the Orange Bowl on Super Bowl Sunday. The site of Super Bowl XIII? The Orange Bowl.

Thomas Henderson had done a lot of talking before the NFC championship game about how good he was and what we were going to do to the Rams. This doesn't accomplish anything positive and can be self-defeating if it serves to fire up the opposition. Just before the game ended, Too Tall Jones, smiling at the television cameras, walked over to where Henderson was sitting. Unfortunately, the network did not pick up what Too Tall said: "Thomas, you're going to have to shut up, man. You're gonna wear us all out. We had to come out here and work ourselves to death just backing up all the things you said. I'm tired and wish you would just cool it. Keep talking like that and we'll have to play so hard against Pittsburgh in the Super Bowl that it'll take us a week to recover."

But Thomas Henderson didn't stop talking. He delighted in entertaining the press with what we intended to do to the Steelers. It got Thomas a lot of publicity. One paper called it "the Henderson Super Bowl." Thomas got his picture on the cover of *Newsweek.*

I hurt my hand in practice the Thursday before the Super Bowl, and was listed as "questionable" for the game. "The loss of Pearson," wrote the Associated Press, "would be crucial to the Cowboys, who use him effectively as a pass receiver on third-down plays."

Tom Landry expressed concern that I might not be able to play. "It would hurt us," he said, "because he's a specialist and extremely valuable to us."

The thing is, I wasn't worried about missing the game. And I mean, *the* game. It was tremendously important to all of us, but I think to no one more than me.

A number of Cowboys talked to the press about the rough tactics used by the Steelers in Super Bowl X. A lot of this was to get it out in the open, in the hope that it would not happen again. "I was just a few feet away," said Drew Pearson, "when Glen Edwards hit Golden with a knee and broke his ribs. An official was right there and he didn't throw a flag. I couldn't believe my eyes. The Steelers were hitting and holding us all the way downfield. Even under the old rules a defender could only bump a receiver two or three times, but that didn't bother them. They were all over us. We're not concerned about these officials letting them get away with what they did in that Super Bowl. There have been a lot of rule changes the last three years and the officials have been caught in a lot of controversy. If the Steelers try to bump us all the way down the field, they'll have to call it."

Fans could take some of what Drew said with a grain of salt. We *were* concerned about it happening again. We mentioned it so that the officials, and especially the public, would be aware of what had happened. We didn't want a repeat. The purpose of saying we weren't concerned about "these officials," the new ones, was so they wouldn't take it upon themselves to "get" us. No sense in making them mad.

Our respected tight end Billy Joe DuPree spoke up: "The Steelers were the most penalized team in the NFL that season. It was miraculous how they got so clean in those two weeks before our game."

The press was interested in the story. They asked Chuck Noll about our charges, and his answer was an affront to the common sense of anyone who witnessed Super Bowl X: "I resent the question in a way," he said. "There is intimation that because we weren't penalized we were successful in getting away with something beyond the rules. We don't play that kind of football. In that game we simply played good solid football."

Coach Noll knew better than this. We don't play that kind of football? He's the coach of that outfit. He knew exactly the type of tactics the Steelers used, and so did everyone else in the league.

Coach Landry even spoke up. "If I were Chuck," he said, "I'd be feeling the same way. They got away with a good thing in 1976. Let's just hope it doesn't happen again.

"The new rule which allows the one chuck at five yards or less will change things—they can't continue to bang a receiver around all the way downfield in an attempt to keep him out of his route.

"And, we're supposed to have the finest officiating crew available for this game. The officials with the best records over the season are going to be calling the game, so you have to assume they'll do a good job. If our best can't handle the pressure of a game like this, then we're in trouble."

Landry and Drew Pearson were doing the same thing. Saying we got a very bad deal from the officials in Super Bowl X, warning that we didn't want to be victimized again, and then assuring that we weren't worried about the current crop of officials who would be working the game, because they were "the best." What was that group in 1976? The worst?

Even Commissioner Pete Rozelle had to respond, and this august arbiter virtually admitted we'd been treated shoddily in Super Bowl X. "I believe Tom's half right," Rozelle said. "Well, three-fourths right. But this is more than a problem for the officials. It has to start by all the coaches in the league controlling their players."

This last was ridiculous. Chuck Noll didn't want to "control" his players, and why should he? They were getting away with fouls which they thought, probably correctly, helped them win a Super Bowl. I agree that a coach should control his players. Landry did. But when the coach refuses, it is the job of the officials to assess appropriate penalties.

Charlie Waters joined the growing chorus that was hoped would give us a fairer shake in Super Bowl XIII. He said the Super Bowl X officials "choked," and "if that happens again Sunday, the Cowboys will know what to do. If they don't call it, we'll play their game."

I thought, *If only this were true.* We could handle the Steelers. We could have taken care of ourselves three years ago, and were an infinitely more capable team now. But I was afraid Charlie's outburst was more smoke than fire. He knew what Coach Landry was telling us: Don't crawl into the sty and slosh around with the Steelers. Landry was hoping that by putting everyone on notice, he was forcing the hand of the officials. It was a good idea, what we were doing. Probably it was the mature thing to do. There was just one problem: I knew it wouldn't change the Steelers, and I had reservations about how stiff the backbones of the officials would be. The Steelers were a frightening team. You could really believe they would kill you, the way they talked and acted on the field. They could kill you with their bare hands with just a short burst of violence. I have to believe the men in the striped shirts had this in the back of their minds.

It was a gray Sunday afternoon for Super Bowl XIII. A depressing day. Not the kind of atmosphere one would think would provide the most spectacular offensive show in Super Bowl history. But that was what would happen in this thrill-a-minute game.

I knew we were well prepared for the game of our lives. We were defending champions, but holding on to the title would be vastly more difficult than winning it in the first place. We knew if we defeated the Steelers we'd be remembered as one of the game's great teams. This was important to us. You don't sacrifice as much as professional football demands if you don't have dreams and the highest goals.

Coach Landry talked to us as he had before Super Bowl X: "We know what they're going to do. We know how to respond to it. Just don't lose your poise and concentration. Okay."

Pittsburgh had derided us in the two weeks prior to the game, intimating we were a "pansy" team. In Steelerese, this means we didn't try to turn everything into a brawl. We figured the plain-thinking Steelers would be looking for us to come out with something tricky, so after returning the opening kickoff to our 28, we ran Tony Dorsett at them 3 times. He gained 9, 16, and 13 yards. Take that. Right down their throats.

Now that we had them thinking run, we decided to use the razzle-dazzle. We were at their 34, and Staubach handed to Dorsett, who handed to Drew Pearson, who was going to throw to a wide-open Billy Joe DuPree for the touchdown that would jump us out in front. But the usually reliable Drew fumbled the ball. It was the first of many times when a break could have gone either way, and it went to Pittsburgh. The Steelers recovered on their own 47, and Bradshaw promptly drove them 53 yards in 7 plays for a touchdown, the score coming on a 26-yard pass to John Stallworth.

Pittsburgh 7 Dallas 0.

Bradshaw had truly matured as a quarterback. He'd grown up, at least as an athlete. This day surely will be remembered as the greatest he ever had. He would be voted the MVP of Super Bowl XIII, and he deserved it.

The Steelers hadn't changed, though. They were the same

snarling, lips-curled, threat-issuing, rules-breaking outfit we'd remembered from Super Bowl X. And, of course, no one would think of giving tit for tat, because no one would disobey Coach Landry. Already the Pittsburgh secondary was mauling Drew Pearson (I guess they chose him because Golden Richards was gone). The game would become a nightmare for Drew. Still, I thought it might work out. We were a much better team than the one they had manhandled three years earlier.

We scored on the next possession after the Steeler touchdown. On third and long from the Steeler thirty-nine, beating a frenzied, scream-filled, all-out Steeler blitz, Roger hit Tony Thrill Hill streaking down the left sideline. Drew got a good shield block on Mel Blount and Hill went all the way.

Pittsburgh 7   Dallas 7.

Both times we had the ball we moved it. It was a sign of what would happen all day. "This one was a fight all the way," Joe Greene would say. "In that last Super Bowl it really wasn't that equal. We had a class team and the Cowboys were a young team that used a lot of flim flam. But this bunch out there today wasn't playing pansy football. They were *playing*."

I would hope so. I respect Joe Greene (who doesn't?), but I question what he calls "pansy" football in Super Bowl X. We almost won that game. And we didn't have the officials on our side.

Early in the second period the Steelers got a dose of Dallas toughness. Bradshaw rolled to his right, hit Franco Harris on the hip with the ball, regained possession, and was grabbed by Hollywood Henderson and Mike Hegman. Mike tore the ball loose at the thirty-seven and ran untouched into the end zone!

Dallas 14   Pittsburgh 7.

We were atop a Matterhorn of adrenaline. It took Bradshaw only three plays to bring us down from the cliff. On the third he tossed a seventy-five-yard score to the brilliant John Stallworth, sixty-five of the yards coming after Stallworth broke loose from Aaron Kyle.

Dallas 14   Pittsburgh 14.

The Steelers continued their illegal tactics, especially against Drew Pearson, but the *Cowboys* drew the personal-foul penalty. It was called on Billy Joe DuPree, a very clean player, and this started the Steelers going on a touchdown with just

twenty-six seconds remaining in the half. Bradshaw hit Rocky
Bleier for the score from seven yards out.

Pittsburgh 21   Dallas 14.

Our touchdown against Pittsburgh in the first quarter was
the first they'd allowed in that period in eighteen games. The
thirty-five points scored in the first half were the most ever in a
Super Bowl. Terry Bradshaw had passed for 253 yards, a record
for the Super Bowl, and there was still half the game to play.
There had been so many ups and downs, so much excitement.
One writer called it the "superest of Super Bowls." Even more
was yet to come.

The Cowboys dominated the third quarter. The Steelers
never did do much on the ground, just 66 yards total for the
game (Dorsett outrushed the Pittsburgh *team,* gaining 96 by
himself), and Bradshaw managed only about 60 yards passing
the entire second half.

We should have tied the game in the third quarter. The reliable veteran Jackie Smith, of all people, dropped an easy pass
in the end zone that would have tied the game. It was just a
short lob. Smith was all alone. And he dropped it. Roger, seeing
Jackie Smith by himself, threw the ball more easily than he
normally would have, and it was a bit low, but it was the kind of
pass even youngsters should hold on to. I feel bad for Jackie. He
had a great career, and at least in Dallas he is largely remembered for that ball he would have caught 999 times out of 1,000.
We settled for a Raphael Septien field goal.

Pittsburgh 21   Dallas 17.

That was the score as we entered the fourth quarter. This
one I felt we would win. We had momentum, and I think every
one of the more than 100 million viewers in America could sense
we were the stronger team. I felt ten-feet tall. I knew beating
the Steelers in the Super Bowl would be more than anything
else I could accomplish in my athletic life.

We did get in a fight with the Steelers. Actually, I did. I
couldn't take it anymore. Drew had been brutalized throughout
the game. On this particular play he was hit from behind by
Mike Wagner and knocked down. Then I watched with rising
anger and incredulity as Wagner dragged Drew along the
ground, trying to bounce him on his head. He just kept dragging
and bouncing. I was too old a head to expect any penalty flag.

I raced at Wagner from behind, trying to break his collar-bone with a shot. He started to swing at me. I'll never forget what he said: "You didn't have to hit me. I was going to stop."

When?

Violate one of Tom Landry's rules and you can expect a healthy fine, or maybe to be looking for a new place to play. But he never said anything to me about my run-in with Wagner. I know I felt good about what I'd done. The idea of the Steelers, coldly calculating, had been to do to Drew Pearson what they had done to Golden Richards. It wasn't right to let it happen.

Early in the fourth quarter, with the Cowboys getting stronger, two things happened: The Steelers got lucky (call it getting on a good roll, if you want), and field judge Fred Swearingen cost us the Super Bowl (or *gave* it to Pittsburgh, if you prefer).

Terry Bradshaw, *trying to throw the ball away,* threw a long pass over the head of Lynn Swann. Fred Swearingen threw a flag and called pass interference, giving the ball to Pittsburgh on our twenty-three. I think the play could have been called one of two ways. First, it could have been ruled no foul. Second, Swann could have been called for offensive interference. No one, not even Lynn Swann, thought he had been interfered with. The television replay, shown endlessly, revealed that no foul whatever had been committed.

It was not even Swearingen's job to call the interference. He didn't have a good look at it. An official standing much closer to the action did nothing, but I have little respect for this man also. He could have stepped in and overruled Swearingen. It happens all the time. He should have said, "I saw the whole thing. I'm sorry, but there wasn't any pass interference." He said nothing, and Pittsburgh, which had been back on its heels, was set up on our twenty-three with beautiful field position.

But the Steelers should be given credit. They took advantage of the break. Franco roared up the middle for twenty-two yards and a touchdown, a touchdown the Steelers never should have had.

Pittsburgh 28   Dallas 17.

Let Benny Barnes describe the play that ultimately was the difference in the game: "Swann ran right up my back. When

I saw the flag, I knew it was on him. I coudn't believe the call. Maybe he needs glasses. Maybe he was for Pittsburgh."

The Steelers got another break on the ensuing kickoff. Roy Gerela intended to pound the ball into the end zone, but he kicked the ball poorly and it went dribbling in the direction of defensive tackle Randy White, the last man we wanted to field the ball. He was playing with a broken thumb, though in the best of circumstances we didn't want Randy handling the ball. He was supposed to lateral it to a back, but he had such difficulty picking it up there was no time. He fumbled. Pittsburgh recovered. Terry Bradshaw promptly hit Lynn Swann with an eighteen-yard touchdown pass.

Pittsburgh 35   Dallas 17.

The score indicated a rout, but actually we were outplaying them. And outhitting them too. But those two lightning-quick touchdowns, neither of which should have occurred, gave Pittsburgh fourteen points. The first was set up by the terrible interference call. The second by Randy White's fumble. White would not have fumbled if the Steelers had not been kicking off. They would not have been kicking off if Benny Barnes hadn't been penalized unfairly.

We were eighteen points behind (Pittsburgh scored fourteen points in nineteen seconds) and just six minutes, fifty-one seconds remained when the Steelers kicked off again. Most teams would have quit. We didn't. Not only that, we still thought we could win the game. We had all the pride America's Team should have, and we took it right to the Steelers. I was out in the middle of all of it, proud of my teammates, and catching a couple of passes also. Before this game was over the Steelers were wondering from which direction the truck that hit them had come.

The Cowboys drove down the field, scoring on Roger's seven-yard throw to Billy Joe DuPree.

Pittsburgh 35   Dallas 24.

Ho hum, I could see some of the Steelers thinking. They had been openly celebrating on the field with six minutes, fifty-one seconds to go.

We recovered an onside kick. Again we went into the end zone, this time on a four-yard toss to Butch Johnson.

Pittsburgh 35   Dallas 31.

There were less than thirty seconds remaining as we lined up for another onside kick. We had the attention of the Steelers now. I looked at them again, those feared monsters of the seventies, and they looked tired, beaten. They were ready to be taken. We had come at them again and again, resisted fighting with them (except for my tiff with Wagner), outgutted them despite a world of adversity, and *they* were the ones who were physically exhausted. We could have played forever.

Pittsburgh recovered the onside kick. There were twenty-two seconds left. My last memory of Super Bowl XIII is Terry Bradshaw falling on the ball two times after taking snaps from his center, cuddling the ball close to his body, fearing, no, *knowing* that if we got it back, we would score and beat them.

This game hurt more than any other. I was more angry than anything else when it was over, and told reporters exactly what I thought of the officiating: "We can't beat another team that's got fourteen or more players out there. That call [the interference penalty against Benny Barnes] took it all away from us." Being angry allowed me to vent emotions. For the rest of my days, the hurt will grow much deeper. I try to explain what happened to people, people who don't remember how it was, who say, "The Steelers took you twice, huh?" But already I grow weary. I certainly don't want to seem a poor loser filled with alibis. Before I was quoted about "fourteen or more players," the reporter had gone out of his way to describe me as "a restrained, controlled sort who normally does not lash out."

Nor does Roger Staubach normally "lash out." Here is what he wrote in his book, *Time Enough to Win*:

> I never could figure out how Benny could be running fullblast downfield and intentionally trip a receiver *behind* him, which is where Swann was. The whole thing took place near our bench. I was standing right there and saw it. When I saw the flag I thought it was interference on Swann for pushing or something like that.
>
> The official right on the play was back judge Pat Knight. He made the first signal, waving his arms back and forth for an incompletion. Then here came

the flag from over in the middle of the field. All our guys started yelling because they thought it was interference on Swann. Incredibly, field judge Fred Swearingen saw the play differently from everybody else in the Orange Bowl . . .

That whole chain of events was ironic. Swann's play was the biggest of the drive yet wasn't the result of anything he did. It was some idiot official throwing a flag when he's out of position to see the play right. And another official standing on top of the play allowing himself to be talked into a penalty that wasn't there.

To understand how bad the call was, one needs to know Roger, and how unlike him it is to call someone an "idiot." But, then, even NFL Commissioner Pete Rozelle publicly admitted that the interference penalty was a horrible call.

These things should not be allowed to happen. This is the most important sporting event in the United States, and the outcome should not be determined by an official. The players should decide which team is best. I won't make suggestions about how future injustices should be remedied, but the NFL needs to find a way.

The Steelers are hailed as the Team of the Seventies. They won four Super Bowls. But they were given one of them (and maybe two) by the officiating. Had it been different, the Cowboys would have won three (maybe four), and we would have been voted the decade's best. Surely we were in more playoff games in the 1970s than Pittsburgh, and our overall record was superior.

But I've had my say, and I'll let it rest. I try to tell myself that in a just world we would have won that game, but the record says otherwise, and the book is closed.

16
Looking Back— and Ahead

Linda was driving me to the airport. I was heading back to Dallas for the 1979 season, my thirteenth, but neither of us was thinking about that. We were both lost in our own worlds, yet our thoughts were the same.

"I'm going to get a divorce," she said quietly.

I thought that over. I tried to get close to how I felt. This really wasn't a surprise, and all I could think was that I was relieved someone had finally said it. We'd been living together for half a year each season ever since I'd come to the Cowboys, but our worlds were different all year round.

"Okay," I said.

There really wasn't anything to add. This was best, and despite a thousand conflicting emotions (how could it be different? Linda had been my college sweetheart—we had shared so much together), I knew I would have to accept it. She liked Pittsburgh and the life she'd built there. I was certain I'd found my place in Dallas. Of course, later there would be many regrets on my part, but they need not be gone into here. We were able to behave in a civilized manner where the children were concerned, not a common experience if what I've seen with other

divorces is the norm. Greg and Matthew Jay stay with me sum-
mers and as many holidays as possible, and I visit whenever I
can in Pittsburgh. The rest of the time they live with their
mother.

The 1979 season (11–5 win-loss record, knocked out in the
playoffs, 21–19, in a heartbreaking loss to Los Angeles) may
have been my best yet. They don't keep track of this record, but
I think I hold it: I caught 26 passes in 1979, and either scored a
touchdown or made a first down on *23 of them.* In the contest
that decided the Eastern Division championship, a thrilling
35–34 last-second win over Washington, I caught critical passes
of 22 and 25 yards to set up the game-winner.

Incredibly, Gil Brandt wanted to *cut* my pay for the next
season. "You caught forty-seven the year before. Just twenty-
six this year."

"Twenty-three of those were crucial plays," I said. "Those
are the kind of plays I get called on to make. I'm the best you've
got in the clutch."

"You're not playing as much as you used to." Forget sentiment in the NFL. I could have been contributing to the Cowboys for a century, and it wouldn't mean a thing. Of course, I
didn't expect to be paid for what I'd done in the past.

"It's not my fault I didn't play more. Landry only brings
me in for key downs."

"You're not a regular." Gil Brandt is not a warm-hearted
man.

"Look at it this way, if you can. The Yankees don't ask
Goose Gossage to take less money because he doesn't pitch as
many innings as a starter. Gossage is more valuable than any
starter. He comes in when the game is on the line. That's what I
do. Try to think of me as Goose Gossage."

"That's baseball."

Good grief, I thought.

We finally worked it out. It was *illegal* to cut my pay, but
this was impossible to explain to Gil Brandt. I finally went on
TV to explain my case, and the unwanted publicity persuaded
Brandt to give me a 10 percent increase.

I've never checked it out, but I think my career may be the
longest a running back has ever played in the NFL. I don't know
how many years Bill Brown of the Vikings competed. It seemed

a long time. He's the only running back I can think of who might have played longer than I did.

We went 12–4 in 1980 (Danny White had taken over for the retired Roger Staubach) and defeated Los Angeles and Atlanta in the playoffs. We had to go to the last forty-nine seconds to defeat the Falcons, a drive in which I caught a key pass to keep us going. The last game I would ever play, though I didn't know it at the time, was a 20–7 loss to Philadelphia in the NFC championship.

Because I have spent so many years in the NFL, people ask me many questions about the pro game. One that comes up frequently is, "What is a game plan?" The mysterious, magical game plan is something every TV commentator talks about, but no one ever sees one. At least *I've* never seen one in public print, nor has anyone I know. I've decided to reprint the following actual game plan so that fans can see for themselves what one looks like. When it was given to me, it was neatly typed on two plain, white sheets of paper. Many game plans take up only one sheet of paper, but this was composed by Coach Landry, and his are reputed to be among the more elaborate:

OFFENSIVE GAME PLANS-49ERS-10/12/80

RUSHING

TOSS 49/28 FB LD	I/FB MOT
(W.REV.)	
TOSS 38/39 (32/33 G″)	BR.SLOT-X DIV.AC/4
	REC.
TOSS/DIVE 37/36	I/BR.FLIP HB MOT/4
GEORGE	REC.
TOSS 33/32	I W.DIV.AC
FAKE TOSS R/L CO.	
32/33 DO. X	I
DIVE 49/28 TW. FB LD	BR. FLIP
21/40 SPECIAL DO. X	I FLIP
H 21/40 FOLD	RED EA. (+5)
	ROV.DIV.AC.

20 TRAP   RED W.SH.DIV.

SL. 38/39 / F 94/95 / DIVE   J.H.
  33/32/G

SL. 34/35 (Y REV.)   BROWN

SL. 24/45   DO. X   I R FLIP

SL. 43 FB WHAM   R.R.

TAKE OFF RT.   I.R.

PO. 45/24 "O"   RED

PO. 47/26 NOP   I W.SH.DIV.

PO. 47/26 G-OPT   RED

PO. 49/28 WGO   RED EA. ROV. + 5

FIRE PASSES

FIRE 26/47 Y S.O., Y-9   X OPP/3 REC.I FLIP
                                          SLOT X SH. MOT.

FIRE PO. 47/26 NOP W-3

                    DO.X   BROWN

FIRE ROLL RT/LT

                    4 RECS   BR.FLIP HB MOTION

FIRE ROLL LT/RT Y S.O.,   RED/RED EAGLE ROV.
  T.O.   OPP.

FIRE PO. 47/26 NOP QB   I W.S.D.
  PASS, Y BENCH, Y
  POST

FIRE SL. 47/26 B SHOOT   RED W.S.D.
  QB PASS HB DELAY

FIRE PO. 49/28 WGO   RED FLIP
  BOOTLEG SPEC.
  LT/RT DO.X

FA 41/20 Q.S.LT/RT Y/W   BROWN/RED EAGLE
                                          ROV. OPP.

DECEPTIVES

DRAW LT/RT FB   BR. & I/BR.EAGLE
  SLANT/ROV WHAM   ROV.OPP

DRAW RT/LT   J.H./RED

DRAG ST/WK   I/3 RECS.RED FLIP SLOT

16 SC.	BR./3 RECS RED FLIP SLOT

RUN SITUATION PASSES

81/51/61	RED/J.H./3 RECS. RED FLIP SLOT
82 X SL.OUT B CIRCLE	BROWN
SPEED 83/83, 63	RED X OPP/J.H. & RED X OPP.
63 WAGGLE LT/RT	RED FLIP X MOT
HOT 74/L/R 64	I/BROWN
SP 54 A TURN IN/59 A CO.WAGGLE LT/RT	J.H.
L/R 66	J.H.& BR/3 RECS.BL.FLIP SLOT
15 WAGGLE RT/LT/16 WAGGLE LT/RT	I/BR
L/R 16 Y BENCH/R/L 16	BROWN/RED
L/R 16 Y & X CORNER W ZOOM	RED FLIP W MOTION
CUP 87/67 X POST	J.H.

PASS SITUATION PASSES

3RD 3, 4, 5

81/61 AUD 17 VS DOG	RED
16 Y&X CORNER W ZOOM	RED FLIP W MOTION
12 A CROSS B OPT	SP ORANGE
HOT 17	SP OR TI FB HI

3RD 6-12

HOT/SPEED 12 S.Ls/POST	SP ORANGE
R/L 84 W BENCH/W TURN IN	SP OR TI FB HI
HOT 17	SP OR TI FB HI

L/R 16	SP OR TI FB HI
L/R 64 Y BENCH/Y TN.IN	SP ORANGE
PO.49/28 EGO (W. REV.LT/RT 4 RECS.	SP ORANGE
L/R 15 DO. S.L.	SP BR UP
L/R 66	SP BR UP
L/R 18 DO. CORNER A & X CROSS	SP BR UP

SHORT YARDAGE/G.L.

SHORT

Dive 33 Rov. Wham	Blue Rt Rov Sh. Div.
SL 22 FBLD	Br. Lt. Rov. Opp
Fi. Sl. 36 B Swing X Delay	Br. Rt. Rov Div Ac.

GOAL

20 Pinch Rov. Wham	Red Rt Rov. Sh Div.
Po. 49 EGT Special	Red Rt.
Fi. Sl 47 B shoot	Red Rt Rov Sh. Div.

2 MINUTES

3-2

Blitz 83,63		Sp. Or. Ti. FB Hi.
Blitz 12 A & B S.L.	(Man)	Sp. Or.
L/R 64 Y Bench	(Man)	Sp. Or.
L/R 66/L/R 65		Sp. Or. Ti. FB Hi.
R/L 84 W. Bench	(Man)	Sp. Or.
16 Waggle Lt/Rt		Sp. Or. Ti. Do. Hi.
R/L 16		Sp. Or. Ti. FB Hi.
Hot 17	(Man)	Sp. Or. Ti FB Hi.

DEC

65 Middle Screen	Sp. Or.
Drag Wk/St	Sp. Or.

Draw Rt/Lt   Sp. Or. Ti FB Hi.

K.C.

R/1 84 W Bench   Sp. Or.

L/R 64 Y Bench   Sp. Or.

81/61   Rally

4-0 & NO SUB

Use 3rd Down Plays

20 YARD LINE IN

RUNS

SL 34/35   Br. Flip

SL 43/22FBLD   Red Flip

Pi. 20/41 T Trap   Red

Po 47/26 NOP   Red Flip

Di. 49/28 TW FBLD   Br. Flip

20-15

RUN SIT.

L/R 14 X Cor Y Post (X   Br. Flip
   Man Key)

L/R 16 W-8 Y-7 (Y & W   Red
   Key)

PASS SIT.

L/R 11 Option   4 Rec.   Sp. Br Up

14-10

RUN SIT.

Fi. 47/26 Y & X Cross   Br. Flip

Fi. Sl 34/35 A Shoot & Go Y
   Rev. Sc. Lt/Rt FB   Br. Flip

PASS

Hot 17   Red

9 IN

RUN SIT.

Fi. Sl. 41/20 T Trap Bootleg   Br. Flip

Fi. Po 49/28 WGO Bootleg   Do. X.
   Spec.

                                    Red Flip

PASS SIT.
Speed 82 Do Sl. Out B
   Circle   J.H.
Hot 82   Red

    This must have been a good game plan; we used it to crush
the 49ers, 59–14.
    Let me explain just one of these plays, the "Fake toss R/L
CO. 32/33 DO. X I." It would be called as follows by the quarterback in the huddle: "I—fake toss right, counter thirty-two,
on two. Ready. Break."
    The play calls for the fullback—the "3"—to run to the "2"
hole, which is between left guard and center. The "fake toss"
means the quarterback will first fake a lateral. "DO. X" stands
for the fact that we'll be using two tight ends, and players know
this, not from the quarterback saying it in the huddle, but because the messenger coming from the sideline is shouting
"Double X!" and also holding up a clenched fist. The fist is in
case the crowd noise is so loud his teammates can't hear him.
The "I" means we'll be running from the I formation.
    The game plan attacked San Francisco defensive back Eric
Wright, who was young and had not yet acquired his great tech-
niques. Of course, this 49er team bore no resemblance to the
great club that demolished Miami, 38–16, in the 1985 Super
Bowl.
    The 49ers this year were weak against the run, and we sent
Tony Dorsett at them right away. A little later in the game we
ran misdirection plays, set up by earlier traps, and the inexperienced and not particularly well-coordinated San Francisco
linemen often found themselves hopelessly out of position.
    The game plan also featured numerous play-action passes,
which worked just as they were diagrammed on the blackboard
once we got them looking for the run. Nor could the 49ers cope
with all the motion we threw at them. When Landry became the
first coach in Cowboy history, he didn't have a lot of top players, so he tried to compensate with a great deal of motion. When
the Cowboys did reach the top, he just kept using it. In this particular rout, we not only were much better than San Francisco,
but also much trickier.

*   *   *

In 1980 I had one of my few unpleasant experiences with Tom Landry. Along with Kellen McClendon and Steve Sokol, I was a member of Consolidated Management Enterprises, a firm assisting athletes in, among other things, contract negotiations. We had represented Scott Laidlaw and Butch Johnson, and now were assisting Tony Dorsett. A lot of Tony's pay had been deferred and he wasn't pleased with his present contract, so Consolidated Management Enterprises was retained to renegotiate for him.

Because I was still an active player with the Cowboys, I stayed completely out of the negotiations. Steve Sokol handled them. At Tony Dorsett's instructions, Steve Sokol told Gil Brandt that Tony might have to leave training camp if something couldn't be worked out. That night, Brandt called Sokol. "You guys have a surprise coming," Brandt said.

The next morning Brandt called Sokol again. "Tom says," Brandt said, "that if Dorsett walks, then Preston Pearson is gone."

I thought this was totally unfair. This put me in the middle, where I didn't belong. I'd carefully avoided having anything to do with Tony Dorsett's contract renegotiation. Why should I be fired because Tony Dorsett was unhappy? It was also a way to put unfair pressure on Sokol, who was a business partner of mine. The matter bothered me so much I couldn't concentrate at practices, and I decided to talk to Landry.

I told him the facts as outlined here. He said, "Okay," in a noncommital voice, but I felt he didn't believe me. The fact that he didn't deny what Gil Brandt had attributed to him indicated to me that he had indeed been part of the pressure to get Dorsett to settle by threatening me. It left a sour taste in my mouth.

I didn't really retire from football. Coach Landry made it clear I didn't fit in with the team's plans. He said he wanted to get a punter to relieve quarterback Danny White of that duty. He never did get his punter.

I could have caught on with a number of other teams, and at high pay. But that would have meant leaving Dallas, and I had a number of business enterprises going. It didn't make sense for me to pack up and go to another city. I thought everything over carefully and decided the time had come to call it a career. I knew I wouldn't miss the hurt. I would miss the excitement of the big games, and especially the camaraderie with teammates. I'd made a lot of good friends, and they would stay friends. That was the best part of it all.

It was necessary to call my own press conference to announce that I was leaving the Cowboys. A number of times I had heard players complain of the treatment they'd received when, after years of service to the Cowboys, it suddenly was all over. They felt deserted and alone. Management wants loyalty to be shown by the players, but often doesn't return it. There was all-pro Rayfield Wright, for example, who, after thirteen years, just wasn't asked to come back, and he finally cleared waivers and signed with the Philadelphia Eagles. It looked as though the Cowboys had abandoned him, dumped him. There was no big press conference for Rayfield when he retired. But when Roger Staubach retired (Roger, for whom Rayfield blocked), it seemed every reporter in the world was on hand. The Cowboys reserved the posh Stadium Club so that Roger could say good-bye. I know the great Lee Roy Jordan was another who wasn't treated as he should have been just before he quit.

Anyway, after I'd called my own press conference, the Cowboy front office said they had been planning one. I'd like to believe this was true. For six years I'd been an important part of the organization. All six years we made the playoffs, and three times we went to the Super Bowl.

But I'm still a Dallas Cowboy at heart. The good memories far outweigh the few bad ones. And I didn't spend much time worrying about my career once I decided to end it. So many players when they retire suffer what can only be called shock. They withdraw from the world. They live in a world only they inhabit. I was fortunate. I had a number of business operations (I'd been very careful to ensure that something would be waiting when the football ended), and these kept me busy as many hours as I cared to work. And that was a lot: I've always been someone who needs to keep doing.

I think Daddy helped me the most when I finally knew it was over. I was feeling sorry for myself and called him. "Keep your head up," he said. "Look to new horizons, Preston. You've got your health, and your brains aren't scrambled like some of them. You're lucky. Be proud of what you've done."

He was right. Lucky I had been. Lucky to have ever gotten into this league. Lucky to have had so much success. Lucky to have been a Cowboy. And lucky now, because from the perspective of fourteen years, I can sit back and remember the great ones I played with. I can even choose, as I do now, to name the All-Time Preston Pearson NFL Team (composed solely of those who were teammates), and just reading these names opens up a torrent of good memories:

PRESTON PEARSON
OFFENSIVE TEAM

Player	Position	Team
Roger Staubach	Quarterback	Dallas
Franco Harris	Running Back	Pittsburgh
Tony Dorsett	Running Back	Dallas
John Stallworth	Wide Receiver	Pittsburgh
Ray Berry	Wide Receiver	Baltimore
John Mackey	Tight End	Baltimore
Jon Kolb	Offensive Tackle	Pittsburgh
Jim Parker	Offensive Tackle	Baltimore
Blaine Nye	Offensive Guard	Dallas
Sam Davis	Offensive Guard	Pittsburgh
Mike Webster	Center	Pittsburgh

PRESTON PEARSON
DEFENSIVE TEAM

Player	Position	Team
Ed Jones	Defensive End	Dallas
Bubba Smith	Defensive End	Baltimore
Joe Greene	Defensive Tackle	Pittsburgh
Randy White	Defensive Tackle	Dallas
Lee Roy Jordan	Middle Linebacker	Dallas
Mike Curtis	Outside Linebacker	Baltimore

Player	Position	Team
Jack Ham	Outside Linebacker	Pittsburgh
Bobby Boyd	Cornerback	Baltimore
Mel Blount	Cornerback	Pittsburgh
Cliff Harris	Weak Safety	Dallas
Jerry Logan	Strong Safety	Baltimore

The choice at quarterback was a tough one between Roger Staubach and John Unitas. Each had a great arm; each was tremendously competitive. I felt Roger ran better than Unitas did, was a better athlete, and of course both were much smarter players than Terry Bradshaw.

At wide receiver I believe Ray Berry and Drew Pearson were very close. Both were very smart. Both were brilliant catching passes over the middle. Neither was exceptionally fast. I chose Berry because I believe he ran slightly better routes than Drew, which means Berry's routes were perfect.

I think the defensive front four could be more than an all-teammate selection. These men—Bubba, Mean Joe, Too Tall, Randy White—could be the four greatest ever to play their positions. Three outstanding players had to be left off: Ernie Holmes, Jethro Pugh, and Harvey Martin.

Thomas Henderson wasn't selected at outside linebacker because he didn't play enough years at the top level of which he was capable. As I've said, Thomas had enormous potential. He wasn't a team player, however, and football is most definitely a team game.

Of the three coaches I played under, I would have to choose Tom Landry to coach this imaginary aggregation, though Don Shula has many qualities to recommend him. Chuck Noll's I-know-it-all attitude disqualifies him, in my opinion. I like the way Landry trusted his assistants, and as far as being a creative innovator, he is in a class by himself. Great as Shula is, you don't see in his teams what I describe as a spark of genius. Watch the movement of the Cowboy offense closely the next time you can. There is so much more there than the casual eye can see.

* * *

My mother died October 2, 1982, from a massive stroke. She had been in a coma for a month. Nevertheless, it came as quite a blow for me, and I vowed as I headed for Freeport that I would try to be strong for the sake of others. It didn't work. I looked at her lying there in the church, and I started to cry. So many memories passed through my mind. Especially clear was the day she stood at the back of our little house watching the train that was carrying me to college go by. She'd had a hard life, but it was good, and filled with love.

Daddy also tried to be strong at the church—like he always was strong. But it wasn't long before he was going for his handkerchief. He took Mom's death terribly hard. He had to give away things that had belonged to them all their lives. They brought back memories too sweet to bear.

Rufus broke down at the church. I think Mom's death hit him the hardest of all. Yet he would have made Mom proud. She always tried to help others, and now so did Rufus. Realizing how alone Daddy would be, he started to take care of the house, and of our father too. I gave Rufus a big hug before I had to come back to Dallas. We both had tears in our eyes.

Mom was so honest and hard working. I think, yes, that with many of her old-fashioned values, she was wise. She didn't see very much of the "bigger" world, but she knew how someone should behave in it. She knew how to prepare her children. I think Mom knew how much we loved and treasured her. She left us suddenly, and I'm left with the eternal lament: *if only I'd told her more often.*

When I stopped playing football I had a business to go to, which I'd formed with five other guys: Aaron Kyle, Ed Jones, Butch Johnson, Benny Barnes, and Billy Joe DuPree. Aaron Kyle left the company when he was traded to Denver, and Billy Joe DuPree now has his own business, but the rest of us are doing quite well. We have seven Kentucky Fried Chicken franchises, a janitorial services company, and we've promoted some important concerts: Michael Jackson, Quincy Jones, Lakeside, Stevie Wonder, Angela Bofill, Aretha Franklin, Rick James, and Kool and the Gang.

I also have my own company, PPI/PSA, which has promoted college football games and the NFL/NBA Tennis Challenge, and arranges personal appearances for athletes and others. This company also has produced caricatures on cups, caps, and T-shirts. One of the cups, distributed by 7-Eleven, had sales of more than four million dollars. In addition, I have the right to establish Wendy's franchises, I am an original shareholder in the First National Bank of Pittsburgh, the first black-owned bank in that city.

It was always important for me to have a life other than football, and I think preparing for this *while* I was playing has paid off. I was the host of the television show *Sports View,* seen in 6.5 million homes on Warner Amex Cable and Black Entertainment Television. I'm learning a lot in all of these ventures, but I think I'll do all right. I had a lot to learn about football, and that worked out pretty well.

I try to be involved with as many community projects as I can. I'm active with the Dallas Sickle Cell Anemia Foundation, sit on the board of the Junior Black Academy of Arts & Letters, and have served as honorary chairman of the Cystic Fibrosis Association. One of my favorite jobs is talking to organizations of young people on the dangers of drugs and alcohol, and the positive alternatives available to them.

Each day presents a new challenge. It was the same in football, especially for me, someone who, just as in the business world, wasn't even supposed to be in the game. I expect to accumulate as many good memories in my present life as I have from football.

Something Tom Landry once said is one of my memories. He is not given much to praise, but he once referred to me as a "quality veteran."

It wouldn't be bad if, when my life is over, all of it could be summed up that way.

Index